D0856095

COMMANDO

Hit-and-Run Combat in World War II

COMMANDO

Hit-and-Run Combat in World War II

KENNETH MACKSEY

Scarborough House/*Publishers*

NORTH COUNTRY LIBRARY SYSTEM
WATERTOWN, NEW YORK

Scarborough House/*Publishers*
Chelsea, MI 48118

FIRST PUBLISHED IN THE UNITED STATES OF AMERICA IN 1990

Library of Congress Cataloging-in-Publication Data

Macksey, Kenneth.
    Commando : hit-and-run combat in World War II / Kenneth Macksey.
        p.   cm.
    Includes bibliographical references (p.   ).
    ISBN 0-8128-2973-5 : $23.95
    1. World War, 1939-1945—Commando operations.   I. Title.
[D794.5.M33   1990]
940.54'86—dc20   89-70351
                                                              CIP

CONTENTS

LIST OF ILLUSTRATIONS

All the illustrations are reproduced by kind permission of the Imperial War Museum, with the exception of Nos. 9, 10, 13 and 15, which are reproduced by kind permission of the United States Marine Corps.

ABBREVIATIONS

A
AFHQ	Allied Forces Headquarters (Mediterranean)
AJF	Anti-Japanese Forces
Amphib (Phib) Recon Patrol	Amphibious Reconnaissance Patrol
Amtrack	Amphibious tracked vehicle (see also LVT)

B
Bde	Brigade (British)
Bn	Battalion
Brig	Brigade (US)

C
C	Director of the Secret Intelligence Service (symbol for)
CAS	Chief of Air Staff
CCO	Chief of Combined Operations
CCS	Combined Chiefs of Staff
CD	Executive Director of SOE (symbol for)
Cdo	Commando
CIGS	Chief of the Imperial General Staff
C-in-C	Commander-in-Chief
CNS	Chief of the Naval Staff
CO	Commanding Officer
Co	Company (US)
COHQ	Combined Operations Headquarters
COI	Central Office of Information
COPP	Combined Operations Pilotage Party
COS	Chief of Staff
COSSAC	Chief of Staff to the Supreme Allied Commander
CTC	Combined Training Centre

D

DCCO	Deputy Chief of Combined Operations
DCNS	Deputy Chief of Naval Staff
DCO	Director of Combined Operations
DDCO	Deputy Director of Combined Operations
DDOD(I)	Deputy Director, Operations Division (Irregular)
Div	Division
DNC	Director of Naval Construction
DNI	Director of Naval Intelligence

E

ETO	European Theatre of Operations
EPS	Executive Planning Staff

G

Gee	A radio navigational aid
Gestapo	Geheime Staatspolizei
GS(R)	General Staff (Research) Branch

H

HLI	Highland Light Infantry

I

Indep Coy	Independent Company
IO	Intelligence Officer
ISTDC	Inter-Services Training and Development Centre

J

JCS	Joint Chiefs of Staff
JIC	Joint Intelligence Committee
JPS	Joint Planning Staff

L

LCA	Landing Craft Assault
LCI	Landing Craft Infantry
LCM	Landing Craft Mechanised
LCN	Landing Craft Navigation
LCP	Landing Craft Personnel
LCS	Landing Craft Support
LCT	Landing Craft Tank
LRDG	Long Range Desert Group
LSI	Landing Ship Infantry
LST	Landing Ship Tank
LVT	Landing Vehicle Tracked (Amtrack)

M

MAS	Motoscafo Anti-Sommergibile (Italian MTB)
MEW	Ministry of Economic Warfare
MFV	Motor Fishing Vessel
MGB	Motor Gun Boat
MIR	Military Intelligence Research Branch
ML	Motor Launch
MO	Military Operations Branch
MTB	Motor Torpedo Boat

O

OG	Operations Group
OSS	Office of Strategic Services

P

PT Boat	Patrol Torpedo boat
PW	Prisoner of War

Q

QH	Gee receiver set

R

RA	Royal Artillery
RAF	Royal Air Force
RAN	Royal Australian Navy
RANVR	Royal Australian Naval Volunteer Reserve
RE	Royal Engineers
RHLI	Royal Hamilton Light Infantry
RM	Royal Marines
RMBPD	Royal Marines Boom Patrol Detachment
RN	Royal Navy
RNR	Royal Naval Reserve
RNVR	Royal Naval Volunteer Reserve
RNZNVR	Royal New Zealand Naval Volunteer Reserve
RWK	Royal West Kent Regiment

S

SAS	Special Air Service
SBS	Special Boat Section
SEAC	South East Asia Command
SGB	Steam Gun Boat
SIS	Secret (or Special) Intelligence Service
SOE	Special Operations Executive
SOG	Special Operations Group
SSRF	Small Scale Raiding Force

U

UDT	Underwater Demolition Team
USAAF	United States Army Air Force
USN	United States Navy
USMC	United States Marine Corps

V

VCCO	Vice-Chief of Combined Operations
VCNS	Vice-Chief of Naval Staff

W

W/T	Wireless Telegraphy

X

X craft	Miniature submarine

INTRODUCTION

The majority of the campaigns conducted by the Western Allies during the Second World War were, at their start, Combined or Joint Service operations. In the aftermath of that war many books – some fact, some fiction – described individual battles with a plethora of detail concerning acts of individual gallantry by the men of special organizations. The name Commando, which had stimulated popular imagination and raised the hopes of a hard-pressed British people in the desperate days of 1940, had by then gained world-wide acceptance as symbolic of elitism among fearless and ruthless fighting men. And yet, among the Official Histories published on both sides of the Atlantic, not a single one describing the work of the Combined Operations Organizations was commissioned. Instead the story was deliberately merged with Campaign Histories. As a result the numerous minor hit-and-run operations which featured in all theatres of war were either totally omitted or reduced to a footnote, treatment which, in terms of history, was both an injustice and an obfuscation. For no matter how lightly separate raids may have weighed in the scales of a total war, or how localized the impact on friend or foe of pinprick skirmishes, the accumulated effect of raiding was important – at times vital. By the same token, the omission from most histories of the intensive but frequently abortive attempts to launch all manner of raids has left behind an impression of irrational inactivity in the prosecution of the war, which was quite untrue and demands explanation.

It is also often forgotten that the causes of shortcomings in the publication of recent history are often the result not only of the demand to protect national security, but also the need to avoid defamation of living individuals. Much that should be revealed in the interests of clarity and of history has to be suppressed; and the primary losers are those among the generation who made that history, who are denied a full understanding of what it was about. Of course the rules which, to all intents and purposes, banned examination of official records of the First, let alone the Second World War had largely been relaxed by 1973 on both sides of the Atlantic, and the more recent publication of the British Official History of Intelligence has performed another important service. Meanwhile the death of many of those concerned minimizes the risk of libel actions against historian or publisher.

Documents about the intrigues, vacillations, misunderstandings, prejudices and political as well as military confrontations which were the daily chores of Combined Operations Headquarters and the bedevilment of even the smallest operation are available to demonstrate why it was that many hitherto inexplicable dramas occurred. Repeatedly it is the negative aspects which are the most revealing. Certainly, in the context of amphibious hit-and-run raiding, the unpublicized stories of the raids which did not take place often throw more light on the causes of hesitations and apparent contradictions than do current explanations of those which did.

At the root of rejections or cancellations of planned raiding operations is to be found the underlying weaknesses of the Allied position: the doubts of leaders at all levels; faults in training and equipment; inadequacies of technique; the corrosive ramifications of departmental jealousies and competition; and the restrictions upon uninhibited combat imposed by politico-humanitarian principles. Consider, for example, the inhibitions placed upon even the smallest attempt to carry the war to the enemy and steal the initiative by the Prime Minister, Winston Churchill. His ingrained memories of Gallipoli in 1915, with its heavy loss of life on fire-swept beaches, as well as his dread of inflicting avoidable hardship upon friendly people in enemy-held territory, made him chop and change his mind. Note the concern of President Roosevelt and the American Chiefs of Staff that a plethora of minor diversionary operations would militate against a concentrated war-winning effort. Bear in mind the legitimate objections of the Intelligence Services to any operations which might interfere with their vital function of gathering information. Add to these the worries of Admirals, loaded with the burden of winning the war at sea, upon which everything depended and to which all else gave pride of place. Finally do not forget the weather's depredations, nor those of enemy resistance, either of which could halt an action after all the preliminaries had been settled.

History calls for a definitive account of Allied Combined Operations in the Second World War. Practical publishing and the tyranny of space make this unlikely. The best that can be done is to fill gaps amid the existing books and bring to notice material which has hitherto been locked away. In this book I concentrate on the field of the smaller raids, set against the background of their causation, in the hope also of highlighting the contribution of forgotten top-grade people who, for a variety of reasons, have been misjudged or whose acts of courage and sacrifice have been overshadowed by the glare of a few highly publicized celebrities. Just as it is time to record smaller operations in greater detail, in addition to those at St Bruneval, St Nazaire and Dieppe, so it is right to pay tribute to the work of Admiral of the Fleet Sir Roger Keyes alongside that of Vice-Admiral Lord Louis Mountbatten, Colonel W. J. Donovan and Rear Admiral R. K. Turner. Similarly it is desirable to mention not only the famous – the Lovats, Stirlings and Carlsons – but to expand upon the lesser known Appleyards, Pinckneys, Berncastles, Edsons, Boyds and Kennedys of raiding fame, and to link their courage and determination with that of the sailors who took them to their rendezvous with destiny. And when the telling of the story can be contemporary, in the fighting men's own words, that is better than projections of distant hindsight.

I have focused my research on the archives held by the Public Record Office, London, the Library of the Ministry of Defence and the various National Archives of the United States Navy and Army in Washington, DC. I have also consulted the Imperial War Museum, London, the Royal Marines Museum, Southsea, and the US Marine Corps Center, Washington. As a deliberate policy, however, in my endeavour to use mainly contemporary records, I have interviewed few survivors and have been wary of post-war written memoirs. Old men tend to forget, prejudice can intrude, politics do enter into the subject, and high literary merit sometimes conceals a wealth of error. In any case I have a preference for the 'flat' action account rather than the highly embroidered narrative. I am, however, indebted to Captain G. A. French, RN, for providing me, in discussions, with invaluable insight into Allied and Joint Service Planning during the formative period 1940 to 1942; to Colonel P. A. Porteous VC and Captain P. Gardner VC for anecdotes, guidance and assistance; and to several landladies and barmaids whose recollections of fighting men at play and in repose were valuable in understanding atmosphere and the under-pinning of morale. To all those institutions and contributors who have helped, I wish to pay full acknowledgement and give heartfelt thanks for making their documents and memories available. I would recommend to anybody who is sufficiently enthused by my discoveries (British and American) to visit the Public Record Office at Kew and study in detail, as I have done with the unfailing help of the Staff there, the superb (and far from over-weeded) collection of documents relating to Combined Operations in Europe and the Pacific and Far East. They are to be found scattered throughout CAB, ADM, AIR and WO Records but concentrated to a remarkable extent under DEFE 2, to which I have made the most frequent reference in assembling this book. And among these, none are more rewarding than the 36 thick files of the COHQ War Diary which show how power in the hands of dynamic innovators can compel innovation against even the stiffest reactionaries. For, in the final analysis, the events described here are the products of a relatively small number of very determined and intelligent men who knew how to get their way, be it in London, Washington or against the declared enemy on several hundred different beaches, in every theatre of war.

Finally I wish to express my indebtedness to Chester Read, who drew the maps; to Felicity Northover, who read my scrawl and typed the manuscript; and to Bill Woodhouse, who read and criticized the draft with his usual thoroughness and critical good sense.

MAPS

NORTH-EAST
FRANCE
TO THE
NETHERLANDS

Scheveningen

H O L L A N D

Walcheren

Zeebrugge

Ostend

7 miles

ANTWERP

Bray-Dunes

Ghent

Dunkirk

les
Hemmes

Gravelines

B E L G I U M

Calais

BRUSSELS

Ambleteuse

Boulogne

Hardelot

Plage Ste. Cécile

LILLE

Le Touquet-Plage

Etaples

Merlimont
· Plage

F R A N C E

Quend-Plage
les-Pins

St Valery

Cayeux

Onival

It

Abbeville

River Somme

AMIENS

0   10   50   100

Miles   Miles

FRANCE

AND THE

ENGLISH CHANNEL

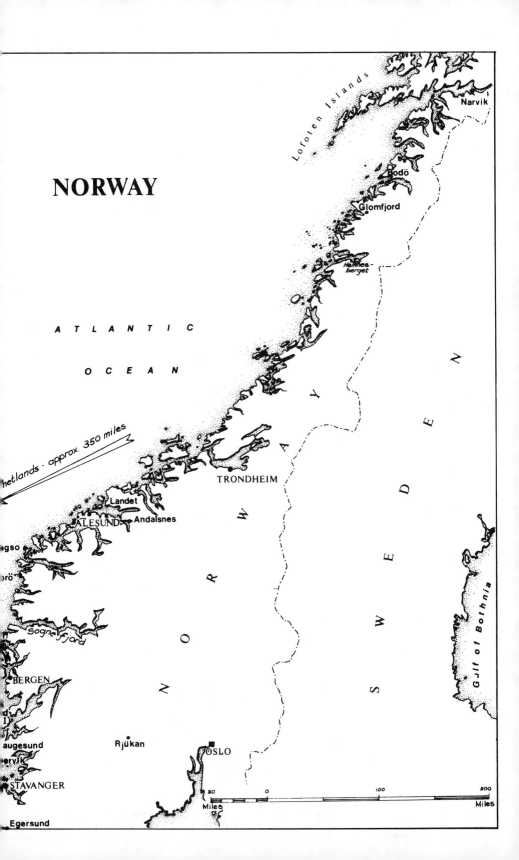

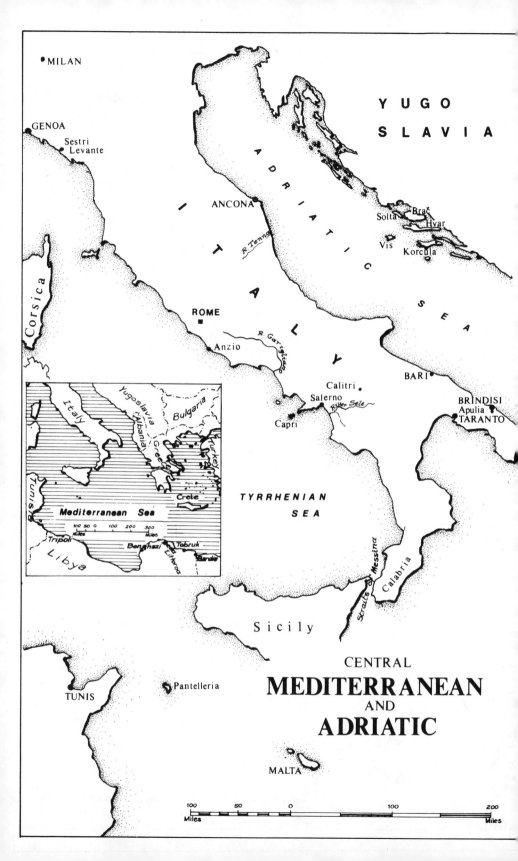

MILAN

GENOA
Sestri
Levante

Corsica

ANCONA

R. Tenna

ADRIATIC

YUGO
SLAVIA

Solta
Vis
Korcula

Brač
Hvar

SEA

ROME

Anzio

R. Garigliano

Capri

Calitri
Salerno
River Sele

BARI

BRINDISI
Apulia
TARANTO

Italy

Yugoslavia
Albania
Greece

Bulgaria

Turkey

Tunis

Mediterranean Sea

100 50 0   100   200   300
Miles   Miles

Crete

Tripoli

Benghazi

Tobruk

Bardia

Libya

TYRRHENIAN
SEA

Straits of Messina

Calabria

Sicily

CENTRAL
MEDITERRANEAN
AND
ADRIATIC

Pantelleria

TUNIS

MALTA

100   50   0   100   200
Miles   Miles

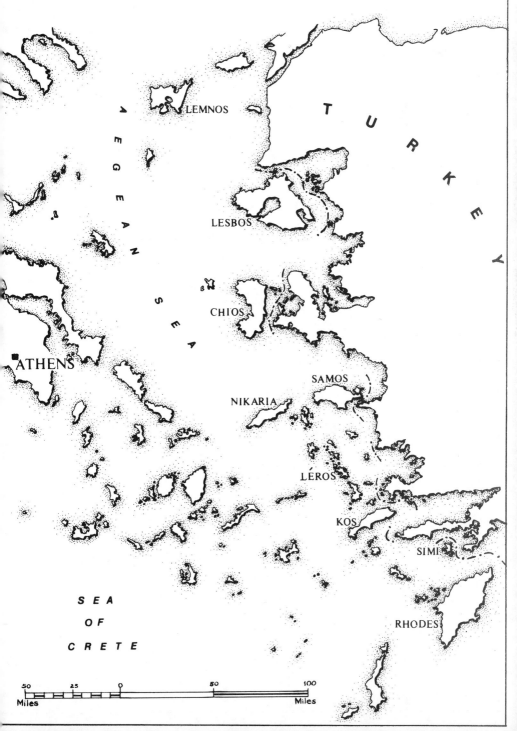

THE AEGEAN

LEMNOS

TURKEY

AEGEAN SEA

LESBOS

CHIOS

ATHENS

SAMOS

NIKARIA

LÉROS

KOS

SIMI

RHODES

SEA

OF

CRETE

50   25   0   50   100
Miles   Miles

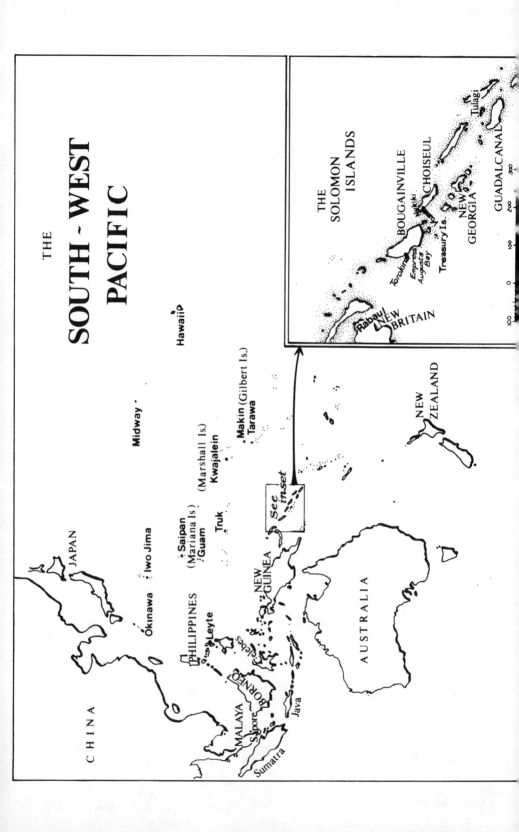

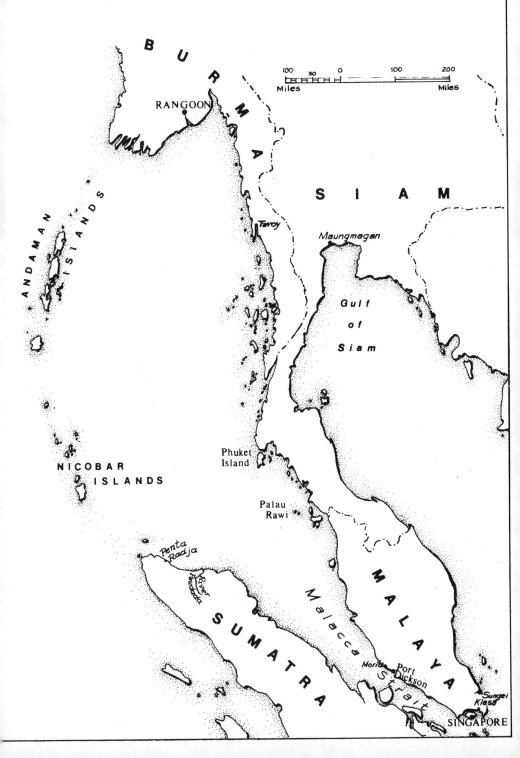

SOUTH - EAST ASIA

B U R M A

RANGOON

100 50 0 100 200
Miles   Miles

S I A M

ANDAMAN ISLANDS

Tavoy

Maungmagan

Gulf
of
Siam

NICOBAR
ISLANDS

Phuket
Island

Palau
Rawi

Penta
Radja

River
Pandeza

SUMATRA

M A L A Y A

Malacca

Morilta Port
Dickson

Strait

Sungei
Klesd

SINGAPORE

CHAPTER 1

Beside the Seaside

It came as a shock to the British people, particularly those who lived within sight of the channel, that by the end of June, 1940, they found themselves in the front line of a major war. Because the Second World War began so soon after the First, millions of people naturally assumed that this latest outbreak would be, with the feared addition of severe air raids, similar to its predecessor – a long campaign on land with occasional naval battles and U-boat warfare. To amphibious warfare the British had not paid much consideration since 1918, and that went for the Germans too, with the result that when the latter, to their surprised delight, conquered Western Europe, they were no better prepared to launch an invasion of England than the British were to prevent it. Of course there had been the Norwegian campaign, but in that case the German invasion by sea and air had been, initially, virtually unopposed. It was known by a few experts that, far away in the Pacific Ocean, the Japanese possessed amphibious forces with recent practice in the art, but that was of small account to the British when their homeland was directly threatened. Anything happening East of Suez lay in the laps of the Gods and the Americans. The Japanese were their main threat, but, starved of resources, they had given careful consideration to the likelihood of amphibious warfare in a vast ocean arena dotted by islands.

So far as the British were concerned, domination of the quadrilateral formed by the northern tip of Norway, the Isles of Shetland and Scilly and the town of Biarritz in south-west France was all that mattered. No longer that hot summer could the coasts be regarded as friendly holiday resorts. Where parents had built sandcastles with their children in 1939 a hostile presence now ruled. Barbed wire entanglements spread their tentacles, mines were being buried and pill-boxes and entrenchments loomed over esplanade and pier. Bandstands, amusement arcades and miniature rifle ranges stood empty and silent, many of their clients now in uniform and manning the defences in readiness for full-bore shooting against an invader who was expected any day. Already overhead one form of raiding had begun, even before the last man returned in defeat from France. The Luftwaffe's machines bombed and machine-gunned and were held at bay by forces which were barely capable of defence, let alone attack.

Early defeat for Britain did, indeed, seem a certainty and the down-trodden victims of Germany's conquests endured in despair under the jackboot while the rest of the world looked on and pondered only the prospects of one last, hopeless, back-to-the-wall struggle ending in ignominious surrender in the face of overwhelming might. Only a few RAF bombers provided the means to strike out at the enemy land forces, aided in the coastal regions by bombardment from ships of the Royal Navy. Although there was talk of a great day when the enemy would be ejected from his ill-gotten gains by a great invading British army, there was scant reason in June, 1940, to have much confidence in that dream, and no hope at all had it been known that less than a score of specialist landing-craft were at that moment in existence.

All the more surprising and up-lifting was it then, when an announce-ment on 25 June said British troops had landed on the enemy-occupied coast, inflicted casualties and withdrawn unscathed, soon embellished by hints that this was but one of several such sorties. And soon the public began to hear about a new kind of soldier whose special role it was to carry out these amphibious hit-and-run strikes – Commandos, selected for their ruthlessness, superior physique, cunning and prowess in combat. Quite a lot of them were ex-criminals, it was rumoured – and with the smallest hint of truth. Well-equipped, too, with tommy-gun and knife, and carried to their stealthy work by fast boats manned by skilled sailors.

In fact they were amateurish in concept, and the Commando strikes of 1940 bore little resemblance to the bar-room tales. But they gave a boost to morale and they made those abroad, particularly in America, start to believe in Britain's chances of survival. If a nation could still attack while in deepest adversity it might win through in the end. And if Commandos were forces to win inspiring victories, then these were forces worth emulation.

By the time of the Battle of Britain it had already became apparent that this was a new kind of war in which specialists would play vital roles. Controversial as they were bound to be in the eyes of traditionalists, the Commandos, as they began to form and train beside the seaside, were adopted by the public, along with RAF fighter pilots, as saviours – shining examples of supreme courage who held the key to the survival of the nation. It was hard luck on the members of the older fighting arms that their best endeavours were overshadowed by men they viewed as upstarts. The fact remains that the name and meaning of the word Commando, copied from one of the basic organizations of the Boer Army of the South African War, would soon attain worldwide fame as the epitome of the deadliest kind of infantryman and founder of a dynasty of professional combat units derived from them.

CHAPTER 2

First Strike

As the last survivors from Dunkirk were coming home and three weeks before France bowed out of the struggle, leaving her entire coastline in German hands, the vital spark of aggression, motivated by the political as well as military need to maintain an initiative, however slight, had been struck by certain unorthodox people scattered around Whitehall. Their existence sprang from a move in 1938 to examine means to influence German opinion by 'attacking potential enemies by means other than operations of military forces' and this led, among other avenues of approach, to the General Staff at the War Office forming a research section called GS(R) and consisting of one General Staff Officer Grade 2 and a typist, to study subversion and sabotage. Under Major J. C. F. Holland in the months preceding the outbreak of war in September, 1939, GS(R) began to expand rapidly both in size, influence and activity. Holland had experience of guerrilla warfare in Ireland and attracted others with enthusiasm for explosives, unorthodox weapons and irregular methods – men such as Major C. McV. Gubbins who had also seen service in Ireland and in Russia during the Revolutionary War in 1919. And it was in his first pamphlet, called *The Art of Guerrilla Warfare*, that Gubbins pronounced the vital doctrine of this kind of subversive combat:

> Guerrilla actions will usually take place at point blank range as the result of an ambush or raid ... Undoubtedly, therefore, the most effective weapon for the guerrilla is the sub-machine-gun.

But it was Holland who provided the driving force at GS(R), which was re-named MI(R) in 1939. As Professor M. R. D. Foot wrote in *SOE in France*: 'Holland was both brilliant and practical; he was also quite unselfish. He saw MI(R) as a factory for ideas: when the ideas had been worked up to the stage of practicality, his aim was to hive off a new branch to handle them. . . . Early in the war he and his lively and enterprising staff launched interesting and secret organizations.' These included escape lines, 'mosquito' sabotage parties and much larger fighting forces known as Independent Companies – a typically British last-minute improvization to cope with circumstances for which the nation, having neglected the armed forces in peacetime, had done nothing to prepare. The Independent Companies were intended to stage amphibious guerrilla attacks against the Germans invading Norway in April – a task which the War Office was compelled to undertake because, as Lieut-General A. G. B. Bourne, the Adjutant-General of the Royal Marines, wrote,

There were no Royal Marines available at that time. The strength of the Corps at the outbreak of war was roughly 10,000, the sea commitments for the war roughly 11,000. . . . Actually, when I took over, apart from 260 officers and men sitting on sandbags waiting for anti-aircraft guns in the Middle East, I had 95 officers and men on which to raise the Mobile Naval Base Organisation of 250 officers and 5,000 men, and 50 of the 95 were mounting guns for the Army on the coast of England.

Ten Independent Companies were recruited from volunteers drawn mainly from Territorial Army infantry divisions stationed in the United Kingdom.

Each Brigade found a Platoon and each Battalion a Section. The Sections were led by officers . . . There was no 'Q' side proper, but between 50 and 60 tons of stores of all description were allocated and administered by Headquarters. The idea was that each Independent Company should be organized as a ship-borne unit. The ship was to be their floating base and to take them to and from operations. For this reason they were not provided with any transport. The Force became operational very soon after formation and was called "the Gubbins Force" after the name of its commander, Brigadier Gubbins.

Gubbins Force, consisting of six companies, landed at Bodö, south of Narvik, and was almost at once involved in a rearguard action under heavy air attack and much skilful enemy pressure by Alpine troops. Yet the action at first went in Gubbins Force's favour, 'so much so that we disputed the order to retire when it came'. There was indeed a remarkable spirit of individual gallantry bordering upon a bravado which some might have called amateurish. 'The trouble with the Independent Companies,' as one of the founders of the Commando Force who was present was soon to minute, 'was the low quality of their personnel, as no Regulars were included'. The officer concerned was, of course, reflecting the ingrained scepticism of nearly all Regulars for irregulars at that time. Failures there were at all levels, and the men of the Independent Companies were just as scathing in their criticism of the Regulars they fought alongside – but even at this early stage there emerged a spirit of sacrifice which was to become typical of the Commandos, as the Independent Companies would soon be known. Take, for example, the report on a platoon commander of No 1 Company when under attack by three or four hundred Germans:

> He caused a lot of casualties to the Germans, but suffered severe losses himself and when he realized that it would only be a question of time before he was wiped out, he gave the order to withdraw to the northern shore of the peninsula on which Hemnesberget stands. Before leaving, he ordered Private Howie, a Signaller, to destroy the local telephone exchange. . . . Howie ran up the hill towards it and was at once pursued by two Germans who opened fire on him and ordered him to stop. By this time he had reached the telephone exchange. He made no attempt to return their fire, but instead turned his back upon them and emptied his revolver into the telephone apparatus. He was shot and killed.

The campaign in Norway was not the most meritorious of those conducted by British forces, severely damaging though it was to the German naval forces involved. But by the time the remnants of the six Independent Companies returned to Scotland at the end of May, this setback had merged into the pall of disaster which had overcome the Allied armies in Europe. Yet already Holland, at the request of the Chiefs of Staff, was casting around for ways of sticking pins into an enemy who was all too obviously armed and armoured with such strength as to make him almost invulnerable.

No sooner had the Germans reached the Channel coast west of Abbeville on the evening of 20 May and begun to advance northwards towards Boulogne than, by the quite illegal employment of prisoners of war, they began to erect defences and mount batteries to fend off the raiders from the sea who they expected at any time. They had but a short time to wait. As the rearguard was sailing away from Dunkirk on 2/3 June a trawler commanded by Lt-Cdr J. F. W. Milner-Gibson was going in the opposite direction, bound for Boulogne, to drop off three officers in a rowing boat to spy out the land ashore. It was a pity that two of the party were lost and a stroke of luck that the third, after rowing hard for thirteen hours, was picked up in mid-Channel on the 10th. But it was contradictory as well as churlish for the Prime Minister to call this escape a 'silly fiasco', for already Winston Churchill was looking forward to the day when a great Allied armada would place vast armies ashore in France. A start had to be made somewhere, sometime, and, to begin with, by a few courageous individuals.

One such was Lt-Col Dudley Clarke, the Military Assistant to General Sir John Dill, the Chief of the Imperial General Staff. How much assistance he ever gave to his Chief at this period is hard to gauge. As Bourne wrote:

> He was, I am told, detailed from the War Office to give instructions to the Army Officer going to Andalsnes. This he was supposed to do in the train going to Scotland. He decided that . . . he had not given sufficient instructions so he sailed for Norway. After a short time there he was recalled to the War Office. A few days later a Marine Officer at Andalsnes was told that an individual was floating about in the fjord in a rubber boat. He was brought ashore and turned out to be Col Clarke who had been apparently deposited by seaplane. When asked why he had come back, he remarked, 'I left my sponge behind', which was a fact but a poor excuse for getting into the front line.

In London on 4 June Clarke reflected upon the disastrous situation in which Britain and her armed forces found themselves and recalled his own experiences in 1936 when 'a handful of ill-armed (Arab) fanatics' had been able to 'dissipate the strength of more than an Army Corps of regular troops'. That night he jotted down a plan for small forces raiding across the Channel and next morning presented it to the CIGS who mentioned it to the Prime Minister. Permission was instantly granted 'and Clarke was given a free hand provided . . . that no unit should be diverted from its essential task, the defence of Britain . . . and secondly that forces of amphibious guerrillas would have to make do with minimum arms.' Attached to this permit came two orders: first to mount a raid across the Channel at the earliest opportunity; second to set up a new branch in the War Office called MO9 to control 'uniformed raids'. One suspects that the CIGS was slightly relieved to see the back of his belligerent MA and there is, indeed, ample evidence that he was opposed to the specialized 'shock troops' which Clarke now strove to form and launch prematurely into action.

It was to Nos 8 and 9 Independent Companies (which had not gone to Norway) that he turned for volunteers. Within a week those volunteers had been formed into a new No 11 Company.

We moved to Southampton and spent some ten days firing on ranges and practising embarking and disembarking from Royal Air Force high speed launches. These were very fast and did not hold more than six to eight men. One day we were told to bring haversack rations as we were going to be all day on the ranges. We were taken there in buses, but they did not stop and the next thing we knew was that three parties of us were at Dover, Hastings and Ramsgate.

Strictly in line with the CIGS's restraining conditions, the Army gave minimum support, the twenty Thompson sub-machine-guns supplied being 'on loan' only from a central pool of these weapons which consisted at that moment of only forty. But the Second Sea Lord welcomed an opportunity to strike back at the enemy at a time when all else was defeat, and the Royal Navy rose to the occasion. Without delay a strange collection of craft, mostly private motor boats of dubious sea-going qualities, were assembled under Captain G. A. Garnons-Williams to join the trawler which was going across the Channel every other night under Milner-Gibson's command. The RAF 'crash' speed boats were pressed into service because the rest of the motley fleet were too slow. In the same way in which the Independent Companies were recruited from part-time soldiers, the naval crews were mainly made up of part-timers, some from the RNR, most from the RNVR, among them a number of capable small-boat men with knowledge of inshore waters. And to control a force which, from the outset, *had* to be joint Service a new organization had to be created under General Bourne.

I was told on 12 June that the Chief of Staff had decided that I should be in command of Offensive Operations, as it was called at that stage. . . . I got, as being the quickest method of starting, an allotment of four rooms in the Admiralty and Captain L. E. H. Maund RN and Captain Garnons-Williams appointed. . . . Next morning I arranged for Major A. H. Hornby, RA to be put on my staff . . . and later the Senior Air Officer became S/Ldr Knocker.

On 17 June Bourne received the directive which was to carry him and his successor through the formative months in the life of what was already becoming known as the Combined Operations Directorate:

1. You are appointed Commander of Raiding Operations on coasts of enemy occupation and Adviser to the Chiefs of Staff on Combined Operations.
2. The object of raiding operations will be to harass the enemy and cause him to disperse his forces, and to create material damage, particularly on the coastline from Northern Norway to the western limit of German-occupied France. . . .
4. Six Independent Companies and a School of Training in Irregular Operations have already been raised by the War Office. These and irregular Commandos now being raised will come under your operational command. . . . In addition the War Office has taken preliminary steps to raise parachutist volunteers of whom a number will be placed under your command. . . .
6. Certain raids by the independent companies have already been planned. . . .
7. Irregular actions of various types are undertaken from time to time by the Service Intelligence Departments. There must therefore be close touch between your staff and those departments in order that your several activities shall not interfere with each other and that, on occasions, co-operation may be possible.

MI(R) had already struck; one of its agents, with the aid of half a dozen British soldiers and a Verey pistol, had put the torch to 200,000 tons of oil at Gonfreville, near Harfleur, on 9 June. And Operation COLLAR, Clarke's first strike using 11 Indep Coy, was well advanced in preparation. The idea was to land fighting patrols between Étaples and Boulogne on the night 23/24 June on terrain already spied out by Milner-Gibson, who was placed in command of the six RAF crash boats, intended to save airmen shot down at sea and manned by civilians. The Commandos (as No 11 Indep Coy already liked to be known) were under the command of Major R. J. F. Tod, but, needless to say, Clarke would not be left out and was allowed to go, providing he did not set foot ashore. Wrote Lieutenant Evill:

I chose the roughest and toughest men possible. Three of them were Scotsmen. The plan was that we should land at three different places on the coast and carry out a reconnaissance of the German defences. We were armed with Tommy-guns and grenades and there was a Bren mounted on the motor boat as anti-aircraft protection. . . . We eventually got in sight of the French coast at 2 a.m., but we did not land because we did not know where we were. As we were arguing in low tones about our whereabouts there was a terrific roar and a German seaplane took off almost beside us. With difficulty we prevented one of the Scotsmen from shooting it up with the Bren gun which would have betrayed our presence.

After trying without success to get ashore in a rubber dinghy, Evill and his party returned home. Company Sergeant-Major Parker's party, on the other hand, did get ashore, shuttled there three at a time in a little wooden dinghy. 'We ran across 250 yards of beach and formed a bridgehead. We sent out two patrols, one of which ran into a Jerry patrol on bicycles. Neither the Germans nor ourselves opened fire and the only enemy I saw that trip was a huge rat.'

Lieutenant Swain's party also got ashore, but at Hardelot, which was not his proper destination.

He had some tough men with him, three of them gaol birds. They got into Hardelot and saw one or two trucks. . . . Then they ran into a Jerry patrol of two men on the beach. Swain called on them to halt; they opened fire. Swain's pistol jammed. Two of his gaol birds fought the Jerries on the beach and killed them both. On the way back the engines of the launch failed and they got stuck on the sandbank and had to swim for it. Eventually they got off the sandbank and returned to Folkestone on one engine. There they were refused permission to enter harbour and lay off the boom covered by the guns on shore, wet through and slightly tight, having drunk the contents of two jars of rum. When they did get ashore they were arrested by the Military Police.

Near Boulogne a party under Major Tod had also been fired on and Dudley Clarke, standing up in the bows of the boat, had his ear nicked by a bullet, making him the only British casualty of the night. But at Plage de Merlimont, south of Le Touquet, the Germans suffered quite heavily, two sentries being killed outside a heavily wired house near the beach and many more hit when grenades were thrown through the windows of what was taken to be a headquarters but seems to have been a dance hall with French people present.

The boats which returned to Dover, unlike the ones at Folkestone, were cheered by those ashore who knew what was afoot, and who, like everybody else in Britain, were desperately in need of something to cheer about. So Bourne, who was there to meet them, gave an euphoric, impromptu Press Conference which was blazoned across the newspapers to the disgust of the Prime Minister, the approval of the Minister of War,

Mr Anthony Eden, (who defended Bourne in the Cabinet) and the delight of the populace for whom Commandos, like RAF fighter pilots, had become a symbol of hope.

The Prime Minister's initial enthusiasm for small raids was already on the ebb. It was, he said, 'unworthy of the British Empire to send over a few such cut-throats', and he began to seek fresh means of control and execution. Meanwhile Bourne did the best he could with the improvizations he and his staff were compelled to adopt while still working part-time for the Royal Marines and rarely getting anything like a full night's sleep. Quite apart from shortages of weapons and craft, there were such minor deficiencies as camouflage face-cream (solved by using greasepaint supplied by a 'Wardour Street costumier') and escape maps, which to begin with were made up and sewn into the men's uniforms by the ladies of DCO's Admiralty office.

It could not go on for long like that. Even as Clarke was preparing another foray, crucial decisions for change were impending – and not all for the good of raiding.

CHAPTER 3

'Fourth Arm' or Ministry of Defence

General Bourne lunched with Churchill on 2 July and afterwards unburdened himself of his difficulties – the easily remedied matter of trying to do two jobs at once in a time of crisis and the need to put the waging of irregular offensive warfare on a firm footing, linked to the general strategic conduct of the war.

> I was much struck with the lack of co-ordination between the various Departments such as CD, CI(R), Ministry of Propaganda etc. . . . I therefore put up a paper suggesting co-ordination of the whole of these various activities and including combined operations because raids had to be part of war policy and the boats and shipping of combined operations were required to effect the purposes of the other Departments. This was agreed by the Chiefs of Staff. At the meeting I was asked what type of person I had in mind and I said, 'Someone like Lord Loyd (*sic*)'.

As Colonial Secretary and a personal friend of the late T. E. Lawrence, a great commander of guerrillas in the previous war, Lord Lloyd might well have filled the role admirably. The joint organization which Bourne preferred was in line with similar proposals already put forward by the Director of Military Intelligence (DMI). At a crucial meeting after the lunch with Churchill, Lloyd indeed voiced the need for 'a Controller armed with almost dictatorial powers', one who Dr Hugh Dalton, the Minister for Economic Warfare (MEW), felt ought to be 'independent of the War Office Machine'. No less, in fact, than 'A Fourth Arm', as Dalton later termed it, a new body in which the emphasis of command and control would be more under political than military management. It took a fortnight to reach departmental agreement for the setting up of what would be called 'Special Operations Executive' (SOE), with Dalton, at Churchill's request, in charge but with Combined Operations excluded. Indeed the divisions of responsibility were so blurred at the edges and so couched in secrecy that it was hardly surprising that for the next year or more, as Foot remarks, 'The prickly personalities of ministers were faithfully reflected among some of their subordinates, leading to a year-long series of pitched paper battles between the Foreign Office and Ministries of Information and of Economic Warfare.'

It would be pleasant to record that the Combined Operations Director-ate, through its exclusion from the SOE net, escaped a similar chain of confrontations. That this was to be far from the case has to be laid at the door of Churchill, regardless of what his apologists may say. He it was who appointed Dalton, a notoriously ambitious Socialist, politician and intri-guer, to head SOE on 15 July; and he who overruled the approval of the Chiefs of Staff for Bourne's plan for a single Directorate (SOE) to control all types of raiding. The fact that, as Bourne wrote, 'Sir Roger Keyes did not agree with the inclusion of the Combined Operations Directorate in this Organization, saw the Prime Minister and immediately had it taken out,' in no way absolves Churchill from the responsibility for doing so, true as it undoubtedly was that, as one disgruntled senior Army officer put it, Keyes was 'hanging around for employment'.

The influence of Keyes upon Churchill was indeed strong, as will be seen . But so, too, was Churchill's determining power over Keyes, as will also be seen. What should not be overlooked at any point in the development of British amphibious operations is Churchill's instinctive reluctance, born of the setback to his political career by his responsibility for the fiasco of Gallipoli in 1915. 'The iron of Gallipoli', as Keyes called it, was ever in his mind, warping his decisions. It was therefore natural that he should desire to place amphibious operations in the hands of Keyes who, as the mainspring of the raid against Zeebrugge in 1918, was the one man he regarded an expert on the subject. It was also inevitable that his misgivings about Bourne and his concept should be aggravated, after the 'unworthy' Operation COLLAR, by the all too obvious incompetence of Operation AMBASSADOR on 15/16 July.

AMBASSADOR's target was the Island of Guernsey, its intention to capture prisoners. It was guided, however, by false intelligence, steered by a defective plan and executed by sailors and soldiers who were inad-equately equipped, poorly trained and suffering from rather more than their share of bad luck. A party of men from the recently formed 3 Commando, led by Major J. F. Durnford-Slater, RA, were by no means ready for their task and those of Tod's 11 Independent Company, despite

the experience of Boulogne, were hardly any better qualified. Carried in
the destroyers *Scimitar* and *Saladin* to the vicinity of the Channel Islands,
the raiders then transferred to crash boats manned by crews who 'were
RNVR volunteers of a most cheerful and happy-go-lucky disposition.
The first thing we discovered as we left the destroyer was that they had
forgotten to adjust their compasses which were many degrees wrong, so
we had to guess at our landing place.' That was probably why CSM Parker
of 11 Independent Company arrived at Sark instead of Guernsey and had
to sheer off when picked up by a searchlight. The remainder of the
Company failed to get ashore because their crash boats broke down and
the whaler put at their disposal was 'full of bullet holes, the destroyer
having recently been in action. They paddled about for some time in the
darkness, but so much time had been lost that they thought it necessary to
return to the destroyer. They failed to find her in the darkness and all
transferred from the whaler to the broken-down crash boat. . . . As they
were doing so they saw a black shape rushing through the darkness; it was
the destroyer and they were picked up.'

The party from 3 Commando did slightly better. As least they got
ashore and in the right place, wading through 3½ feet of water. A barracks
they visited proved empty; they spoke to a few residents 'most of whom
were too frightened to talk properly' and 'one man who was apparently
insane'. They were ashore for just over two hours, but when they got back
to the beach to re-embark, 'a heavy swell had got up and the speed boats
(Nos 323 and 324) could not come nearer than about 50 yards, so we all
had to swim for it.' Then it transpired that three men who had said they
could swim could not, so they had to be left behind. Meanwhile the party
loading the Brens and Tommy-guns into a rubber dinghy were pitched
into the water, drowning one of their number.

> At this critical moment the Germans also came to life and started
> machine-gunning. . . . We all had an exhausting swim through the surf
> but . . . eventually reached the speed boats. One of these (324) then
> broke down (and was destroyed), and aboard the other one the crew
> were not very good at making up their minds . . . even the engine-room
> attendant emerged to take part in the discussion with the captain. . . .
> By this time we were nearly an hour late for the rendezvous with the
> destroyer and . . . we could just see her disappearing at high speed.

Flashes from a torch brought her back, most gallantly since it thus
exposed her to air attack as day broke; but by a miracle they got away with
it and returned safely to Dartmouth. They left behind, however, the two

British officers they were meant to pick who had previously visited the island in plain clothes as spies. They now had to find uniforms, surrender to the Germans and spend the rest of the war in prison.

It was the outcome of this bungled raid which confirmed Churchill in his resolve to make a radical change at the top in the month-old Combined Operations Directorate. His selection of Keyes for the job was a natural one from their point of view, if not from that of the Services upon whom the new DCO was about to be imposed. They were of an age – Churchill 68, Keyes 67 – and they had long been in collaboration. When Churchill was First Lord of the Admiralty in 1915 and pressing ahead with the amphibious operations to force the Dardanelles, Keyes had been Chief of Staff to the Admiral in Command. Moreover, Churchill was a keen admirer of Keyes for his immense fighting spirit and determination to get things done. Keyes, for his part, as a Member of Parliament had been a staunch supporter in Churchill's wilderness days when he was excluded from office. It had been Keyes, during the Norwegian Campaign in April and May, who had tried to push Churchill (once more First Lord of the Admiralty) into overriding the advice of the First Sea Lord, Admiral Sir Dudley Pound, and of the other Chiefs of Staff, into storming Trondheim Fjord and into letting him lead the force in person. And it had been Keyes who had stood up in Parliament, wearing the uniform of Admiral of the Fleet, to castigate Chamberlain's Government and help to bring about his replacement by Churchill.

Churchill's postwar comments on Keyes reflect romantic admiration for a favourite. 'In him burned a flame,' he wrote in his *History of the Second World War*, thereby casting an innuendo upon some sailors and many soldiers whom both regarded as obstructionists. But in his directive of 17 July, written immediately after AMBASSADOR, Churchill made it plain that he had in mind something much larger for Keyes than the execution of amphibious raiding. For he retained both Bourne and the original directive to him, along with the injunction that it should be explained why the change had been made:

Owing to the large scope now to be given to these operations, demanding an officer of higher rank in charge. . . . Pending any further arrangements, Sir Roger Keyes will form contact with the Service departments through General Ismay as representing the Minister of Defence [Churchill himself].

Clearly this was another way, by an indirect route, to give substance to the so-called Ministry of Defence which, in fact, was but a secretariat without authority over the Service Departments. For many years similar proposals had been under discussion but had been successfully resisted by the Admiralty, War Office and Air Ministry, who obdurately defended their traditional autonomy. In May Churchill had asked another of his admired strong men, Marshal of the Royal Air Force Sir Hugh Trenchard, to become Minister of Defence. Trenchard, sensing difficulties, declined, leaving Churchill to take the appointment himself. Keyes, who was senior to all three Chiefs of Staff, and who treated the First Sea Lord as just another Staff Officer, as he had once been to Keyes, was being placed (no doubt with his full approval and possibly at his suggestion) in a position from which he could co-ordinate and possibly control the three Services. Such a move was bound to stir up as much departmental resentment as did the creation of SOE, and some idea of how Churchill envisaged it working can be obtained from a letter he wrote on the subject of raiding (which was about all the Armed Forces were capable of in terms of initiative at this time) to Mr Eden, the Secretary of State for War, on 23 July.

2. It would be most unwise to disturb the coasts of any of these [occupied] countries by the kind of silly fiascos which were perpetrated at Boulogne and Guernsey. The idea of working all these coasts up against us by pin-prick raids and fulsome communiqués is one to be strictly avoided.
3. Sir Roger Keyes is now studying the whole subject of medium raids – i.e., by not less than five nor more than ten thousand men. Two or three of these might be brought off on the French coast during the winter. As soon as the invasion danger recedes or is resolved, and Sir RK's paper-work is done, we will consult together and set the Staffs to work upon detailed preparations. After these medium raids have had their chance there will be no objections to stirring up the French coast by minor forays.
4. During the spring and summer of 1941 large armoured irruptions must be contemplated.

Quite apart from the almost total lack of trained men, suitable equipment, shipping, air power or a developed technique for their joint employment, the logic of a strategy which started early with medium-sized operations and was then watered down by minor raids is difficult to comprehend. That this was Keyes' idea is possible but not documented – his previous involvement with raids was on the medium scale. What was crystal clear from the outset was Keyes' intention to free himself and his organization for Admiralty supervision and control. At once he left the offices at the Admiralty and took up residence at the other end of Whitehall in offices in Richmond Terrace. Inherently there was strong opposition to these changes both inside and outside Combined Operations. Foremost among the critics was Captain Maund, Keyes' Naval Assistant, who until quite recently had been Chief of Staff to Lord Cork while the latter was in command of operations in Norway and who, therefore, had been included in Keyes' stinging criticism of the Navy's performance. Maund held that:

> There was one thing that governed what could and what could not be done, and that was the number of craft available and suitable. . . . It was quite clear in these circumstances that the main task ahead of the DCO was to build craft, convert the ships to carry the craft and train the crews. What few people seemed able to appreciate was that the years 1940 and 1941 could only be years of building ships and craft and collecting crews. It would have been better to have had no Commandos at this time, no troops with which to whet the appetites of imaginative planners; then perhaps we should have been able to concentrate better upon the real object of DCO at the Admiralty.

There spoke the sailor who saw all things maritime as difficult and specialized and all things connected with soldiers and land warfare simple and easily assimilated. Not every soldier would have agreed with Maund, but many would (and did) concur with his views over the dangers of the move from the Admiralty to Richmond Terrace:

> From the material, naval personnel and psychological aspects, separation at this particular time, when everything depended upon Admiralty effort, was a misfortune and led, as the days went by, to a good deal more than separation. The day of the private navies and armies had dawned and the office of the DCO became one with which the Service Departments had not much wish to play.

With imminent invasion threatened and a dire shortage of resources for anything, let alone raiding, Combined Operations were bound to take a low place in the order of priority and more time was spent cogitating, scheming, plotting and intriguing than might have been the case if it had been allowed to partake in real instead of paper battles. But with small raids outlawed and medium ones virtually beyond its scope, it was to this that it was reduced while the Commandos trained without, for the next seven or eight months, getting to grips with the enemy.

CHAPTER 4

Men, Weapons and Craft

Eight weeks after Clarke had put forward his scheme and ten days after Keyes took over as DCO, there were 750 men in the Independent Companies and 500 in Commandos, in addition to the crews of Garnons-Williams's diverse flotilla of small craft. Already, apart from the change in raiding policy effected by Keyes and Churchill, the nature and style of the land element of Combined Operations was changing. For while the principle of volunteering for this special force remained inviolable, the method of recruiting had been altered and the qualifications tightened up. The formal organization was in course of preparation by a War Office which insisted upon traditional methods. Within a few months the Commandos would be officially called Special Service troops – a term which, in its abbreviated form of SS, sounded far too like that of the German SS. Yet the men rejoiced in their own, self-assumed title of 'Suicide Squads'. The initial insistence that officers and men must be physically fit, ready trained and proficient swimmers remained in force, but could not be relaxed although extra emphasis was being placed upon good character. Being an individualist and a volunteer were not necessarily sufficient reasons for acceptance. Each man had to become part of a team and it was with that in mind that Commanding Officers, when appointed, were given powers to select their own officers who, in turn, chose their own subordinates.

'This is how I got into it,' wrote 2nd Lieutenant J. G. Appleyard:

(Gus) March-Phillipps was selected by Col Lister as 'B' Troop Leader. He was told he could have a free hand in picking two volunteer subalterns from the whole of the Southern Command (about 30 volunteered) for his two section leaders. . . . Each section has 23 men and so the whole strength of the Troop is 50 men. . . . We have about

200 'volunteers' from which to pick the 47 for our troop. *Everything* depends on the men we choose. We ourselves select the men and have the right to take from this list of volunteers any we like. . . . On parade and on a job there must be rigid discipline. Off parade there will be a great fellowship. At all times there must be absolute trust and confidence. There will be no punishments – a man is either IN or OUT. . . . There will be no paper work, no administrative work. No billeting problems, no feeding problems as we feed and billet ourselves. Every man gcts 6/8 a day above his normal pay for this purpose, every officer gets 13/4 a day extra.

All of which sounded splendid when written in the euphoria of his joining on 1 August, 1940, and before the snags had been discovered. Obviously *somebody* had to do the administration! Those in opposition had closed ranks against the Commandos, and they included many influential people, among them Sir John Dill, the GIGS, Lieut-General Alan Brooke, the GOC-in-C Home Forces, and the COs of most regiments, whose men, by order, could not be denied the opportunity to volunteer for the Commandos if they chose to do so. At the root of the objections to the Commando idea lay reasoned fears that the Army's discipline would be undermined and that units would lose their best men upon whom they depended for future leaders. Without denying the need for a few special 'shock' troops, Brooke, for example, thought they should be restricted to a single company in each division. With their pride injured, COs naturally insisted that their particular units could do anything Commandos could do, provided they were given the same priorities which already were being granted to Keyes' *corps d'élite*; but they overlooked the fact that, among the recalled reservists and newly recruited conscripts filling their ranks, many were by no means genuine volunteers and therefore lacked the spark of hearty aggression. But later in the war a shortage of leaders did afflict the infantry.

By 27 September all the Independent Companies had been absorbed by the Commandos which now numbered ten, with a total strength of some 8,000 men, including 500 potential parachutists, of whom only 100, as yet, were learning how to jump. They came from almost every Corps and Regiment in the British Army and already included a few Royal Marines and Americans. Besides these, there was 10 (IA) Commando, consisting of one French Troop, one Dutch, three Belgian, one Norwegian, one Polish, one Yugoslav and one Troop of enemy aliens, such as Sudeten Germans. And while efforts were being made from on high either to have them disbanded, brought into line with regular forces or at least deprived of the special lodging allowance, the Commando units themselves were acquiring that electric spirit which, of necessity, set them apart from those who did not have to practice amphibious warfare. The deliberately acquired habits of independent thought worked marvels in inculcating reliability allied to flexibility of execution when in action.

It soon became the rule, when any movement of the Commando was necessary, to dismiss the men at one place at, say, six in the evening, with orders to be on parade at six in the morning the next day at some other place, often many miles distant. How they reached it was their own affair, providing they did so. By this practice a Commando soldier might travel sixty, seventy, or even a hundred miles in twelve hours; and the number who failed to reach the new rendezvous was infinitesimal.

To which it could be added that the number who were absent without leave or who deserted was also well below the average for the Army as a whole.

Of the men who offered themselves for a type of service which was far more exacting than that in normal units, about 25% failed the medical examination. Others could not keep up the pace of training. The rule about swimmers was not rigidly enforced since 'it was found that to refuse them would lead to the rejection of too large a number of men otherwise fit to be Commandos'. They simply had to learn as quickly as possible. Lieutenant Pip Gardner, RTR, (who was later to win a VC after he had been returned to his own Regiment because trained tank men were badly needed in tanks) recalled being paraded on the end of Weymouth pier:

> Somebody shouted, 'Alright! Everybody jump in the sea'. So we did and then had to rescue the four who had claimed they could swim and who, quite obviously, could not.
>
> Today's programme has been typical, [wrote Appleyard]. Reveille 6.30, training run 7 (about a mile) followed by PT, breakfast 8, parade 9, inspection, route march 8–10 miles (with arms, in battledress, belts etc) at fast pace, including cross-country work, map-reading, compass work, moving through cover etc. Lunch 1, swimming parade 2.30 for 1½ hours swimming, running, exercising etc. Tea at 4.40. Lecture by M-P (his OC) for three-quarters of an hour at 5. Free for the evening at 6. . . . Later on, of course, there will be weapon training, range practice, cross-country runs, hare and hounds, treasure hunts, mock operations, night operations, etc.

Living in civilian billets did, of course, add to the attractions of being a
Commando. Undeniably there was competition among Commandos to
find themselves the best accommodation and a genuine desire among
many landladies to have Commandos in preference to other soldiers. The
testimonies speak for themselves.

Commandos: At no time during my service with the Commandos can I
truthfully say that I have lived in a rotten billet. Indeed, on the contrary I
have friends all over the country from Brighton to Beddgelert from
Seaford to Scarborough, from Dover to Dumfries.

Billets in some places were just second homes.

Landladies and Barmaids, who soon got used to having rifles on the
hatstand in the hall and grenades lining the sideboard:

I was at that time a barmaid at the Queen's Hotel off the Weymouth
Station and a building next door was taken over by squads of different
regiments – the Kosbies, the Suffolks and another I can't remember.
Then there appeared a mob of slap-happy and wild men who turned
out to be quite a smashing mob. They called themselves the SS Squad,
Suicide Squad. A lot of training was done locally but once, I remember,
they all trooped into the bar and said they had to get to Cornwall
(Land's End). No money, no food, no transport. Beg, borrow or steal
and had to be back by Saturday. They left on Monday. They were back
by Friday night very excited but on their knees, all shouting, "We've
done it" – and were they glad of their beer.

I loved to see the boys wash and shave and get ready for parade and
then put their hands up the chimney and black their faces with a sooty
hand! Their favourite dinner was toad-in-the hole, mash and a tin of
baked beans mixed with a tin of tomatoes. One, Stan, spent his
honeymoon at our house and the lads soldered several bells and things
under the bed-springs for the First Night and we had a helluva job to
get them all off. They put the mattress on the floor that night. Mum was
WVS and had to look after the neighbours in air raids and the lads were
really helpful when they were there. They used to go to Lulworth Cove
and do their cliff climbing.

Ours were Army Commandos, one Irish, one a Londoner, each
wearing different hats and badges. Their standards of cleanliness were
immaculate – in dress and in their rooms. They were always armed and
they never left anything behind. They would go off in the morning and
would come back looking dishevelled and tired. They would sometimes
ask for sandwiches the night before – which was not always easy what
with the rationing. Usually spam or something like that. They walked to

and from work. They were very careful about security: when some girls asked them about their work nothing came out.

Security was, of course, of overriding importance. For example, 'A separate uniform was mooted (in 1940) but was rejected as men might be sent back to their units to rest after a raid and it was not desired to draw too much attention to them.' But there were other reasons for denying any form of special dress, as became clear in a War Office letter to DCO in June, 1941:

> The [Army] Council regrets that they are unable to agree that a special head-dress is either necessary or desirable for S.S. Units. All the men in Commandos come from units which, on average, have over 100 years' tradition behind them, and the Council feels sure that these men, so far as their personal inclinations are concerned, would certainly rather carry the badge and insignia of their own regiment than a newly-invented head-dress which appears to savour somewhat of an accoutrement of the Blackshirts.
>
> When the Commandos are actually engaged in operations the question of a uniform head-dress does not arise, as a steel helmet of a uniform pattern is already available. On the other hand, when the SS Troops are not in fighting kit, there would appear to be a considerable advantage from the security point of view in allowing the men to wear the head-dresses of their own regiments, and thus render it difficult for enemy agents or others to estimate what a particular detachment is really likely to consist of.

The CIGS's antipathy to Commandos was unrelenting. In September, 1940, he made a determined attempt to cancel the Lodging Allowance and thus do away with the privilege of living independently of barracks and camps. Keyes played the politician and successfully held out by dealing direct with the Secretary of State for War. In a letter to Eden he pointed out the triviality of the CIGS's complaints about misuse of the Allowance, saying that to remove LA would be regarded as a breach of faith and that probably the existing system was less expensive than the normal arrangements.

The War Office's attitude to weapons was also sometimes akin to its feelings about dress. Although there was general agreement over the use of the standard rifle, Bren light machine-gun, pistol and No 36 grenade, and rejection of the bow and arrow (despite its silence of operation and the effective use of one in the hands of an expert at Dunkirk in May) the selection of close-combat weapons was more debatable. For while the carrying of a fighting knife was considered sensible (and also useful for preparing food), the sub-machine gun was frowned on by many soldiers of the old school. In 1938 the Birmingham Small Arms Company pressed the War Office for an order to manufacture the Thompson sub-machine gun for which it had acquired a seven years' option from the USA. They let the option lapse upon receipt of a pompous letter saying that 'the British Army saw no need to equip itself with gangster weapons'. As a result, panic measures had to be adopted in 1940 to acquire a few of these reliable, if somewhat heavy, .45 guns with their excellent stopping power at close range.

The problem of acquiring suitable men and weapons for the Commandos was, however, as nothing to the difficulty of finding and training the sailors and airmen who would carry them to war and the craft in which they would travel. There were, indeed, few enough ships, boats and aeroplanes with which to fight, let alone for training purposes, and the reason for this could be laid squarely at the door of those who, before the war, had paid little more than lip-service to future amphibious operations. For example, almost every proposal to build mechanized landing craft was stopped by lack of funds or lack of interest.

An exercise held in 1938 at Slapton Sands showed how out-dated British methods and facilities were at a time when the Japanese had already demonstrated, in an opposed landing against the Chinese at Tientsin, a technique involving many landing craft transported to the beach area in a 10,000-ton landing-craft carrier, the entire operation supported by air power and warships. At Slapton the troops paddled ashore at night in rowing boats launched from destroyers – a technique no further advanced than that used at Gallipoli in 1915. As a summary of a paper dated 30 June, 1939, put it:

> The problems left to us in 1918, which had been only successfully solved in respect of a relatively small raid on Zeebrugge, had scarcely been touched. We had no means of putting an army ashore in face of opposition and the technical problems of a greater rate of build-up than the enemy scarcely received any attention at all.

It was therefore unrealistic, almost ludicrous, when Churchill wrote to Keyes on 25 July, 1940:

> I am hoping that you will shortly present me in outline . . . with three or four proposals for medium-sized action (i.e. between five and ten

thousand) of the kind which I mentioned to you verbally. I certainly thought we should be acting in September and October.

For there were available no personnel ships, no tank-carrying ships, just four Mechanized Landing Craft (MLC), each capable of only 7½ knots and of taking a 14-ton tank, sixteen small Assault Landing Craft (ALC), six motor boats, four punts (for use from submarines) and thirteen horse boats. As for suitable aircraft to lift the 100 parachutists under training and the 400 standing by, only a few unsuitable Whitley bombers were to be had at once and the War Office refused to allow these to be used until remedial measures were taken after two fatal accidents in July and early August.

Ambitious plans were afoot at the Prime Minister's and Keyes' urging to convert five fast ships of between 10,000 and 3,000 tons as personnel carriers; to convert two train ferries and four Turkish horse ferries to carry tanks; and to build a fleet of Tank Landing Craft, each of which could take three 40-ton tanks at 10 knots, and many assault landing craft of which a quantity were to be bought from the US. But the ship-building industry could not complete plans and set up production over-night, and, in any case, the demands on the shipyards for warships and merchant ships to replace losses, let alone to increase strength, were insatiable. No priority was given to landing craft. But at least there was then a will within the Admiralty to get things moving, and fewer serious instances of obstruction occurred there than elsewhere. According to Keyes, in a letter to Major-General Sir Hastings Ismay, Churchill's chief staff officer at the Ministry of Defence, it was not the same in the other two Service Ministries. On 27 August, listing the difficulties raised by the War Office and the Air Ministry to thwart his attempts to raise and train paratroops, he wrote:

The truth of the matter is, the Army has raised some irregular troops, but has not equipped them yet, and the War Office never lose an opportunity of expressing their disapproval of 'shock troops' in principle.

The Navy is trying to train these irregular troops and Regular Brigades, but though we have been at war for a year, it has failed to provide the ships and landing craft to prosecute amphibious warfare. It is not easy to get on with the war. I haven't bothered the Prime Minister again, as there is really nothing he can do, unless he starts afresh and gets two or three ardent offensive spirits – free from everlasting Committees – to help him do so.

Depressing though it sounded (as it most certainly was at the height of the Battle of Britain with invasion expected at any moment), the months of August and September did witness a most remarkable laying of foundations for the future. Meetings sponsored by MO9 and DCO discussed ideas and placed demands for development of a host of devices and techniques. The War Diary of Combined Operations abounds with ideas and the drive to put them into action. At one meeting the Director of Armoured Fighting Vehicles (Major-General V. V. Pope) would be laying down specifications and plans for tanks which waded and tanks which swam, ways and means of getting tanks ashore through minefields, and tanks which flew or could be carried in gliders. At another the problems of the means to transport men and equipment by air was considered. Stated MO9 on 2 August:

If airborne raids are to be carried out, operational transport will be required to lift 1,500 men. . . .

The *immediate* requirement . . . is the provision of aircraft for training parachutists. The Whitley [with its hole-on-the-floor exit] is now generally accepted as unsuitable . . . both from a psychological and an operational point of view. It is agreed that for operations a door exit is required.

A final need is for some machinery and technical establishment to develop Army air transport requirements. There is a pressing need for some progress in the problems of transporting troops, guns and AFVs by air and in landing – and sometimes evacuating – them on various surfaces by means of parachute, gliders, helicopters and normal aircraft etc.

At which point it is worth interjecting that the British were as yet unaware that the Germans had used gliders operationally in the taking of Fort Eban Emael, in Belgium, on 10 May; and that the door exit for parachutists was already leading to an imminent decision to request procurement of the latest American Douglas DC3 airliner as the most suitable for the task – the machine which would become famous as the Dakota.

This was the ideas and paper war. The real war would not wait, and Winston Churchill, for all that he was now fully aware of British inadequacy for the prosecution of amphibious operations, searched eagerly for means to prove that the lion could still roar. He soon found several bold approaches for doing so and 'setting the Staff to work'. But the medium raids policy introduced fundamental problems which Churchill cannot possibly have foreseen – and these, to a large extent, were counter-productive and, would be damaging to almost everybody connected with Combined Operations in the autumn of 1940.

CHAPTER 5

From TOMATO to DUDLEY –
The Winter of Frustration

Desperate as the British situation appeared, the Prime Minister was ever ready to divert forces from defence if it could be shown that offensive action, even on the periphery of the European battle area, would contribute to survival and to building up confidence in Britain abroad, above all in the US. Ultimate survival would depend upon keeping the sea-lanes open, particularly those connecting Britain with the east, either via the Mediterranean or round the Cape of Good Hope, which became all the more difficult when Italy entered the war on the Axis side on 10 June. Operations designed to guard or open up convoy routes thus came to be regarded with particular favour – such as occupying the Spanish Canary Islands, the Portuguese Azores and the French West African colonies which lay across the route to the Cape and might easily fall into Axis hands. Simultaneously, the examination of ways to keep the Mediterranean open led to consideration of hitting Italy hard enough to ensure her collapse.

On 23 June the first of a series of concurrent and conflicting plans aimed at one or other of the peripheral objectives was set in motion, a process which, ironically, was to stultify Combined Operations for well over a year. Fearing that the Germans, 'with Spanish connivance', might fly troops to the Azores, the Chiefs of Staff Committee initiated Operation ALLOY, later known as BRISK, as a means of pre-empting any attempt to violate the soil of Portugal, Britains' oldest ally. Next came Operation SHRAPNEL, later re-named PILGRIM (and still later to acquire a subsidiary title, PUMA), aimed at seizing the Canaries from Spain if Spain took Gibraltar. Each of these operations was in competition with the other because they drew on the same meagre force of battleships, aircraft carriers, cruisers and destroyers of the Royal Navy, then deployed at Gibraltar and off West Africa, but tasked to fight at any moment in the

Mediterranean or in the English Channel if the Germans invaded. The only troops available at once belonged to Force 101, consisting of the Royal Marine Brigade, No 10 Independent Company and maybe four Commandos, all to be carried in five ships (when they were ready in mid-August) and put ashore by dribs and drabs in fifteen assorted mechanized landing craft and rowing boats.

But as BRISK and SHRAPNEL were gradually developed on paper and repeatedly postponed in the pious hopes that Spain would resist Hitler's overtures to share the loot with Germany and Italy, an opportunity to strengthen the West African route by seizing the important French port of Dakar presented itself.

When the Vichy French Government signed an Armistice with Germany in June, General Charles de Gaulle raised his standard under the name of Free France and gathered round him the few among his nation who wished to continue the struggle against Germany. A few days later the French people and Government were antagonized when the British neutralized or attacked those parts of their Fleet which would not join the Free French. The heavy loss of life and destruction of French ships almost drove France into Germany's arms. The Vichy French Government passed sentences of death on de Gaulle and made plain that attempts to take over French territory, at home or abroad, would be resisted.

De Gaulle, for his part, aimed to seize as much overseas territory as possible, and high on his list was the port of Dakar in West Africa, where lay important elements of the French Fleet. He suggested the operation (then named SCIPIO) to Churchill in July and at the beginning of August serious consideration was given to the project (now named MENACE) by the Inter-Services Planning Staff and accorded first priority. The forces being gathered for ALLOY/BRISK or SHRAPNEL/PILGRIM were ear-marked for MENACE, which was approved by the Chiefs of Staff on 21 August, without much consultation, it seems, with DCO. The story of this mis-managed operation, which was to end in failure on 25 September, need only be considered here in respect of the methods employed and its bearing upon the future of Combined Operations. Whichever way one looked at it, chaos was beginning to reign supreme due to lack of firm co-ordination from the top.

There was a difference of opinion between the First Sea Lord (Pound) and the CIGS (Dill) as to who should command. The Navy insisted it was their prerogative, as of tradition, but the Army won the argument on practical grounds, since a sailor at sea could not control a battle on land. When it came to the crunch, there was no land battle because the French resisted doggedly with ships and coastal artillery, the latter having the upper hand, as had so often been the case in the past, most recently at Gallipoli in 1915. So no attempt was made to put Free French troops, the Marine Brigade or No 10 Independent Company ashore. Which was, perhaps, as well. For one thing fire control was tenuous and, at a crucial moment, the Military Force Commander (Major-General N. M. Irwin) was arbitrarily removed from the scene when the cruiser *Devonshire*, in which he was sailing, was whisked away on a purely naval occasion to engage the French Battle Squadron. And, for another, the dire shortage of mechanized landing craft would have seriously handicapped the assault forces. The fifteen ALCs and two MLCs were quite insufficient to lift the entire force ashore at once in the first flight and then allow a quick follow-up by strong reserves. It was therefore proposed that three ALCs should carry in a company in the first flight; three ALCs towing seven lifeboats would bring in the second flight, consisting of the Construction Company and the Beach Detachment; five ALCs and fourteen lifeboats would carry the marines in the third flight. Three ALCs and three lifeboats would carry Brigade Headquarters and the infantry's carriers would be ferried ashore piecemeal by the MLCs.

How badly they would have fared has to be left to the imagination, particularly since the preparations had been so rushed that only four days' training of the assault force was possible before it sailed from Britain. Security, too, was lax, particularly in respect of the Free French Forces, some of whose officers had been heard talking carelessly in public in England about where they were going, a lapse which probably did not actually jeopardize the operation but which sowed seeds of suspicion of the French. Such mistrust was frequently to bedevil joint operations with de Gaulle's Free French. In conclusion, MENACE prompted an immediate re-appraisal of the ships and assault craft needed in the future.

Of crucial import was the post-operational opinion of MENACE's Military Force Commander, who pointed out: 'There is a need for a central organization to co-ordinate combined operation,' adding the suggestion, instantly seized upon by Keyes, that DCO's staff should form the nucleus of such a headquarters. After discussion, the War Office produced on 12 October a revised Draft Directive to DCO which bore, in fact, a pronounced resemblance to the original version of June and did not satisfy Keyes. The next six months would be spent by committees in a struggle radically to re-draft an out-moded concept. In the meantime Keyes would have to battle on under the initial directive (modified by the 5–10,000-man codicil and the embargo on small raids) and suffering from what he took to be deliberate obstruction by individuals and the three Service Ministries.

In the aftermath of MENACE, the Marine Brigade was retained in Freetown, Sierra Leone, poised to land either on the Azores or the Canaries, or to partake in a yet another new project, the attempt to seize the Italian island of Pantelleria in the central Mediterranean – Operation WORKSHOP. In the meantime two other fairly large-scale operations were being studied by the planners. On 24 July they looked at CHURCH – a proposal to send a force of brigade strength up a ten-mile fjord to destroy the port at Petsamo from which Finnish iron ore and nickel was exported to Germany. Lack of suitable ships was, as usual at this time, the insurmountable obstacle, but the risks of enemy interception were also high and the game was thought not worth the candle. Early in September Churchill put forward yet another new idea of his own, under the name of Operation TOMATO, to 'destroy or make prisoner all the enemy in the Channel Islands'. Fantastic as it may seem – and remembering that there were no special landing craft available, that all crash boats were in use for saving airmen, that there was a singular lack of reliable intelligence and no way of providing continuous fighter cover at extreme range – the plan was given careful study, probably in order to placate the Prime Minister.

'In favour,' decided the planners. 'It would provide a moral fillip in England. . . . Against is the main fact that if we occupy the islands for twenty hours and then abandon them, the repercussions will affect the local population who were abandoned in the first instance and are to be abandoned again' – a valid and recurring point in the years to come.

TOMATO was pushed aside and the DCO was left to concentrate on projects which were every bit as risky but more likely to be actuated, since they promised, if successful, to alter the course of the war. Ambition knew no bounds in Richmond Terrace. The central object was nothing less than knocking Italy, Germany's weakest ally, out of the war, or, at least, creating a situation which would deflect the Germans from whatever else they intended to do in 1941 – probably the assault on Britain or, maybe (as was already suggested by intelligence sources) the invasion of Russia. Italy looked vulnerable. In the Middle East and East Africa attempts by the Italian Army to invade adjoining territories had been checked or thrown back. At sea her Fleet was getting the worst of it, to the extent that the besieged island of Malta was holding out strongly and the passage of the Mediterranean was still a reasonably safe operation for strongly escorted British convoys. Tempted by so many indications of frailty, Churchill's mind turned to an attack on the Italians. It is, perhaps, worth pointing out that many of Churchill's ideas were sparked off by midnight conversations with the semi-official Kitchen Cabinet he had gathered round him in his Wilderness Days – such controversial and, at times, eccentric figures as Professor Lindemann, Major Morton and Sir Roger Keyes himself. Each morning a fresh flurry of directives and 'prayers' ('Pray tell me . . .') would be dictated.

> In September [Keyes wrote] the Prime Minister asked me if I had ever considered the possibility of capturing the Island now known as WORKSHOP [Pantelleria] . . . [Not until early in November did the Chiefs of Staff consider this proposition in relation to others against the Dodecanese then] but declared their preference to WORKSHOP . . . In spite of this approval the J.P.S. [Joint Planning Staff] and E.P.S. [Executive Planning Staff] raised every possible objection and persistently derided the operation to my staff, declaring that strategically it would have no effect on the conduct of the war and did not fit in with the War Plan: operationally it was hazardous; it would be quite impossible to land a second flight of troops, and they condemned generally my views to my staff.

Resistance was maintained by the planners who preferred BRISK and who allocated more and more troops, including four Commandos and the Marine Brigade, to it. When Keyes told the Prime Minister of the delays, Churchill summoned a meeting of all three Defence Ministers and the Chiefs of Staff at which 'my proposal was unanimously approved and the Prime Minister told me that he wished me to command the operation' – a request which originated from Keyes himself.

But still the Central Staffs resisted, throwing up a barrage of valid objections on the lines that it must not prevent BRISK, that it was a risky operation, and that, even if successful it would create the need to garrison the island with forces which could not be spared. Throughout December the arguments raged and the Chiefs of Staff vacillated, withdrawing their original approval and supporting their planners in castigating Keyes' outline plan as 'immature and sketchy'. To which Keyes retorted that he did not expect 'to be criticized by the comparatively junior staff officers, who I knew were responsible for making these suggestions to the Chiefs of Staff'. One day the operation would be 'on', with the ships loaded at Lamlash in Scotland; the next it would be 'off', due to objections, bad weather or a mechanical breakdown in one of the ships. Early in January, when WORKSHOP, in the light of Italy's defeats in Cyrenaica, East Africa and Albania, might well have stood a chance, Pound, as Chief of Naval Staff, declared that no convoy would pass through the Mediterranean that month. WORKSHOP would have to be postponed until February, but by then it would be too late. A German air corps moved into Sicily and demonstrated by some extremely accurate dive-bombing that the passage of the narrow seas would, henceforward, be a hazardous undertaking, thus giving notice to Keyes and the Chiefs of Staff that WORKSHOP was off.

So BRISK and PILGRIM reassumed their priority while the staffs and their Chiefs haggled and the sailors and soldiers did what they could with inadequate resources to develop landing techniques. WORKSHOP's chances of success belong to the realms of conjecture, but conjecture is always fascinating. What might have happened if Operation DUDLEY (sometimes known as 'The Roman Holiday Plan') had come off? Designed by DCO's Captain Garnons-Williams and dated 21 October, 1940, its aim was 'To punch Italy out of the war by the capture of Rome' in early February. Ironically it received a measure of encouragement from those who denigrated the more practical WORKSHOP. A very detailed scheme was prepared with the idea of landing 5,000 Commandos and a handful of tanks in the ships allocated to WORKSHOP at the Lido de Roma to 'capture the city, Government, Broadcasting Centres and Mussolini'. The stakes, as the proposal admitted, 'were the loss of 5,000 men and perhaps the ship against the chance of knocking Italy out of the war.'

There is an air of compulsive realism about this hardly known and inspired gamble which commands respect in hindsight , even though its ultimate scope was probably unattainable – 'Sudden paralysis of her (Italy's) vital nerve centre, followed by a week of concentrated offensives against her national morale, in the hope that in this period she can be induced to accept armistice terms,' – because, no matter how the Italians behaved, it was unlikely the Germans would have stood by and done nothing. It might well have been possible for each carefully schemed phase of the operation to make headway – the approach by sea; the air bombardment and Fifth Column work in Rome the night before the attack; the dawn landing and rapid advance of seventeen miles to the centre of Rome; the neutralization of the garrison, allied to the capture of the centres of Government and its communications; the occupation of a 'keep' in the centre of Rome and its defence during a period of intensive attacks upon morale. Certainly the prospects of the Mediterranean Fleet and Force 'H', reinforced, engaging the main Italian Forces, were mightily enhanced for, as Garnons-Williams suggested: 'Not even the Italian Navy could lie down under an attack on Rome.'

It is, however, worth quoting the remarks of Major-General M. B.

Burrow, the Military Attaché in Rome until May, 1940. He thought
DUDLEY had 'great chances of success', but as a far-reaching blow to
Italian morale was 'more doubtful of it', arguing that, 'if the 5,000
troops were ultimately captured, at the expense to Rome of a few
damaged buildings, the affair might well be presented as a "harebrained
British scheme" and "a victory for Italy". 'He also envisaged problems in
capturing Mussolini, who might not be at his home or office (as assumed)
but 'probably busy with a light-of-love elsewhere in the city at the time
of the raid'.

Of course, the arrival of the Germans in the central Mediterranean and
the imminent despatch of the Afrika Korps to North Africa to help
retrieve the Axis situation there put paid to DUDLEY just as it put paid to
WORKSHOP. Nor was there to be action for BRISK or PILGRIM. The
march of events, coupled with disagreements and intrigue in London, led
to a winter of frustration for the Special Forces. It was no consolation to
volunteers whose main desire was to fight an irregular war at once to
discover that, bit by bit, they were being reformed by the War Office into
something which looked remarkably regular. For in November the loose
collection of individual Commandos were grouped into the Special
Services Brigade of five battalions, each of two Commandos, commanded
by Brigadier J. C. Haydon. Nor did an increase in strength of two
additional Commandos placate those who found themselves on anti-
invasion duties, filling sandbags and looking out to sea for an enemy who
had failed to appear. A regime of intensive training, broken by false alarms
of impending battle, was mightily discouraging to the eager in spirit. This
was a time when a few Commandos began to earn themselves a bad
reputation, occasionally appearing in the Civil Courts after brawls with
civilians and men from other units, and, more damaging, when enthusiasm began to flag and standards of performance slip.

Inaction was also most discouraging to Keyes and his staff, who not only
found themselves prevented from going to war but also the target of a
growing series of attempts to disband the Commandos and the Combined
Operations Directorate along with them. Yet, as the internecine departmental war was waged with increasing bitterness, Admiralty and War
Office were steadily assembling the craft and resources which would
divert energy from internal squabbles and towards action against the real
enemy.

CHAPTER 6

The Shadow of Abolition

Immediately after the collapse of Operation MENACE the Prime Minister called a conference with DCO and the Admiralty to give urgent consideration to the ocean-going ships that were bound to be needed to land large numbers of tanks and heavy equipment directly on an enemy shore after a long sea voyage – a requirement which, Churchill stated, would 'constantly recur and no offensive would be possible until it was solved'. Told to produce, as a matter of urgency, what were later known as Landing Ships Tanks (LST), the Director of Naval Construction (DNC) was obliged to start from scratch upon what were known at first as 'Winettes' while casting around for some ready-to-hand ships for conversion. Three light, shallow-draught oil tankers which had been specially designed to cross the bar of the Maracaibo River in South America were selected and made ready by June, 1941, but they proved unseaworthy in bad weather, had a fault in their bow doors and could only land tanks on very steep beaches.

In the months to come DCO and, to a greater extent the Inter-Services Training and Development Centre (ISTDC), which had been set up in 1938, drafted the specifications for many different types of landing ship, landing craft and special devices which, it was envisaged, would be needed for raiding and, later on, major invasions. Principal among these were:

Landing Craft Tank (LCT) – a ramped, flat-bottomed craft designed to carry three or four tanks in an open hold at 10 knots, the first of which was completed in November, 1940, and an order for 200 placed in April, 1941.

Landing Ships Infantry (LSI) – converted merchant ships to carry Landing Craft Assault (LCA) and soldiers to the operations area at a range of 1000 miles. The first of these were the three Glen ships and two Dutch cross-Channel steamers which were used during MENACE.

Landing Craft Infantry (LCI) – a smaller type of LSI capable of ocean-going and direct beach-landing and not as vulnerable as its big sisters.

Landing Craft Mechanised (LCM) – (some partly armoured) capable of landing a light tank or a platoon of infantry on a beach, with a speed of about 10 knots.

Landing Craft Assault (LCA) – a partly-armoured ramped craft of low silhouette, with a speed of 10 knots, capable of beach-landing 35 men.

Landing Craft Personnel (LCP)* – of which there were several versions designed specifically for raiding. The first, and perhaps most celebrated was the Eureka, designed in 1926 by a brilliant American, Andrew Higgins, for use by trappers and oil drillers and alleged, with its high speed of 20 knots, to have been used by rum-runners off the coast of Florida. Without a ramp, unarmoured and rather noisy, until silencers were fitted, they proved magnificent sea boats and were capable of jumping a bar or a submerged log. They had, moreover, been adopted by the US Marine Corps after exhaustive tests in 1938 and 1939.

From the outset it was realized that the lack of surplus shipbuilding capacity in Britain made it inevitable that the vast majority of all types of landing craft would have to come from the USA. The initial order for fifty Eurekas was but the first of hundreds of all classes. It represented in addition to construction of aircraft, the first major involvement of the US in Combined Operations in a war which, as 1941 advanced and the Japanese became more bellicose, it became increasingly obvious she could not avoid. With their eyes fixed anxiously on the Far East and the Pacific, the military authorities, particularly the Navy and the Marine Corps, were only too pleased to exchange views and experience with the British and, with characteristic vigour, exploit the lessons learnt. The extent of this collaboration will be seen later.

To train, maintain and develop a vast new fleet and the paraphernalia of equipment related to combined operations, an equally enormous growth in shore establishments had also to take place. At Inverary on Loch Fyne in Scotland the first Combined Training Centre (CTC) was opened in August, 1940. Here the landing craft flotillas could carry out joint training with the Army on a large scale. Thereafter, all round the coast of the

---

* Henceforward I adopt the abbreviations used for landing craft later in the war, although until 1943 LCT were known as TLCs, LCMs as MLCs, LCAs as ALCs, and so on.

British Isles, but mainly in Western Scotland, East Anglia and along the South Coast, there sprang up scores of bases to house a plethora of organizations which came into being to satisfy the rapidly expanding demands of amphibious warfare. Revised operational requirements called for new techniques and new technology which had to be controlled and run by people who had first to be recruited and trained. Hand in hand with this routine had to go a constant critical analysis of lessons learnt on exercises and in battle, which, in turn, would generate fresh demands for experiments, trials or radical changes of organization, machinery and methods. With such resounding names as HMS *James Cook*, *Brontosaurus*, *Squid*, *Newt*, *Arbella* and *Haig*, they played the essential back-stage role in creating the forces which would raid and eventually invade on an unprecedented scale. To the raiding forces the Raiding Training Centre at Warshash, Hants (*Tormentor*), the Parent Ship of Raiding Craft Flotillas at Brightlingsea, Essex (*Helder*), the Tank Landing Craft training Base at Bo'ness (*Stopford*) and the Special Training Establishment at Acharacle, (*Dorlin*) were to become the most familiar. But to Commandos nothing was more celebrated, respected or dreaded, than their own training centre, opened in 1940 at Achnacarry on Loch Eil, which was to become their Depot under the command of a very tough and thorough officer of the Royal East Kent Regiment (The Buffs) called Lt-Col C. E. Vaughan.

Around Achnacarry Castle there grew a legend which Vaughan, with his uncompromising enforcement of rigorous, almost brutal training methods, single-mindedly fostered in order to give the Commandos the edge over their equally professional enemies. It was a means to 'be cruel to be kind' in order to enhance each soldier's chances of ultimate survival. It was perfectly correct to say, as did one Commando, that, 'It was all normal infantry training, but just a little harder, a little tougher.' Throughout the Army, notably at the Infantry Battle Training School at Barnard Castle in County Durham, the principle of training hard under realistically simulated battle conditions was adopted. Live ammunition was preferred to blank, the men manoeuvering while bullets kicked up around them or zipped close overhead. At any of the schools being wet, cold, uncomfortable, frightened and exhausted was the rule rather than the exception, a state of misery which extended to hours spent in tents between exercises, even in deep midwinter. Assault courses were of the most physically exacting, cross-country movement over the coldest streams, through the stickiest bogs or up the steepest slopes and cliffs, by day and night, come what may, in all kinds of weather. But when the normal infantry instructors decided to call a halt, there was a tendency on the part of their

Commando cousins to call for one additional effort – and then march back to camp and be expected to have every item of kit spotlessly clean with badges and brasses as bright as a new pin.

Some 25,000 men experienced the Achnacarry course throughout the war, the new arrivals reading the epitaphs on mock tombstones lined up at the entrance, each relating lapses which had brought about the early demise of some imaginary Commando allegedly buried beneath: 'He failed to keep his head down'; 'He failed to shoot first', and so on. In the end some forty occupied real graves as a result of training accidents and the exacting conditions which total war alone justified. Of course, there were those who 'could not take it' and their fate demonstrated one of the marginal differences between a Line infantryman and a Commando. The former might live it down without loss of pride; the Commando never, since, for him, failure meant Return to Unit (RTU), the ultimate disgrace, which was also the principal means of enforcing discipline among a military élite which imposed self-discipline and made minimum use of the Army Act.

Commandos, nevertheless, represented only a small proportion of the number of troops put through the mill of Combined Operations training. Making the point that conventional Field Force units would, as often as not, bear the brunt of assault from the sea when the time (and the equipment) for major operations arrived, the Admiralty and War Office collaborated to send 1st Guards Brigade on a two-day exercise at Inveraray in February, landing them from LSIs in some twenty LCMs and thirty-six LCAs of the latest production, and ferrying their guns and vehicles ashore afterwards. In bitter cold the lessons of beach traffic control and logistic support were drummed home, in addition to learning the hard way how to get in and out of boats from ship to shore. In March the tempo of training increased when the Marine Brigade was brought back from Sierra Leone to begin a long stint at Inveraray with the Navy, developing the techniques of sailing landing craft in formation, fire support, communications, beach control and a hundred and one other subjects. Then came the divisions which one day would lead the assault in North Africa and back into Europe – 4th Division, 3rd Division, 6th Armoured Division, the Canadians, Americans and many more.

What was being demonstrated was the clear distinction in amphibious operations between a major invasion by regular formations, whose every intention was to stay ashore and hold ground, and hit and run raids by Commandos. And since the latter, through Churchill's decree, were being denied the opportunity to take part in small raids, and frustrated when allotted to larger operations, there existed a strong feeling in

Whitehall that they might just as well be disbanded. It was against this backwash that the revision of DCO's Directive, in the aftermath of MENACE, took place.

CHAPTER 7

New Directive, Change of Direction

General Irwin can hardly have guessed at the cat he was putting among the pigeons when, in his MENACE report, he recommended the need for DCO to form a centralized organization to control combined operations. Nor can Keyes have imagined the furore which would inflame the debate about revision of his Directive. For the arch-opponents of the Combined Operations Directorate and its leader – not just the Commandos, upon whom, historians have concentrated in the past – now swarmed purposefully to bring about their destruction. At the head of the Philistines stood Captain Maund who, according to Keyes in a well documented series of papers he assembled on the subject, resented Keyes' strictures on the amphibious campaign in Norway. The matter came to a head when, again according to Keyes, Maund:

> was responsible for circulating in the Admiralty, and secretly in my office . . . a paper suggesting that my Directorate was redundant and should be abolished, and recommending that he should be the authority on combined operations at the Admiralty.

It went without saying that when, in January, the paper at last came to Keyes' notice, the Director exploded, told Maund exactly what he thought of him and reported him to the Vice Chief of Naval Staff (VCNS):

'Having been found out, he applied to go to sea, and although the CNS told me later that he had been well scrubbed, he was actually rewarded by being given the command of the *Ark Royal*', which meant he was sent to Gibraltar where he continued to conspire in high places against Keyes and, in particular, Keyes' influence with the Prime Minister.

In fairness to Maund, his motives, however mischievous they may appear, were full of good intentions. He sincerely believed that the

Directorate of Combined Operations was a cause of friction which should be removed in order to allow the existing organizations to function as of old. The paper suggesting this on 11 December, 1940, was not only most ably argued but also clearly the work of numerous other people in several departments who shared Maund's opinion. Fundamentally, the paper argued in favour of 'a clear and natural system' in which every function – operational, technical, training and administrative – connected with Combined Operations was taken care of either by the Admiralty, the War Office or by one of the various establishments springing up all round the country from Achnacarry to the South Coast. It was, no doubt, embarrassing, so far as Keyes was concerned, in its timing, in that he was away in Scotland training the WORKSHOP force. On the other hand, it was not unreasonable to expect Keyes to remain close to the centre instead of oscillating backwards and forwards in pursuit of command in battle which could well have been left to somebody less senior. But then Keyes did have an ultra ego which persuaded him that he alone knew about combined operations.

Keyes should have been aware that much was in course of change among the Armed Forces at that moment, and not confined to Combined Operations. For example, there was a controversial proposal under consideration by the Prime Minister, the CIGS and the GOC-in-C Home Forces (Brooke) to create an armoured army, led by a commander with a seat on the Army Council, which, in effect, would have produced an army within the Army. This, and all off-centre proposals, CIGS and GOC-in-C were successfully resisting, while making moves to take over the infant airborne troops who, some 500 in number, were still Commandos and therefore under DCO control. For, if Dill and Brooke held strong reservations about Commandos, they were extremely enthusiastic about the Airborne Forces at a time when the parachutists were nearly ready for their first operation, and there existed a strong body of opinion which favoured the mass landing of airborne troops and equipment by glider.

Simultaneously attempts were being made to clarify the lines of demarcation between Admiralty, Intelligence, Combined Operations and SOE, with particular reference to raiding. Although an informal arrangement was made at a meeting on 16 December, 1940, between the interested parties 'that SOE would handle small raids, say up to thirty men, and all raids far behind the coastline,' while COHQ would handle the rest, this, due to impracticability, was never implemented. But the Intelligence people were 'against Raiding Parties, as they might interfere with their organization for getting agents into occupied territory'. This was a crucial matter. The contentious Admiralty paper of 11 December also touched on the demarcation issue, pointing out that 'the area in which DCO can raid is not defined' and that 'the execution of any raid is given to one of the Home Commanders-in-Chief to carry out'.

The clash of interests and granting of 'licences to raid' would not be resolved for many months, but airing the subject at this sensitive moment in the life of the Directoriate of Combined Operations re-emphasized the urgent necessity to redefine responsibilities if any form of raiding was to be approved, let alone activated. Yet logical as Maund's views appeared, they failed to specify how, or by whom, the wrangles between Ministries and Departments were to be resolved expeditiously without allowing urgent operational matters to become bogged down in committees.

To cut a long and somewhat murky story short, a new Directive was promulgated on 14 March as the result of negotiation and strong intervention by Churchill in response to Keyes' pleading, along the lines of his letter of 2 February:

> I know you meant me well and intended that my unique experience in combined operations should be made use of. . . . I am very grateful to you for your effort to employ me. I really have been very patient and done my best to work with the Naval Staff. They and their committees made it quite impossible and my position is intolerable.

Keyes won – for the time being. The intention of the Chiefs of Staff that DCO should be restricted to organizing training of amphibian forces was set aside; now DCO had increased responsibility and power to include surveillance and authority over the entire range of Combined Operations with the exclusion of airborne forces.

These, on 27 March, were taken away from the Commandos to emerge as a separate parachute unit, under War Office control. At the same time the redundant Commando 'battalions' were abolished. Keyes, eager for personal action and the operational employment of 'my amphibian force', was well satisfied by the saving of the Commandos and the sub-paragraph which specified his task for:

> The initiation . . . and the planning and execution of operations by the Special Service Troops, reinforced if necessary by small forces – naval, military and air – which are not normally under his command,

along with the provision that assistance from the Joint Planning Staff should be given. Raids involving up to 5,000 men were those the Prime Minister had in mind, and that:

The general policy for raiding operations will be laid down from time to time by the Chiefs of Staff in accordance with the direction of the Prime Minister and Minister of Defence.

The way looked clear for raiding to prosper. It had been decided to send three Commandos (7, 8, and 11) in the Glen LSIs to the Middle East under Brigadier R. E. Laycock. These, DCO assumed, would stand a better chance of employment there since the GOC-in-C Middle East, General Sir Archibald Wavell, was reputed to encourage irregular forces of the sort then operating in the desert and in East Africa – the forerunners, in fact, of all raiders in that part of the world. Soon Layforce was in business. 7 Commando staged a raid against the port of Bardia on 19/20 April, but the operation miscarried; a Folbot canoe (Capt R. J. Courtney) belonging to the Small Boats Section (see below), which was meant to paddle ashore from a submarine and guide the Commandos in, was damaged on launching and unable to fix its guiding lights; LCAs were delayed in launching from the LSI; only slight damage was inflicted on the enemy; there were accidental casualties and loss of men who failed to find the re-embarkation point and were taken prisoner. Even more damaging to the Commando reputation, the largely inexperienced men 'halted or lay down as soon as fire was opened' and did not press on with their task with the boldness expected of them.

Almost at once the dismemberment of Laycock's brigade began. At a time when the threat to the Middle East was great and the forces to hold it meagre, 11 Commando was sent to reinforce the garrison in Cyprus and 7 and 8 to Crete, where they were soon heavily embroiled in the massive German airborne invasion and, fighting as ordinary infantry, roughly handled during the retreat and evacuation from the island. 11 Commando was then sent to Palestine and committed to a seaborne landing against a defended, surf-swept beach in the rear of determined Vichy French forces, defending the frontier of Syria, when the British opted to eliminate German influence in that strategically important country. Pitched untidily into a battle which was intense from the beginning and in which the lack of heavy support weapons was a severe handicap, the Commandos lost 123 men. From this moment the run-down and dispersal of the force was accelerated, although the leaders of 8 Commando managed to persuade the authorities to send them to besieged Tobruk for raiding and garrison duties which they performed with success and laid the foundations of what would become L Section, later known as the Special Air Service (SAS). The rest drifted into disbandment, many finding their way to regular fighting units, a select few eventually joining the other small raiding units which were then in course of assembly under local arrangements in the Suez Canal Zone.

Underestimated at the time, the attachment to 8 Commando of Capt R. J. Courtney's Small Boat Section (SBS) led the way to a revolution in raiding, despite the setback at Bardia. SBS had been brought into being the previous July as the result of a letter from Lieut (E) G. M. D. Wright RN, of HM submarine *Triumph*, to Captain (S), 2nd Submarine Flotilla, drawing his attention to a Folbot collapsible canoe's capacity to carry, in addition to two men, a load of 200–400 pounds (i.e. 160–320 1¼lb demolition charges). 'Supposing that, in suitable conditions, a canoe so loaded were sent from a submarine into a harbour where enemy ships were suspected of lying, I believe considerable damage could be done.'

He went on to state the advantages possessed by such a canoe – complete silence, low silhouette, easy manoeuverability, seaworthiness and a speed of 4 knots sustained for over an hour by a man in training. He added that, as a member of the Royal Ocean Racing Club with considerable experience with canoes, besides practice with demolitions, he was well qualified to volunteer for such an undertaking.

Without hesitation Keyes formed a Special Boat Section within the Commandos under Courtney. Early trials were severely hampered by the Folbot Company whose products were badly made from inferior materials and often late in delivery. The firm shortly went out of business. An attempt in November to land on the Dutch coast in canoes launched from MTBs was abortive, Courtney coming to the conclusion that 'a submarine was a more suitable craft from which to operate Folbots'. Two officers and men of the section arrived in the Middle East in February, fit and full of enthusiasm, but lacking official support for the three tasks that seemed most appropriate to canoes – reconnaissance, pilotage of raiding craft and attacks on shipping in harbour. Practical experiments against the enemy were essential. Teamed with Courtney was Lt-Cdr N. Clogstoun-Willmot RN, a GHQ planner and the navigating officer designate for a proposed raid on the island of Rhodes. His initial study of beaches through a submarine's periscopes was deemed insufficient, so at the end of March he and Courtney, over a period of three days, made the first beach reconnaissance from the submarine *Triumph*, taking it in turns to swim ashore to obtain samples of the shingle, locate rocks, check gradients, note surf and, incidentally, find out how thinly guarded certain stretches of coast were, on one occasion landing in front of the main hotel. They discovered, too, how difficult it could be for a man who had swum ashore to regain contact with the canoe and for the canoe to find the submarine again.

·The main lesson we learnt was that people not expecting attack keep very poor watch. The only troublesome incident was a dog, which followed me up and down on one side of a wire fence, I being the other. He growled at me but did not bark.

Next came the fiasco at Bardia, which nevertheless proved that pilotage was feasible, followed in May by a successful limpet attack on a merchant ship in Benghazi harbour by Sergeant Allen and Marine Miles. They entered the harbour in their canoe, attached their limpet mines to a ship, which later sank, but unfortunately holed their canoe on broken masonry when on the way out and were captured. Between May and December various operations were carried out. The majority were for reconnaissance purposes among the Greek Islands and along the North African shore and a few against the Italian mainland from Malta, in one of which Capt Wilson and Lt Scolfield blew up bridges and wrecked trains. As an illustration of the initiative of the sort of high-grade soldier to be found in the SBS, L-Cpl Bremner, of the London Scottish, made contact in Crete with 200 Australian soldiers who had been left behind and arranged their escape, the men being pulled to three submarines through the water by grass line.

Not every SBS venture was a success and some men were lost on reconnaissance. An attempt on 7 June by Courtney to blow up an Italian fort at El Brega was foiled by native levies whose work as shepherds made them better watchmen than Italian soldiers. But by the time Courtney returned to England in December, 1941, his original force had expanded greatly and was poised to strike from submarines anywhere throughout the Mediterranean. In the process they had carried out in 1941 more individual operations than the entire Combined Operations organization in England.

CHAPTER 8
Trend Setters

Notwithstanding the embargo on small raids, many proposals continued to be made through DCO and the Planning Committees. Preparations for the three most important ones, moreover, were approved by Churchill and Keyes before the wrangle over DCO's Directive was settled – two with strategic aims, one, on the face of it, tactical.

Operation COLOSSUS was experimental in nearly every sense. It was to be the first airborne raid, directed from England against an aqueduct over the Tragino torrent near Calitri, on the ankle of Italy. Its object was to create a serious interruption in the water supply of two million people, including the naval base at Taranto and the ports of Brindisi and Bari, through which supplies passed to the Italian Army under heavy pressure from the Greek Army in Albania. The assault party was to be thirty-eight strong, drawn from the 500 trained parachutists, every one of whom volunteered to go, despite being told there was 'little chance of extraction'. In command was Major T. A. G. Pritchard. Included were three inter-preters, one of whom was a waiter at the Savoy, an Italian national who was well aware of the extreme risk he was taking. Eight Whitley bombers were allocated to the operation, six to lift the men and supplies and the others to carry out a diversionary bombing operation over Calabria. They flew from England on 7 February and staged at Malta prior to attacking on the 10th. The five Whitleys which managed to find the target dropped their loads between 50 and 250 yards of it at 2142 hours, but the sixth suffered from technical difficulties and eventually dropped its party two hours later some two miles to the north.

There was no opposition, only twenty-four peasants and children who were rounded up and kept under guard until the men were 'persuaded' to carry the explosives from where they had landed some three-quarters of a mile to the objective. Examination of the aqueduct revealed that the centre pier was made of reinforced concrete, not brick as expected, but by midnight enough explosive had been accumulated not only to blow one of the side piers, but also a little bridge over the Ginestra stream as a way of hampering repairs to the aqueduct and 'for the fun of the thing', as Lieutenant A. J. Deane-Drummond admitted. When the charges were blown at 0030 hours the result was spectacular. The aqueduct collapsed and water flooded down the ravine. 'Large lumps of concrete and rail from the Ginestra bridge fell round Deane-Drummond and L/Cpl Watson who had not got far enough away, and rained down on the roof of the building where the women and children were shut in. The roof held and, though frightened, none were hurt. Deane-Drummond confesses that he had forgotten about them when he decided to blow the bridge.'

That was the high point of their adventure. From now on it was downhill all the way, since the plan for the submarine *Triumph*, which was detailed to wait for them fifty miles away in the mouth of the River Sele, had been cancelled because one of the Whitley bombers had unwittingly chosen this very place to make a forced landing due to engine failure. Inevitably the scene would be alive with Italians examining the wreck. In any case Pritchard and his men failed to reach the rendezvous. Within thirty-six hours of landing they had all been captured and, in due course, the brave Italian waiter was be court-martialled and shot. As for the effect of the raid, it was negligible in so far as the war in Albania was concerned. Repair took about a month and the local reservoirs lasted out that period. To quote the final report:

'It did, however, spread great alarm in Southern Italy and caused a large amount of serious effort to be wasted on more stringent air-raid precautions and on unnecessary guards.' Coming as it did on the heels of the destruction of the Italian Army in Cyrenaica, it had a further effect on Italian morale, while that of the British received a further boost, as usually was the case when raids were carried out with success and then well publicised.

Operation CLAYMORE had, on the other hand, 'an object mainly economic, partly political and only in a very remote degree military.' It was the only successful candidate among several rejected by the Prime Minister in January, 1941, for a raid on Norway. The intention was 'to descend simultaneously on four ports in the Lofoten Islands . . . with the object of destroying the herring and cod oil factories' which provided ingredients required by the German munitions industry and for the nutrition of their people. Maybe it was overlooked that the people of the occupied territories were invariably the first to be deprived by the occupying power of anything in short supply, but, after all, it was almost impossible to carry out any operation against the Germans without friendly folk being harmed in some way or another, as subsequent events would emphasize.

With 4 March as the target date, plans were laid in February for a naval force, under Captain C. Caslon, consisting of five destroyers and a submarine escorting two LSIs (converted Dutch cross-Channel steamers) carrying 3 and 4 Commandos, the Sappers of 55th Field Squadron RE and fifty-two Norwegian soldiers (the land force under Brigadier J. C. Haydon) to carry out the raid. It would be supported at a distance by units of the Home Fleet and was to be, as Keyes remarked, 'a naval occasion' – a prediction admirably justified in the event since the only shots fired in anger came from ships, most of them at the gallant German armed trawler *Krebs* when she pitted her puny armament against a destroyer and was severely damaged. The Navy had it all their own way, destroying some 18,000 tons of shipping either by gunfire or through the demolitions planted by boarding parties drawn from the crews of the battleships *Rodney* and *Nelson*. All the Commandos had to do was land in their LCAs, round up the enemy and help the Sappers blow up the factories and set fire to the oil stocks. An orgy of destruction proceeded in what can only be described as an atmosphere of carnival, tinged with regret at the terrible damage being inflicted on the livelihood of the Norwegian community and by fear of reprisals to come.

> A picturesque diversion . . . was afforded by the sight of hundreds of fishing smacks and small puffers which sailed out while it was proceeding; the fishermen cheering and waving flags in token of their enthusiasm. The comforts distributed by the troops were also matched in many cases by presents from the inhabitants.

Brigadier Haydon recalled an Army officer with a reputation of being a ladies' man:

> Within half an hour of landing he wirelessed for permission to embark three Norwegian ladies. Permission was refused. Half an hour later he again wirelessed that there were eight Norwegian ladies desirous of joining the Norwegian Red Cross – could he take them off? Permission was granted.

A sailor remembered seeing 'the Colonel of 4 Commando with a boat-load of women who had plumped for coming to England; we cheered him as he went past'. In the final count, no less than 314

Norwegian volunteers came away plus twelve Norwegian traitors and 213 very shaken Germans, twenty-five of them combatants, two SS Police and 186 Merchant Navy and civilians. Fourteen Germans were killed in the trawler *Krebs* and in a small cargo ship whose crew attempted to run ashore. The fifteen signallers at the local Luftwaffe air base gave up without resistance and with all their documents intact when a party under Major Lord Lovat (3 Commando) and Capt M. Linge (Norwegian Army) commandeered some cars and drove fifteen kilometres to capture them.

After ten hours ashore and only one brief visit by a single German aeroplane towards the end, the force withdrew unhindered to Scapa, leaving behind 800,000 tons of burning oil, 18,000 tons of sunken shipping and a queasy sensation in German minds that henceforward Norway might be a frequent target for British attentions which had to be garrisoned much more strongly in future. The most valuable prize of all, however, may well have been the capture from the trawler *Krebs* of material which enabled the code-breakers to read the whole of the German Navy's signal traffic for February, and for two successive months, beside providing the basis for further significant progress in the attack on German codes and cyphers.

Operation BARBARIC bore no resemblance whatsoever to COLOSSUS or CLAYMORE, being conceived in February by DCO and approved on 11 March by the Prime Minister purely as 'an Information raid'. Escorted and navigated by six MTBs from the 4th and 5th Flotillas out of Ramsgate, sixteen of the recently acquired Higgins Eurekas were to carry 220 officers and men from 12 Commando from Dover and land them, across a wide front, between Calais and Dunkirk and Boulogne and the Somme bay, on the nights of 20, 21 or 22 March in a hunt for prisoners. The Commando, identifiable by a shoulder title bearing the word 'Twelve' arrived at Chaucer Barracks, Canterbury, on the 18th and was at once, in the interest of security, placed under close surveillance by L/Cpls Aveline and Sim of the Field Security Police. Their shrewd report provides remarkable insight not only into the security-consciousness of the Commandos but also their outlook and eve of battle tensions:

These men are picked not only for dash and toughness but for intelligence. It can be safely said that . . . it is far more difficult to get information from them than from the ordinary run of troops. . . . In some cases, no information was derived at all. A former BSM (now a Cpl and proud of it!) tried to 'lead us up the garden path'. . . . They tend not to mix with other troops, and were never seen forming the centre of groups of civilians. When asked, 'What does twelve mean?'* they usually said, 'Oh, we're one of the Twelve Apostles'.

Their neatness is up to standard. No reports of trouble from CMP or from Civil Police. One of them said, 'We try and keep out of brawls because we know there'd be more than bleeding noses once we started.' It is noticeable that they use very little bad language . . .

They were to be seen outside their hutments trimming (sic) grenades and loading live ammunition. It was easy to move from group to group first discussing weapons and then general subjects. Thermos containers which were used for carrying food were also out.

They had begun to think that something was up but clearly didn't know what it was . . . In the afternoon they were in their huts. It was possible to see them listening in small groups to what their officers were saying.

But it was to no avail. For as they reached Dover, and were within an hour of setting forth, a signal was received cancelling BARBARIC. Once more Churchill had balked at a raid, saying he had serious misgivings. The Operation had been, he said, 'compared to "a trench raid", but the simile was not an apt one. It would have to be accepted that a considerable proportion of the 270 men involved would become casualties, since the force would be almost certain to find the landing places heavily guarded. . . . If the raid had been designed to achieve a worthwhile object he would have favoured it. The capture of a few German rank and file seemed a very small prize.' He apologized to the Commandos, of course, for disappointing them, and it was true that a last-minute let-down had a detrimental effect on morale.

The validity of Churchill's objections, which ran contrary to the approval of the Chiefs of Staff and DCO, are arguable. It was true that the target area was the strongest fortified area in France, with pill-boxes and emplacements on the headlands sweeping the beaches below and guarding the Channel Ports and the long-range guns' positions. But it is equally likely that such a fast-moving, widespread landing at night would have achieved surprise and have come and gone before the enemy had time to react. Moreover, executed so soon after CLAYMORE and COLOSSUS, it might easily have won a cumulative prize by distracting substantial German resources for the improved protection of the entire

---

* This refers to the unauthorized shoulder flash worn by Commandos – itself a breach of security through unit identification, but not seen as such until 1942 – when it was abolished.

coastline at the very moment when the Axis was busy diverting a vast proportion of its strength to stabilizing the Italians in North Africa, invading the Balkans and preparing for the invasion of Russia. Single raids had no impact on a triumphant enemy. Something big, often repeated, was required to make any impact.

Churchill's ambivalent attitude to amphibious operations remained deep-rooted. While he could stomach launching attacks on unprotected aqueducts and against thinly garrisoned islands at a distance from the enemy's main striking power, thoughts of indulging in attritional trench warfare, of the kind which had wasted so many lives in the First World War, and of assailing well-defended beaches were anathema to him and would remain so, with varying degrees of reservations, throughout the war.

After COLOSSUS, CLAYMORE and BARBARIC it was assumed that a landing must have a strategic, political or economic object. Attacks had to be against lightly-held objectives and raiding for raiding's sake, particularly along the Channel coast, was frowned upon. So it was hardly surprising that, for the time being, there was a complete standstill in operations. March remained a false dawn for hit-and-run attacks in Europe, while the war in the Mediterranean heated up, the Blitz reached new heights and the Battle of the Atlantic grew more desperate as German submarines and raiders widened and intensified their depredations. The war was not being won by Britain and the initiative was firmly with the enemy.

CHAPTER 9
Wasting Assets

It would have been perfectly logical for Churchill and the Chiefs of Staff to persevere with Operation PILGRIM and its derivatives in April, 1941, and the months to come if there had been convincing Intelligence to indicate that a German occupation of Gibraltar or the Atlantic Islands, with or without Spanish connivance, was threatened. The records show, however, that only between October, 1940, and January, 1941, were there genuine indications of diplomatic activity in that direction and not a sign of military activity in any form. Indeed, in January positive evidence was to hand of Spain rejecting Hitler's overtures. So it is hard to understand why Churchill and the Joint Intelligence Committee (JIC) harboured such fears and concentrated so hard on PILGRIM, persuading the Chiefs of Staff to double the force originally allocated and, as Keyes pointed out, preventing sufficient forces being allocated for hit and run raids. Speculation must, of need, play its part in the synthesis of Intelligence material and Churchill's powers of imagination were proverbial in their magnitude. High on his list of policy considerations stood the twin aims of winning the Battle of the Atlantic and fostering the American alliance. President Roosevelt, having gained re-election in November, 1940, became bent on a progressively more belligerent attitude to the Axis Powers, safe in the knowledge that a Gallup Poll showed 75% of the American people in favour of supporting Britain even if it led to war. With the passing of the Lend-Lease Bill on 11 March came an assurance that the trickle of American supplies would, in due course, become a torrent without financial restraint. And in a few days' time a succession of announcements made it easier for America to help Britain and hinder the Axis, notably at sea, but always short of war itself. Nevertheless the Anglo-American joint intent was made abundantly plain when unheralded staff talks between them started early in 1941.

Concomitant with material and pyschological aid, America seemed eager to protect herself by assuming duties which relieved the British of the need to garrison or seize key Atlantic bases in order to prevent them falling into Axis hands. The Americans also saw the necessity of stopping the Germans gaining a foothold on the Western hemisphere. Vichy-held Martinique presented a possible German stepping-stone and had to be neutralized by diplomacy; while Greenland became what American newspapers called 'an unofficial protectorate', watched over, like Martinique, by the US Navy. Iceland, after the fall of Denmark and Norway, had been occupied by Britain, but a request by Churchill to Roosevelt for the Americans to take over was acted upon, and US Marines landed at Reykjavik on 7 July, 1941.

Ironically, the commitment of the Marines in the Atlantic was a sign of American military weakness, for these élite troops normally expected to operate in the Pacific where the Japanese needed close watching. But such was the run-down state of their Army that only the US Navy and the US Marine Corps could provide the necessary force; hence their provisional role to land on Martinique, if necessary, and their despatch to Iceland.

Hence, also, the prospective leading role given to the Marines in Operation GRAY, a plan laid in Washington, without British participation, to occupy the Azores in order to deter Axis designs on South America. American Intelligence were as prone as their British counterparts to listen to rumours about threats to the Atlantic Islands, although swifter to overcome their fears when it became plain that the Germans were about to invade Russia. This was a welcome about-turn for the State Department who had been left in no doubt about Portuguese objections to *any* intrusion by *any* foreign power into her territory.

For conflicting and by no means entirely coherent reasons, PILGRIM remained firmly on the stocks, and grew in magnitude, controversy, frictions and technical problems. In April the naval force which began to assemble on stand-by amounted to two aircraft carriers, two cruisers, nine destroyers and several subsidiary ships, plus LSIs and seventy-one LCAs, LCMs and Eurekas, but no sea-going tank landing ships or craft. This armada would carry two Marine brigades, each of two battalions, four Commandos, the 29th (Independent) Brigade Group, a squadron of light tanks and four batteries of artillery. Later a conflict of ideas and interests over command and control arose, a dispute which was to mirror something more than straightforward disagreements over procedures by the inexperienced. It will be described in its proper place.

PILGRIM's most important, if fortuitous, contribution was the boost it gave to training and the development of staff requirements and alterations to ships and techniques in the essential acquisition of the knowledge which would be required one day when major invasions became possible. That it was used as a pretext to prevent small raiding was, in the opinion of some, unfortunate, since raiding, too, was an indispensable way of 'learning lessons by casualties'. Arguably, and there were plenty who so argued, time, as well as opportunities to keep the enemy on the hop, was being wasted by an excess of theoretical debates.

Then, on the morning of 22 June, the Germans changed everything by invading Russia. The war took a violent lurch towards totality. Anglo-American attitudes at once assumed a new direction as the greatest clash in history began in Eastern Europe. It was for Churchill, speaking over the radio that evening, to show which way Britain was going, regardless of any reservations he might personally harbour about Stalin's Russia.

'We shall give whatever help we can to Russia and the Russian people,' he said, adding in private, 'If Hitler invaded Hell I would make at least a favourable reference to the Devil in the House of Commons'. Next day he put raiding back into business.

CHAPTER 10
'Second Front Now'

Within hours of having delivered himself of the British determination to stand by all who opposed Hitler, regardless of race or creed, Churchill addressed his mind to practical means of diverting German forces from their Eastern enterprise. A minute to the Chiefs of Staff on 23 June urged upon them the need to step up air attacks by day as well as by night and also to concentrate attention upon surface raids:

> I have in mind something on the scale of 25,000–30,000 men – perhaps the Commandos plus one of the Canadian divisions. . . . As long as we can keep air domination over the Channel and the Pas de Calais it ought to be possible to achieve a considerable result.
>
> Among the other objectives, the destruction of the guns and batteries, of all shipping, of all stores, and the killing and capturing of a large number of Germans present themselves. The blocking of the harbours of Calais and Boulogne might also be attempted. . . . Now the enemy is busy in Russia is the time to 'Make hell while the sun shines'.

Coming after the cancellation of BARBARIC these contradictions were confusing and so the Chiefs of Staff took them with a pinch of salt and told the Planners to concentrate their energies on small raids across the narrow waters. Captain G. A. French RN, who chaired an important meeting of the Executive Planning Staff to consider the 'runners' a few days later, told me that they usually had before them scores of ideas from which to select a manageable handful. First choice fell on a reconnaissance patrol named CHESS which the War Cabinet Defence Committee adopted on 7 July and Keyes passed to Vice-Admiral Dover for action against Ambleteuse. Another small operation, ACID DROP, was to follow in August, followed by a third, CHOPPER, in September. At that meeting, representing the Naval Intelligence Department, was Lt-Cdr G. Gonin, who took the opportunity of a lull in the formal discussions to mention to French an idea he and his colleagues had had for a raid on the very large dry dock at St Nazaire for which the German battleship *Bismarck* had been making before she had been caught and sunk the previous month and which, any day, might be the destination of *Bismarck*'s sister ship, *Tirpitz*. It is not often one can identify exactly who generated an operational scheme but this one was of particular importance, and for a great many reasons which will appear in due course. For now it was merely referred for consideration and found a place in DCO's diary later in July under the name Operation CHARIOT.

The idea, however, so stimulated Churchill's imagination that he expanded it at once into a concept aimed at 'nipping out the Brest peninsular'. This unrealistic scheme led the Chiefs of Staff into a desperate rearguard action to convince the Prime Minister that a project which would demand six divisions and which, from shortage of shipping, let alone of trained troops, would stretch their resources to the limit, was impossible. One fancies here that, however impractical Churchill seemed (and it is worth recalling that he avoided mention of these follies in his *Memoirs*), his goadings were the products of political expediency as well as sticks to whip the Chiefs and Planners, whose caution he saw as obstructiveness. Already Communist voices which, prior to 22 June, had stood against the 'capitalist and imperialist war', were beginning to agitate for a Second Front *now*, and were painting the demand on walls and publishing it in the papers. Churchill may have later written that 'we did not allow these sorry and ignominious facts to disturb our thoughts', and he did, on 20 July, answer Stalin's demand for a major diversion of Lease Lend Aid from Britain to Russia and his request for vigorous action across the Channel with a well-reasoned paper pointing out how impossible it was, due to lack of shipping and almost everything else.

The fact remains that serious study was made of several ambitious projects in the medium-to-large-raid category in order to satisfy Stalin:

1. Operation RANSACK – a tip-and-run raid of Brigade strength 'to kill Germans and do as much damage as possible' (preferably against a German Security HQ at Le Touquet) without interfering with PILGRIM. The JPS rejected it because only six LTCs (enough to land a single squadron of tanks) were available, and only 600 semi-equipped parachutists. Remorselessly the tyranny of chronic shortages trimmed down the force to a couple of troops from 5 Commando and a company of line infantry, carried in eight

Eurekas, tasked to raid an undisclosed airfield in the Pas de Calais. Like similar designs, including one called IRRIGATE, it was squashed by the Prime Minister for the same reason he had squashed BARBARIC – lack of effect for too much risk.

2. A joint operation suggested by the Russians, which, Churchill reasoned, had to be taken very seriously – an invasion of Northern Norway to clear the country southward and free the sea route to Murmansk along which convoys would soon be taking supplies from the West to the Russians. This was discarded by the Planners as beyond the means available, but stimulated Churchill's insistent and very unpopular proposals to raid Trondheim or Stavanger in the autumn when the nights were longer.

3. Operation GAUNTLET, again at Russia's suggestion, to seize Bear Island and Spitzbergen with a view to liberating the Norwegians and Russians there, destroying the mines and the coal stocks upon which the Germans were drawing, and eliminating German weather stations which were being secretly inserted.

Of the three only GAUNTLET was adopted as a joint British, Canadian and Norwegian venture with the Russians collaborating for the evacuation of their civilians. A force, originally set at two infantry battalions, was whittled down to one (Princess Patricia's Canadian Light Infantry) supplemented by seventeen British officers and 101 men from the Sappers and several different Commandos. Hit-and-run raid that it was in military terms, the whole thing had about it the air of a peacetime policing operation, with the troops sailing in the comparative luxury of the liner *Empress of Canada* and the escort of two cruisers and three destroyers not being called upon to take offensive action. 'So for better or worse ran GAUNTLET', wrote the Force Commander, Rear-Admiral P. Vian, as the soldiers went ashore on 25 August and began the work of assembling the Norwegian and Russian civilians for evacuation, preparing the Russian-run mines for demolition and the burning of 450,000 tons of coal and 275,000 gallons of fuel, and arguing hotly with the mine manager who resisted as staunchly as he could the destruction of his life's work and the future economic well-being of the island. It was a model exercise in peripheral raiding against an undefended target in the absence of enemy detection, a security which was assured by the local Norwegian radio operators who continued to broadcast as if nothing was happening, and totally fooled the Germans as to what was going on.

But not by any stretch of imagination could GAUNTLET be rated as a substitute for a Second Front, even if it did help Russia and harm the

German economy. Nor were the pinprick raids of July and the months to come any substitute. What impact could a few dozen men, spending a few minutes ashore, have on the thirty German divisions in France which were not in the least stretched by occupation of a secure coast line and controlling a population 99% of whom were peaceful, even if secretly hostile? Of course the ineffectuality of very small raids was well understood. Indeed, on 1 July, Keyes had tried to revive the BARBARIC scheme with parachutists and added a few tanks, but this foundered on the same rocks that RANSACK would strike.

So, after all the puff and blow, there emerged Operation CHESS, a raid by sixteen men from 12 Commando, led by an officer who was to become one of the stars of raiding – 2nd Lieut P. Pinckney of the Berkshire Yeomanry. CHESS was important, not because of what was achieved by a landing at Ambleteuse on the night 27/28 July, but for the precedent it set. For the Prime Minister, having, for the moment, been convinced that the large raids he preferred were impossible, reluctantly agreed to small ones 'of the order of ten men', and this, having been formally adopted, became the model for many such to come.

CHESS, like all of its kind, was inhibited by weather, by the phases of the moon and the tide quite as much as by enemy resistance. Wind and surf could arise unexpectedly at any time and hamper landing and re-embarkation; tides and moon tended to restrict raiding to one short, dark period of only a few days each month – and in summer a mere four hours' darkness increased the risks of detection on approach and withdrawal and limited the time which could be spent ashore. Putting a raid together also caused complex problems and included the training and rehearsal of the sailors and troops, the provision and briefing by the Navy of an escort and of MLs to tow the LCAs to the cast-off point, the arrangment of communications and the notification, without breaching security, of all those who needed to know, to prevent, for example, attack by friendly ships or aircraft. Generals who, by the existing rules, held 'the licence to raid enemy sectors opposite their piece of coast' tended to think of each foray as 'trench raiding across a watery no-man's land', and often had no conception of all that was entailed, which was why Admirals attempted to exclude them from the planning process.

There was a sense of occasion on the evening Pinckney's force embarked in the MLs at Dover. Conditions were good and the approach to the cast-off point and transfer to the LCAs went without a hitch. However, the noise of engines alerted the Germans, and when 250 yards offshore they must have been seen as whistles were heard from various places ashore. A lesser man than Pinckney might have abandoned

CHESS there and then, but he was determined to capture a prisoner and was never the sort to give in.

The LCA's ramp was lowered before beaching was made successfully despite the surf. . . . Some 200 yards down the beach a spot to climb the cliff was discovered. Men and myself climbed up with difficulty and found wire. At this moment a star shell was fired and firing broke out. There was no time to get the others up. An MG was firing from the cliff directly above the boat. We got beneath this and threw up grenades. This silenced the MG. I then re-embarked my party.

All very simple he made it sound, but the enemy had scored hits on the other LCA, the tracer snaking across the water to the light of the star shells and killing a naval officer and rating. It was touch and go that they managed to escape and Pinckney was to return with a profound respect for the alertness and competence of the enemy whose reception certainly bore out the Prime Minister's ingrained fear of beach assaults.

Nevertheless CHESS was considered encouraging enough to warrant staging a double event a month later – that being the length of time needed to lay on such raids. ACID DROP and CARTOON were also to be cautious ventures, confined to reconnaissance with no attempt at combat. In the event CARTOON was abandoned at a later stage, leaving ACID DROP to go it alone in two parties of thirty and twenty men to tackle, respectively, beaches at Hardelot and Merlimont on either side of Le Touquet. ACID DROP turned sour from the start. To the men of 5 Commando the LCA crews appeared slap-happy and deficient in training. Officers in white flannels may look engaging on a yacht but do not inspire confidence on a night operation. Then a misinformed naval officer condemned the soldiers to a voyage in the LCAs, squatting in water instead of in the dry of the MLs. In any case they were destined to land wet since the LCAs stayed too far out for fear of stranding and the Commandos were compelled to wade ashore. Fortunately the enemy here were not as aggressive as those at Ambleteuse. There were no obstacles, no mines and no opposition, despite indications that the Germans were aware of a hostile presence when they began whistling warnings to each other among the dunes. But contact there was none, and so no prisoners. It all rather went to show how easy BARBARIC might have been.

Operation CHOPPER on 27 September was quite another story. The Navy had taken the lessons of ACID DROP to heart. Not only were the LCA crews well trained but everybody, from top to bottom in the chain of command, was keen to go. One RN officer asked, 'Why can't we increase the frequency of these things?' – a very reasonable request which pointed to indifferent organization and lack of enthusiasm in higher places. No lack of aggression infected 1 Commando on this occasion, although a mistake in navigation took the two LCAs in Force B three miles off-course from the objective of Courseulles and landed them in front of alerted defences, illuminated by flares and raked by fire. Two men were killed, one badly wounded and an LCA holed so badly that the men had to bail to stay afloat. The Commandos were filled with praise for the sailors on this occasion – their determination to get them out under fire, the way they made their way home despite losing contact with the supporting MGB and the care they took with the wounded – the skipper of LCA 26, in his report 'regretting having to chop up my centre seat to provide splints for a severely wounded man'.

Force A fared better after it landed correctly at Point de Saire on the Cherbourg peninsula. A party from 5 Troop under Capt G. A. Scaramanga penetrated inland, got no answer when they knocked on the door of a shuttered house and then, as their scouts reached a bend in the road:

> A German cyclists' patrol came round the bend going a good speed on low handle-bar bicycles. There were three in a row in front and one behind. Our leading tommy gunners opened fire immediately. I saw the two leading cyclists on my side of the road crumple up and fall on the road. I ordered the bodies of the two Germans to be taken to the LCA; the other carrying party was slow in coming to the fact that one of the men detailed to carry it had been slightly wounded. Time was pressing, being already 35 minutes after the scheduled time of departure. As the two Germans appeared identical, I ordered one body to be left, and everybody embarked. Two men were slightly wounded, possibly by ricochets from our own tommy guns. Afterward one of my men told me that he had seen the body of a third German dead in the hedge. After re-embarking . . . fire was opened upon us with one MG firing tracer. . . . No beach obstacles or wire were encountered. No searchlights or Verey lights were seen. No enemy aircraft were seen.

It was only a pin-prick to the Germans who at that moment seemed well on the way to overrunning Russia and then should be able to turn back on Britain in 1942. The raids did not receive strong publicity in Britain and only passing mention by the German Propaganda Ministry which had its attention held elsewhere. But changes were on the way, and the time was not far removed when the Germans would be compelled to take a lot more notice. Before then, however, the Combined Operations organization in Britain had to be taken in hand.

CHAPTER 11

The New Team

It is sad to record the manner in which, as Anglo-American collaboration as well as their joint war-making resources gathered strength and expanded, Sir Roger Keyes' influence as DCO waned and was finally, quite ruthlessly, extinguished. He may not have used his powerful position with unblemished wisdom or complete success, but it has to be remembered that he had taken on a situation for which there was no precedent. His slide from the pinnacle of authority began peremptorily at a meeting of the Chiefs of Staff on 18 July when, at the behest of Churchill, he was removed, none too gently by the CIGS, General Dill, from executive command of PILGRIM and replaced by Lt-Gen H. G. Alexander. A fortnight later, still in full control as DCO, he was attending the second of two historic meetings between a mission of senior US Marine Officers, headed by Brig-Gen J. A. Smith, with those among the British who were closest involved with planning amphibious operations. Frankly and amicably, eleven British and eight Americans exchanged views and experience over a wide range of tactical, logistic and technical problems, while Keyes held forth vehemently with concepts wedded to his personal feats in the past.

These meetings were the logical follow-up to initial ABC (American, British, Canadian) Staff Conferences which had been held in Washington in January and February, 1941, and marked a further step in American involvement in the war. Comparison of the methods and equipments of the two sides illustrated remarkable similarities of approach and equally clear-cut divergencies of opinion. There was mutual regard for each other's development of ships and equipment, high British praise being given to the Higgins Eurekas, which the USMC had fostered, and considerable interest shown in the unique amphibian tractor (Amtrack LVT which the British would later call Buffalo). This vehicle had first taken the USMC's attention in 1923 when the American, J. Walter Christie, had designed one, but which had only reached practical status in 1935 when a wealthy young inventor, Donald Roebling, had produced his 'Alligator' – for rescue work in the Everglades, Florida. Just a few days earlier, the first production model of this swimming tractor, with a rear loading ramp, propelled on land and in water by its special paddle tracks, had come off the line. In due course it would become a maid of all work for personnel and stores, besides acquiring an armoured combat role with rotating turret and various armaments.

The principal divergencies of opinion centred not upon how but where and at what time of day to land on an enemy shore. The Americans plumped for daylight, reckoning it less confusing and feeling convinced that, however tough the opposition, dive bombers from accompanying aircraft carriers would provide sufficient neutralizing fire support. Keyes spoke, as usual, about his experience of a daytime massacre at Gallipoli and a night-time drama at Zeebrugge, and recalled that 'the Naval bombardment [at Gallipoli] which supported our troops had been quite unable to deal with machine-guns of the defenders'. When Smith asked if it would not be the same at night, Keyes replied dogmatically, 'It would not, as the machine-gun would be less accurate'.

But Keyes' deputy, Major-Gen Drew, put his finger on a vital plank in British ideas and methods: 'In planning operations against enemy positions we did not choose beaches which were virtually "Maginot Lines", but only those which were lightly held. Systematic defence, with crossfire, would prevent our success either by day or night.'

Smith countered by remarking that he 'still felt that tactical surprise would not be achieved by a night landing,' but was contradicted by Keyes saying 'after our experience at Helles, several night landings and raids were successfully carried out'.

Which pointed to the other significant difference between British and USMC methods. For the latter, notwithstanding the historic fact that their first ever operation against the British during the Revolutionary War was in the nature of a raid, gave low priority to this kind of work, other than through routine infantry patrolling. It was all a question of situation, of course. The USMC had no need for amphibious raiding because its doctrine, developed over the past two decades, was shaped to fight in strength at long range in the vast Pacific Ocean from island bases and landing ships. They did not reckon upon having their backs to the wall and the enemy only a few score miles away across narrow seas. It would take a few reverses in battle to compel reconsideration of this standpoint.

No doubt Keyes had this debate in mind when he contemplated the lessons of Exercise LEAPFROG, a large-scale rehearsal for PILGRIM, which he attended on 10 August, and in which the Maracaibo LSTs were to be tried out for the first time. It was, by all accounts, a disaster, and one which, to some extent, had to be laid at the door of the Joint Commanders, Rear Admiral L. N. Hamilton and Lt-Gen H. G. Alexander, both of whom later admitted to their inexperience in such operations. A summary of an operation which began with one LSI breaking down before leaving the Clyde for Scapa Flow and continued in bad weather, and in which the Maracaibos exhibited their fundamental defects as beach landing ships, states:

> In spite of careful training [a compliment to DCO] the mistakes of the past were again apparent. Movement across the beaches was slow, success was not exploited and there were delays in landing the vehicles [which was not surprising considering that only the small LCMs were available]. This exercise confirmed a recommendation made after the Dakar operation – the need for a properly equipped Headquarters Ship [a matter which the Admiralty had failed to tackle and did not resolve until the first such vessel, *HMS Bulolo*, began conversion six months later].

It is inescapable, and confirmed to me by private information, that the humiliating muddle at Scapa, in the presence of the King, where confusion was compounded by the Force Commanders and their staff having no set place in which to work together, as Keyes had said they must, was used as a pretext by the Chiefs of Staff to rid themselves of Keyes and severely reduce the powers of DCO. In a long letter to the Chiefs of Staff Committee on 31 August Keyes rather tediously set out the history of LEAPFROG, accepting 'no responsibility for the miscarriages' but noting that, in a COS paper drafted by the Naval Director of Plans:

> the Joint Commanders [Hamilton and Alexander] have attempted to put the blame for the failure to organize and train the PILGRIM force for the task confided to it on my Directorate and they suggest my elimination as a means of avoiding a repetition of their failures and miscarriages of LEAPFROG. These were mainly Naval, and in any case General Alexander assumed joint command after the Naval arrangements for the Exercise had been made, and these deprived him of the means of executing the military plan.

The campaign of vilification, concerted by those in the Admiralty who detested Keyes, inevitably came before Churchill. He not only had to deal with the matter in Committee, but had also to listen to rumours conveyed to him direct by an emissary from the Maund Faction in Gibraltar and the Embassy in Madrid – rumours which had as their basis resentment of the Prime Minister's interference in Naval matters and the malign influence of Keyes over him. With regret, Churchill was forced to conclude that Keyes had to go. It was impossible to let him continue, no matter how right he might be, if everybody was against him and if friction was endemic. The sorry affair festered throughout September as the factions jostled for position and bad faith sullied negotiations in a bitter struggle for power. In the end Keyes, out of petulance generated by frustration and the realization of his waning influence with the Prime Minister, over-called his hand. Right as he was to call Churchill's attention in August to the need to employ the PILGRIM Force, 'the only amphibious force we possess' and to use it 'to inflict a very severe blow across the Channel or Overseas,' or to 'get rid of the PILGRIM commitment – which is holding up action', it was of no avail.

The Chiefs of Staff put forward a new draft Directive which divested Keyes of his operational control and reduced him to the status of Advisor on Combined Operations, a humiliating proposal they cannot have expected the 69-year-old Admiral of the Fleet to accept, and which he duly refused.

Poor Keyes! With his strong personality and set views, he had been given an uphill struggle when appointed DCO by Churchill, and his replacement was made sadder because he took it so hard and, at the same time, suffered a tragic personal blow. For a while the authorities watched him anxiously as he threatened to expose in the Houses of Parliament what he regarded as weaknesses in the prosecution of the war. An officer from the War Office attempted to impound his papers and he was sent a copy of the Official Secrets Act as a reminder that even Parliamentary Privilege in wartime had its limits. So he chose his words carefully when he explained to the House his dismissal, and departed with dignity, although continuing to write letters to those still in power endeavouring to even scores with those he thought had destroyed him – naming Maund, of course, Alexander and Brooke as among his enemies. Then came news of the death in action of his son, Lt-Col G. Keyes, leading his Commandos in an abortive and desperate raid in Cyrenaica (COPPER FLIPPER) in an attempt to kill the Commander of the German Army in Africa, General Rommel. It was all the worse that this was a mismanaged attack for which Geoffrey Keyes was largely responsible. Landing from a submarine behind the lines never had much chance of success, particularly since the house to be raided was not Rommel's headquarters at all, and in any case, the General was out of the country at that moment. Basic Intelligence was at fault, but the award of a Victoria Cross to Keyes must have been some consolation to his fighting father.

Roger Keyes, as Captain French says, was a 'Blue Water Admiral' of the old school, whereas his successor at HQ Combined Operations, Lord Louis Mountbatten, was both a Blue Water Admiral and a thinker, 'which is very rare'. Nevertheless, in the autumn of 1941 Mountbatten was only a Captain whose reputation with the public was mainly concerned with his exploits commanding the destroyer HMS *Kelly*, culminating in the loss of his ship in battle off Crete in May. This hardly seemed to qualify him to take over a Department which had few friends in Whitehall from an eminent Admiral of the Fleet. Even though he was promoted to Commodore, this gave him little weight in a struggle with the Admiralty, War Office and Air Ministry. Moreover COHQ's responsibilities now excluded an operational function, relegated as it was, under the Chiefs of Staff, to 'technical advice' on all aspects of, and at all stages in, the planning and training for combined operations, 'the study of tactical, and technical developments . . . from small raids to a full-scale invasion of the Continent', and research and development of technical equipment and special craft.

Mountbatten, who was most reluctant to take the job, was of course splendidly qualified to restore COHQ prestige. A brilliant organizer, he had specialized in Communications and was steeped in the regime of the Service. An officer whose father had been First Sea Lord in 1914, and thus responsible for having the Fleet completely ready for war then, he was also a courtier of the Blood Royal whose charm and innate diplomacy made all paths smooth without in any way distracting from his immense natural authority. This time the Prime Minister's choice, backed by the Chiefs of Staff without demur, was unerring. Moreover Mountbatten's arrival in haste at Richmond Terrace from a tour of the US was timely in every way. He was, in fact, recalled from a special mission in the US where, to quote Churchill, 'he was received with great consideration. He cruised with the Pacific Fleet, and on his return to Washington had long discussions with the President, to whom he was authorized to disclose what we were doing in preparations for landings on the Continent. . . . The President showed him the greatest confidence and invited him to stay at the White House.'

The feverish summer of large-scale planning which had culminated in minor results was coming to an end in a chill atmosphere of realism. PILGRIM was disposed of because, it was admitted as the Battle of the

Atlantic swung in the German favour and shipping losses mounted, 'We cannot afford to lock up seven MT ships'. Medium-sized raids of promising dimensions were in course of preparation. But even with Keyes out of the way, COHQ's relationships with the Ministries and Services remained as tense as ever, and worst of all with the Admiralty, which continued to be bent on destroying an organization it had brought to its knees. There was one beneficial change, however, when in December General Brooke took over from Dill as CIGS and assumed the chair of the Chiefs of Staff Committee which he was to fill with distinction for the rest of the war.

As this new team came into being policy changed, as it had need to do. As C-in-C Home Forces, Brooke had been opposed to the idea of large-scale operations in North Norway, at Trondheim or Stavanger, or in the Brest peninsula, and was ambivalent though not obstructive about small raids. But coming to power within a few days of the Japanese attack on Pearl Harbor, he was at once propelled into the upper realms of Allied policy and strategy in which Combined Operations assumed a central role. Nearly every operation of the future was certain to depend on co-operation between sea, land and air forces. Therefore he was obliged to place himself above inter-Service rivalries in the interest of War Cabinet orders to raid more frequently and effectively and in order the better to concentrate upon divergencies between Allies.

CHAPTER 12

Raids Sour – With a Pinch of Sweetness

One of the common military ironies is the sad fate of senior officers who are unlucky enough to be at the top of the tree at the start of a war and, as a result of initial setbacks or disasters, often beyond their control, lose their jobs on the eve of their successors coming to prominence to benefit from the hard work of their predecessors and pick up the glory. It was Lord Mountbatten's good fortune to assume the dual appointments of Adviser on Combined Operations (ACO, when advising the Chiefs of Staff, and Commodore Combined Operations (CCO) when dealing with administration and raids) at the moment PILGRIM was relaxing its grip on shipping and when the supply of craft and other equipment was accelerating. But it was to his immense personal credit that, within two months of taking over from Keyes, he had won the Chiefs of Staff's confidence and persuaded them to issue yet another new Directive on 9 December, restoring to COHQ the important role of planning operations by Special Service troops. This Directive allowed Mountbatten to influence the Chiefs of Staff in the preparation of Outline Plans and to act as guide to the Force Commander, with involvement up to and including its final implementation – the latter function to be augmented by lending experienced operational staff officers to Force Commanders for that purpose.

Backstairs intrigues persisted, of course. It was hardly to be expected that those in the Admiralty who resented the very existence of COHQ would abandon the barricades at once. Indeed, there were those who fervently hoped that the arrival of Mountbatten with a weakened Directive presaged the early demise of COHQ. The bitterness of feeling was abundantly indicated when one Captain RN at the Admiralty forcibly said to a visiting Captain RN from COHQ: 'You think you're bloody clever in Combined Ops, but all you are is a pain in the neck of the Navy. Get out of my office!' Even General Ismay, a soldier with breadth of vision, would at a later date express his hostility when he minuted: 'All these loose ends like SOE and COHQ are anomalous and tiresome'. Nevertheless from the moment Mountbatten took over there was a slow growth in confidence between departments, even between CCO and the Admiralty and Planning Staffs, such as would have been impossible under the previous régime. As Captain French told me: 'Dickie would simply come in for a chat and before you knew where you were a sensible solution had been worked out.' Concurrently Mountbatten set in motion a sweeping reorganization of his own Headquarters to meet the demands of the future. Responsibilities were more precisely defined, Operations and Administration were parted, and the Intelligence Section strengthened and placed within Operations, charged not only with providing information to those doing the raiding but looking acquisitively for raids worth undertaking.

The war did not stand waiting for Mountbatten's reorganization, of course. Indeed, before he took over the pressure applied by the Prime Minister in favour of a major attack on Norway had compelled the Chiefs of Staff to agree to small raids on France and to initiate some kind of larger action, like CLAYMORE, against Norway. The immediate result was SUNSTAR and KITBAG, followed by ARCHERY and ANKLET.

Operation SUNSTAR was commanded by V Corps in Southern Command and was intended as the October raid of the month, but had to be postponed until 23 November. A troop of 9 Commando went to undertake an assault on a specific objective which was, in more respects than one, an experiment in Channel waters. For a start they were to be carried to the launching area in an LSI and there transferred to four LCAs lowered from the LSI's davits. All went well in good weather. Escorted by three MGBs, they made their landing a quarter of a mile from the intended spot and struggled up clay cliffs to tackle an enemy four-gun battery position 700 yards inland at Houlgate, not far from Deauville. What happened next is well described by the Germans.

> Four English boats approached the beach, stopped their engines and let the tide carry them in. . . . They were armed to the teeth. They started to climb the slope, using ropes and climbing irons. . . . Anything in their uniform or their weapons which might make a noise had been fastened with string or rubber bands. The first detachment reached the heights without the slightest notion that a German patrol, having seen the boat, became suspicious and warned the next posts silently. One of the English soldiers' revolver went off. Now hell was let loose. The German field post fired a few warning shots, and when nothing happened the machine-guns opened up. . . . The Tommies suddenly

faced a strong barrage. . . . They disappeared again, much quicker than they had come and with much noise. They simply hared away. . . . They threw everything away – machine-guns, rifles, tommy-guns, ammunition, steel helmets . . . together with a small wireless transmitter.

Forfeiture of surprise at the outset stopped the enterprise dead. In the opinion of the leader there could be no question of moving inland, since he was already behind schedule. The dash for the beach was certainly hasty and re-embarkation at high tide was extremely difficult in breakers which compelled the LCAs to lay offshore and forced the men to swim. Explaining the loss of so much equipment, the CO of 9 Commando reported:

> All losses occurred while swimming the last few yards. . . . Men put their weapons on to the door of the LCA and, while being hauled aboard by Naval and Military personnel already aboard, the weapon would be dislodged by the movements of those getting the men into the LCA. . . . I might quote the story told me concerning one of the Bren Gunners.
>
> This man, being short of stature, was knocked over when he got into the surf. He got up, still with his gun in his hands, and launched himself a second time through the surf. This time he disappeared completely, taken down by the weight of the gun. The Officer thought he was lost, but, while helping the next man aboard, he suddenly saw a boot near the bow of the craft. A sailor grabbed this and, after a struggle (which knocked two rifles overboard) the man was finally got into the LCA more than half-drowned. He had to leave his Bren gun at the bottom, however, and had to be physically restrained from attempting to dive in and have another go at getting it out.

SUNSTAR, nevertheless, was one of those episodes from which all concerned preferred to extract lessons and then forget. It did nothing but encourage the enemy, who made full use of it in their propaganda, and they would have been even more gratified had they known of the failure of the escorting MGBs to make contact with the LCAs, and the adventures of the LCAs after being attacked by German aircraft by daylight in mid-Channel and left to navigate themselves. Eventually they came ashore at Pevensey Bay. 'They crashed through the anti-boat scaffolding,' reported the disgusted Naval C-in-C, Portsmouth, 'without much damage to themselves; this matter of efficiency of the defences is under examination.'

Operation KITBAG, which followed SUNSTAR sixteen days later, was an even sadder chapter of accidents and also illustrated how much there was yet to learn. Planned as a raid by 6 Commando on Florö, north of Bergen, it sought, in the CLAYMORE manner, to seize cyphers and documents destroy shipping, a canning factory, oil tanks and cold-storage plant and bring back any Norwegians who wished to escape. Realizing that some Norwegians would not welcome such destruction, those taking part were instructed to treat their Allies with the greatest courtesy but not allow them to interfere with operations, never an easy command to obey when dealing with friends.

The raid, carried in an LSI, assembled in the Shetlands on 9 December, where the troops went ashore for a rehearsal, leaving a small party on board priming grenades. They were grouped round a table being filmed at work by a cinematograph film unit under an officer who, after the war, was to become a great name in that industry. The RSM describes the scene:

> Gunner P***** jumped up from his seat shouting, 'Duck! The thing is off', at which I saw fizzing coming from the grenade which he was holding. He immediately made for the Forward Emergency Hatch. . . . Actually he dropped the grenade and shouted 'Duck' and his body was between me and the grenade. I saw a Norwegian soldier bend down to pick it up. Gunner P***** was standing, everyone else on the floor. I stood and watched it.

Too late the Norwegian tried to throw the smoking grenade away, but it went off killing him and others and wounding several more. The subsequent Inquiry showed beyond doubt that a box of primed grenades had become mixed with unprimed, probably the result of too few people being left behind for the work and certainly not to be blamed on the film crew, as was suggested at the time. No good was to come of KITBAG, which arrived close by its objective on the 12th only to be cancelled because, due to navigational errors, landfall could not take place on schedule.

Already its successor in Norwegian waters had been conceived and was being planned by COHQ, Rear Admiral H. M. Burroughs and Brigadier Haydon having been appointed joint commanders on 6 December. It was to be a double event: ARCHERY, consisting chiefly of 2 and 3 Commandos, with elements from 4 and 6, aimed at Vaagso, synchronized with ANKLET, another raid against the Lofotens, this time by 12 Commando, sixty Norwegian troops and a party from SOE. But whereas ANKLET was likely to land unopposed, ARCHERY was expected to hit tough opposition when it came inshore on 27 December and, therefore, for the first time in a European raid, was planned as a formal assault supported by naval bombardment and a smoke screen laid from the air. Even so, resistance might have been a lot worse had not the ships managed to enter the fjord before dawn, undetected, and the cruisers and destroyers open fire on the battery at Maaloy Island, taking the garrison completely by surprise. Thus 3 Commando, landing fast, was able to seize the battery with hardly a fight.

The battle for South Vaagso was a very different matter. Here 2 and 3 Commando met a forewarned enemy who prolonged the struggle into the afternoon and fought to the death. Reuter's correspondent on the spot caught the excitement of the house-to-house fighting in the main street and underlined the initiative shown by all ranks:

> One Officer had slipped on getting out of the boat, jammed his leg between it and the rocks but struggled on, limping badly; another encountered immediate machine-gun fire and with his men engaged and killed five of the enemy before setting fire to an ammunition dump. Later he was killed. . . . At one time the entire troop was without an officer in command. Despite casualties, all ranks pursued their task with gallantry both before and after they were reinforced by a floating reserve.
>
> Many Germans were roasted to death in homes they made strong-points and from which they doggedly refused to emerge, even when grenades or a fusillade of shots had set the rooms about them on fire.
>
> While we were still dodging behind boulders and slinking over the first half-mile, and whilst the Norwegian men, women and children, anxious to go to England, were running back to our barges, some in tears, some laughing, all rather scared, two destroyers rode majestically past the town. We stood up and waved, daring the snipers. Heavy gunfire reverberated down the fjord to add to the clamour of explosions and the heat of battle.

Meanwhile the RAF had been busy, combing airfields from which the Luftwaffe might take off to bomb the ships and laying smoke to conceal the approach of the assault wave of LCAs. Again Reuter's man:

> Two single-engine Messerschmitts paid us a brief exciting visit, shot down two aircraft giving us aerial cover and swooped into the fjord, firing their machine-guns into the snow-covered slopes. Gunners of my parent ship accounted for one Messerschmitt and damaged a Heinkel with their Oerlikon guns.

Simultaneously ANKLET was underway at the Lofoten Islands. Here 12 Commando was halved in size because one LSI had broken down. Not that it mattered. There was no resistance and the force spent nearly forty-eight hours ashore, capturing ships, taking prisoners, collecting codes and distributing food to the population, who asked the troops either to stay with them or take them away.

There was a price to pay; there always is in war. At Vaagso, in return for inflicting over 200 casualties on the Germans, destroying much equipment, causing severe damage to industry ashore, shooting down several aeroplanes and dealing with 16,000 tons of shipping, the bill amounted to eight RAF aircraft lost, twenty men killed and thirty wounded. At the Lofotens the cost was of a different kind, but still serious and brought to official attention by a bizarre and emotional incident. During the return voyage two officers of 12 Commando, one of whom was the redoubtable Capt Pinckney, threw overboard a film taken by the Gaumont British Company's camera crew, giving as reason their distress at the treatment of the populace who had suffered harrowing reprisals in the aftermath of CLAYMORE. Initially the people declined to help the Commandos:

When, however, they were given to understand that we should remain until the scale of the German attack became too great, they co-operated to their fullest extent. On our premature departure, they all felt they had been betrayed and they wept and cursed us to a man. This treacherous side of such an ignominious expedition was not filmed. We felt that there was every danger of films and photographs being made public which, apart from its complete deception of the British people, would seriously add to the incredible damage already done to Anglo-Norwegian relations by what one Norwegian so rightly described as a 'very cheap demonstration'.

It left a bad taste, even after the war. In *The Green Beret* it was said that the incident occurred because the officers were 'so inflamed by the exaggerated reporting of their exploits', which often was the case on the media's part, but not on this occasion. The officers concerned were placed under arrest and the incident gave warning to Mountbatten of the necessity to bring Public Relations well under control in the future, particularly since his aim in this raid, and in those to follow, was to make the official communiqué a 'joint' one for all Services and ensure that COHQ 'got a good mention'. In fact the British this time had good cause for satisfaction with the Propaganda exchanges, since, for the first time, the Germans revealed their consternation at what was clearly a defeat by putting out grossly exaggerated accounts of what had taken place without admitting to the damage which had been inflicted. It was, moreover, a timely victory for the Allies since, at that moment, the tide of German advance had been halted as the war entered yet another new phase.

CHAPTER 13

Biting

By coincidence 6 December, the day on which the Joint Commanders were appointed to lead Operations ARCHERY and ANKLET, the war stood on the brink of one of its greatest convulsions. In Russia the Red Army took the world by surprise by launching a massive winter offensive in dreadful weather to throw the Germans back from the gates of Moscow and from their farthest penetrations into the Ukraine. And in the Far East the Japanese put the finishing touches to the preparations which, next day, would be revealed as 'The Act of Iniquity', the surprise air raid on Pearl Harbor which would propel the Americans from co-belligerence into formal war and provoke the Germans also to declare war against the US. If, in the ensuing cataclysmic weeks, everything looked like one enormous unmitigated disaster, in Washington and London the underlying aims of the leaders focused on seizing the initiative, regardless of how badly everything was going at the front. Anglo-American co-operation, which had been closing in comradeship since 1940, now flourished and burgeoned in meetings of decisive importance. Taking with him a strong team of Chiefs and experts, Winston Churchill joined Roosevelt and his upper hierarchy shortly before Christmas for the ARCADIA conferences which were to set up the Combined Chiefs of Staff Committee in a titanic struggle of the United Nations against the Berlin/Rome/Tokyo Axis.

ARCADIA was even more than a momentous meeting of Statesmen and Chiefs of Staff formulating the policy and strategy designed to bring down the Axis and, of vital importance, according priority to the destruction of Germany while allocating sufficient resources to check and, later, throw back the Japanese. It was a forum for joint consultations between Allied military men of which the ground-base issues concerned the amphibious warfare upon which almost every initiative had to be dependent. Hence the presence in Washington at the end of the year of a

Combined Operations Mission to settle operational and technical plans, dealing with procedures and the acquisition of the staggering number and types of assault shipping and craft needed, was fundamental.

When the operational demands of the moment were clarified during ARCADIA they had, when linked to Moutbatten's dynamic energy, an electric effect. Bonded to a demand that, in support of Russia, whose ability to sustain resistance, regardless of her current offensive, was still in doubt, and as part of the strategy of the war, it was decided that 'a series of raids, becoming progressively greater in scale, should be undertaken'. Although Churchill was now in some part neutralized at home by the change of circumstances, and under better control by the Chiefs of Staff, largely through Brooke's grim determination in imposing orthodoxy in matters strategic and tactical, Mountbatten had still to overcome the inertia inherent in divided control of raids between the Naval and the Army authorities and the reluctance of RAF leaders to co-operate fully. Yet by a relentless and disarming process of persuasion and coercion, he was able, within four months, to impose a system very similar to that for which Keyes had fought and failed. When, in May, 1942, the new arrangement of 'licences to raid' had been settled, it had already been tried out and found workable in more than half a dozen operations. In outline, CCO would receive proposals from any source and prepare a plan, sell it to the Chiefs of Staff, allocate the required forces and generally assist during the preparatory phase. Execution would be with the approval of the Naval and Army Commanders-in-Chief concerned, but with the Naval C-in-C, usually with CCO concurrence, making the final decision to sail or not to sail. But command and planning responsibilities changed at the water's edge; there the Army took over. But neither Navy nor Army would be responsible for air support which remained under RAF control at CCO's request. The new system was doubly assured when, in March, Mountbatten was promoted to the joint ranks of Vice-Admiral, Lieutenant-General and Air Marshal and made as Chief of Combined Operations (CCO), a full member of the Chiefs of Staff Committee 'whenever major issues are in question'. This unique solution was designed to help cope with the unique problem of ensuring that the three Services behaved as a team on the eve of their being joined in action by a new and powerful American ally who held definite views and methods of his own. No longer would British Admirals and Generals rule their coastal domains like feudal barons. A stronger hand of Royal descent now laid a firm grip upon their watery battleground and imposed a more responsive system, made all the more reliable by Mountbatten's insistence that there must be 'no back-seat driving'. Although forbidden by

Churchill to go on raids, and 'even reproached' by the Prime Minister 'for trying out an early form of one-man submarine (the Welman), invented by SOE, by himself', Mountbatten made sure that members of the Planning Section went on raids themselves 'to gain experience and, by their presence, inspire confidence in those taking part'. This example was followed by Dr Dalton's secretive people in SOE with whom CCO shared much information and special material and gadgets.

1942 was to be the year of the hit-and-run raid, not only in Europe but also, to a lesser extent, in the Middle East. There the Combined Operations Organization set up in July, 1940, was beginning to play its part and there desert hit-and-run attacks by the Special Air Service (SAS) under Major D. Stirling (an ex-member of 8 Commando), had started in November, 1941. But a transitional stage had arrived due to the dual, and sometimes conflicting, demands of 'raids of progessively greater scale' and 'Second Front Now'. At times, as the calls for the latter grew stronger and more passionate, the dividing line between raid and invasion became extremely blurred. The frequency of raids, however, was inevitably low to begin with and the number of rejections or last-minute cancellations still high. But it was soon increasingly apparent, and not least to the Germans, that a steelier sense of purpose had been injected in the West.

January's 'raid of the month' was CURLEW, an attempt by four officers and eleven soldiers of 15th Bn, the Welch Regiment to land at St Laurent in Normandy in two Eurekas in search of information and 'to gain experience'. This was a departure from previous small raids in that men of a wartime Army infantry battalion were being used instead of Commandos. Run by V Corps in Southern Command it was one of the last raids mounted under the old system, although that had nothing to do with the conclusion. The report said that it was 'from the military point of view ... not a success'. It was not the fault of the raiders that there was a distinct absence of enemy, thus denying anything other than negative information. Experience there was in plenty; one of the three MGBs came to the rescue of a Eureka broached to in the surf; the troops spent an unmolested hour ashore, with perhaps a hint of implied criticism that they did not search too hard for trouble, and the Navy did a fine job getting everybody off, albeit with the loss of three Tommy guns and a Naval Lewis gun.

February might have been a month of stupendous events and, in its closing stages, witnessed one of the classic raids of all time. The 'stupendous' could have come about as a result of Operation AUDACITY which, on the face of it, was simply another Norway venture, aimed this time at Alesund, but underneath harboured optimistic hopes that, this time, the German Navy might be lured to sea to give the Home Fleet the longed-for opportunity to engage it in battle.

AUDACITY was appropriately named when it is realized that, when conceived in December, 1941, strong evidence from decrypts of German signals indicated that Hitler was taking a personal interest in reinforcing the Norwegian theatre for the dual purpose of guarding against the danger of a British invasion and attacking the convoys which sailed to Murmansk through Arctic waters. It looked even more audacious when the battleship *Tirpitz* arrived at Trondheim on 16 January. As conceived, the idea was to put some 2,000 troops ashore for ten hours, carried in seven LSIs and closely supported, as at Vaagso, by three cruisers, destroyers and smoke-laying aircraft, while bombers raided the German airfields, giving special attention to those where the latest FW 190 fighter lived, and the Home Fleet waited over the horizon. The arrival of *Tirpitz* chilled the Planners and finally led to abandonment of the scheme in February as other more pressing operations came to the fore in a black period during which the Royal Navy suffered the loss of a great many battleships and cruisers in the Far East and the Mediterranean. As will be seen, the debate over AUDACITY was to have an impact on the considerations surrounding raiding throughout 1942. But in February the wind stood fair for small raids, and already Mountbatten was pressing ahead with irresistible vigour.

The first hint of BITING in CCO's war diary is to be found on 29 December, 1941, when, as a result of pressing inquiries by his new Intelligence Section, a desire of the scientists to possess a working model of the German 'Wurzburg' radar equipment was made known through the Air Staff. Discovery of a Wurzburg site on the cliff top near St Bruneval and the provision of some very good aerial photographs, plus detailed information from Secret Intelligence Service (SIS) agents in France about German troop dispositions in the neighbourhood, showed beyond doubt that here was an ideal target for a raid – but for a raid with a difference, involving practically every department in the business. The plan which evolved was a trail-blazer. Rejecting a frontal assault across a nearby beach because it was heavily guarded, it was decided to seize both the radar site and the coastal defences from the rear by a parachute drop, before bringing in a beach party by six LCAs, launched from an LSI. The rest of the naval force was to consist of two LCS, five MGBs and two destroyers. On 12 January the Airborne Division was informed and told to detail 120 officers and men who would be carried in twelve Whitleys. There was still a shortage of trained parachutists and Major J. D. Frost, the nominated Company OC from 2nd Bn Parachute Regiment, had hurriedly to complete his jumping course before taking part. Rushed parachute training of two more important members of the force had also to be undertaken – a Sudeten German on SOE's strength, whose job was to shout misleading orders to the Germans, and Flt-Sgt C. W. H. Cox of the RAF, who had never been in a ship or aeroplane before. SOE provided special stores and tools which might be needed to extract the radar set, but it was Cox, a radar mechanic, upon whom much depended. His job was to bring back the radar if possible, or at least gather sufficient information upon which counter-measures might be based. His job was made none the less hazardous when the Army refused him permission to wear khaki, making him look rather conspicuous in his RAF blue.

The raid was planned to take place on 20 February and, like all acts which go fairly well in public, suffered various troubles before the night. There were hitches with communications, and then successive postponements due to bad weather. When, at last, perfect conditions existed on the night 27/28 February the parachutists landed easily in the snow, but incomplete. A platoon detailed to seize the enemy position overlooking the beaches came down one and a half miles from the DZ and faced a forced march over unknown country. Meanwhile Frost and the others stormed the house guarding the site as Cox and Lieutenant Vernon, RE, tackled the Würzburg. It was all very exciting, but made a lot easier for the assailants since the only sentry awake 'was a newcomer who did not know where the alarm telephone was'. Nevertheless, the Germans reacted strongly and swiftly once they realized their peril, and Cox found himself under fire while the sappers dismantled the set and he coolly recorded all that he could see by torchlight inside the radar pit.

The retreat to the cliff top became more dangerous with every step Frost and his men took. And they might have been even more worried had they known that the naval force was at risk, due to the nearby appearance of an enemy coastal convoy, and that, due to the as yet non-arrival of the beach assault party, the cliffs were still in enemy hands. All at once Flt-Sgt Cox found himself a soldier:

> We retired when the Army made us. . . . On coming down the slope we were met by a hail of machine-gun fire from the opposite side of the cliff and we tried to dig ourselves in. Mr Vernon told me to take charge of the Sappers while he went back with the rearguard. We lay on the bank for about 15 minutes and then received a hail from the village that the beach defences had been taken.

They were stormed by elements of the 'lost' party which arrived in the nick of time, after a remarkable cross-country march, to put in a full-blooded assault led by Sgt Sharp shouting the war cry of the Seaforth Highlanders, 'Caber Feidh'.

We made our way down to the beach and found we had to wait. After about half an hour the Navy came [bringing with them thirty-two officers and men of the Royal Fusiliers and the South Wales Borderers] and we got the equipment aboard, with the wounded, and after the rearguard had time to make the beach . . . we pushed off. Slight enemy fire was directed against us from the cliff tops, but was soon silenced by Bren guns in the boats.

The British lost only two killed, a few wounded and six missing, all of whom had been left behind and survived; the Germans lost five killed, two wounded and five missing, of whom two were prisoners, one of them extremely valuable, since he was the radar operator and able to explain how to work it, while the other gave valuable information about conditions inside Germany.

Coming as it did on top of so many Allied disasters elsewhere in the world, and a mere fortnight after two German battle-cruisers and a cruiser had sailed, almost unchallenged, up the Channel, the St Bruneval success gave a timely boost to morale. It would be pleasant to record that, this time, the Ministry of Information and the Press complied with Mountbatten's desire for good coverage. In fact there were all manner of slip-ups, umbrages taken and too much detail given when the use of an LSI to carry the LCAs to the attack was mentioned instead of being kept as a valuable secret of Combined Operations technique. But at least CCO succeeded in obtaining credit for everyone in Home Forces and not just the glamorous parachutists who, he knew, were likely to attract the lion's share of publicity. And the RAF could now operate with greater assurance in the knowledge that the secrets of German radar defences were laid bare and could be baffled.

CHAPTER 14

Masterpiece and Mishap

It is important to bear in mind that, while the programme of progressively larger scale raids was in preparation early in 1942, CCO was also heavily involved in steering the first important British invasion towards its execution some 7,000 miles away. Even before the Japanese entered the war an operation called BONUS had been studied, aimed at seizing Vichy French Madagascar which lay astride the vital convoy routes via the Cape of Good Hope to the Middle East, India and the Far East. When the Japanese conquered Malaya and stood poised to break out into the Indian Ocean, the operation was reactivated early in March, under the name IRONCLAD. IRONCLAD, because it was a full invasion, will not be described here; it was hit-and-stay, not hit-and-run. The interesting point remains that, such were now the resources and flexibility of CCO's organization, that he could despatch a force the size of PILGRIM without cancelling everything else. He could, indeed, launch two major synchronized raids on France, a few smaller raids of significance and carry out a profound study of an operation called SESAME for 'a large scale raid of some duration' in Europe in 1942. These will be described in later chapters.

As usual there were almost as many cancellations or deferments as there were operations. For example, operations HUCKABACK and BACKCHAT, intended for the February–March period, were held over for a year, and Operation BLUDGEON designed to capture Germans and destroy two enemy hotels at Noordwijk on the Dutch coast, just north of The Hague, had to be called off when a minefield blocking the only practical sea lane to the objective was discovered. This re-emphasized the fact that the Dutch and Belgian coasts, with their intricate protective shoals and narrow channels, were inherently difficult to tackle, thus compelling CCO to restrict his choice to Norway and France, with penalizing effects.

Mostly the penalties imposed by fixed enemy defences were slight. The main peril to raiding forces was being caught at sea, rather than on land, after they had disclosed themselves by overt action. It was comparatively easy for SIS and SOE agents to slip in and out of Norway and France by boat. The technique, often employed, was to land unobserved immediately below the enemy posts situated on headlands, instead of on open beaches. The fact was that the Germans still underestimated the threat of amphibious operations and lived, at the start of 1942, in a state of false security. Operation CHARIOT was to change all that.

Since Lt-Cdr Gonin had first suggested the idea of smashing the lock gates at St Nazaire considerable thought had been given to the matter. SOE had it in mind but reckoned that, although the German defences were not by any means impregnable, the placing of the necessary 1½ tons of explosives was impossible by hand of agent. The RAF knew they could not do the job by bombing. That left it to the Navy and CCO, but the Admiralty had already shelved the idea as impracticable. Mountbatten disagreed, and a plan, based on the original notion to ram the lock gate with a ship laden with explosives, was prepared. The primary aim was to make the great Normandie dock, which could take the battleship *Tirpitz*, permanently inoperative; the secondary aim to do as much damage as possible to the port facilities and, in particular, to the great U-boat pens then under construction. It seemed entirely feasible to pass an old American destroyer, HMS *Campbelltown*, fitted as a 'boom breaker', and a flotilla of MLs and MGBs and one MTB across the mud flats at high tide, thus by-passing the main swept channel covered by the enemy's guns, ram the gate, land Commandos and demolition parties to destroy the pumping houses and other key points and withdraw by sea.

The Naval Commander appointed was Cdr R. E. D. Ryder, RN; the Military Commander was Lt-Col A. C. Newman, whose 2 Commando, reinforced by representatives from the Sappers and from 1, 3, 4, 5, 9 and 12 Commandos, plus several Frenchmen, were to be landed from *Campbelltown* and brought off by the MLs, while MTB 74 torpedoed either the inner lock gate or the Old Entrance lock. Throughout the planning stage Mountbatten played a prominent part. When Ryder worried lest the tidal waters would not be high enough, CCO put his mind at rest. When C-in-C Plymouth was advised by his staff that *Campbelltown* would bounce off the lock gate and that the charge fitted in her bow 'would kill everyone within half a mile', Mountbatten produced expert advice rebutting their fears. But when Newman objected to having all his men on

Campbelltown, CCO compromised against his better judgement. He allowed some of the Commandos to be carried in the launches, while giving up the original scheme of having the charge on *Campbelltown* blown on impact. Now the charge would be delayed action, devised by SOE, and the Commandos and crew would disembark across the destroyer's bows to join in the fight ashore. Unfortunately this virtually meant the abandonment of the scheme to torpedo the inner gates. Mountbatten was also thwarted in his efforts to make the maximum impression on the Germans by simultaneously launching Operation MYRMIDON (described below) at Bayonne, unfavourable moon and tide conditions delaying it for a week.

Ryder's force set sail from Falmouth on the afternoon of 26 March, disguising its movements to dovetail with a rumour circulated locally that it was a special anti-submarine striking force. At dawn next day they were sighted, steering westwards, by a U-boat which, although twice attacked, managed to count the ships, albeit wrongly, and get off a wireless report without being sunk. On time and unmolested, the force closed in on St Nazaire as, after dark, sixty-two bombers took off from England with instructions to carry out a prolonged raid, each dropping only one bomb per run, in order to baffle the enemy defences and, above all, distract the Flak gunners from looking out to sea.

Let us follow the raid, which, as Mountbatten said to Newman, 'is not an ordinary raid, it is an operation of war', stage by stage through German eyes, using extracts from their Official Report, confused by some contradictions though it is. Explaining why 'it is certainly true that the enemy did succeed in approaching unperceived to within four miles' the Report remarked:

> In addition, the prevalent poor visibility must be considered. The miscalculations of the enemy's intentions [was] due to the U-boat sighting report received by Western Naval Command at 1330 on the previous day. . . . That the 5th Torpedo Flotilla was at sea can only be attributed to the fact that Western Naval Command assumed from the reported behaviour of the enemy force that it was engaged in mining operations. The 5th Torpedo Flotilla was no hindrance to the progress of the enemy, who steered clear of it. There was lack of air reconnaissance, although the enemy's powerful air bombardment was not maintained, yet from 0300 (?) onwards he did succeed, by sporadic attacks, in distracting attention from the seaward sector.

In fact the thick cloud cover made it impossible for the pilots to identify their targets clearly. So, dropping only a few bombs, they flew round and round throughout their allotted time.

In spite of . . . unusual tactics by the enemy, the possibility of a landing from the sea was hardly taken into account. At that time we were not disposed to believe in the possibility of a surprise attack . . . on strongly fortified points.

The *Campbelltown*, led by MGB 314 with Ryder and Newman aboard, was able, after touching the mud, to sail to within one and a half miles of the gates before being illuminated by a searchlight.

The use of the correct recognition signal by the enemy delayed, even though slightly, our defence measures. . . . Only the artillery was adequate. It was first class . . . against the mass of the enemy's small wooden motor boats; even the smallest anti-aircraft gun had a full effect. Against the destroyer, however, the heavy guns of the Naval Flak Regiment were powerless.

Guns blazing, raked by shot, men falling dead and wounded, *Campbelltown*, led to within a short distance of the lock by MGB 314, rammed the gates at 20 knots. Lt-Cdr S. H. Beattie, her Captain, announced her arrival to Capt Montgomery of the Commandos with, 'Well, there we are. Four minutes late!' The sailors and soldiers leapt to their feet and poured over the ship's bows to get to grips with their task ashore.

In the dockyard the enemy was able to land unhindered since there were no barbed wire defences on the hard, or on the steps to the jetty and the quay. . . . Other unprotected points were the steps leading to the gun emplacements, searchlight stations and bunker platforms, and important targets such as lock gates, pumping plants, engine instal-lations and U-boat bunkers. There were not enough machine-guns and the hand grenades were for the most part without detonators. The ships' companies and others who had gone to the air-raid shelters when the air-raid warning sounded could not take part in the fighting, although they were right in the battle area, as they were unarmed.

More resistance than the German report acknowledged was, in fact, mounted, but quite insufficient to prevent Newman getting ashore from MGB 314, or to stop the surviving Commandos from *Campbelltown* from carrying out all the vital demolition tasks at the pumping and winding stations and against the guns in the immediate vicinity. Nor could they stop MTB 74 firing its two delayed action torpedoes at the Old Lock Gate. But when the men reported to Newman for embarkation orders, the news and the sights confronting them were grim. The scene was lit across the water by burning launches; at that moment only five operated. The German guns had, indeed, been 'adequate'; and now, too, their infantry were proving mettlesome, as the initial shock subsided:

> The passing of intelligence and the alert worked quickly and smoothly. . . . The defending troops, though only partially trained in land fighting, and insufficiently equipped, reached a high level of achievement.

They certainly did. Remorselessly, amid the chaos of battle in the waning hours of darkness, the surviving Commandos were penned into the dock area until Newman felt obliged to give the order to attempt to escape in small groups. Only five managed it. Of the rest, 169 were dead, the remainder prisoners, including Beattie and Newman, each of whom, with Ryder, would receive the Victoria Cross. Also to receive posthumous VCs were A. B. Savage of MGB 314 who kept his 3-pounder gun in action at point blank range against a pill-box, and Sgt T. F. Durrant RE of the Commandos who fought an incredibly heroic action from the decks of ML 306 when she was intercepted at sea by the German torpedo boat *Jaguar.* Long after the ML was wrecked by gunfire, Durrant continued to fire a machine-gun from amid the shambles, refusing to surrender and persisting until he could shoot no more. His was probably the first VC awarded to a soldier for a naval action on the recommendation of an enemy officer after the war.

Campbelltown lay embedded in the lock gate, the time-fuse within her set, the charge in the crumpled bows intact. At 1000 hours, as German officers and men stood upon her and on the quayside, the big bang came. Some 400 died and, thinking there was a renewal of the raid, the Germans began shooting in the town again, killing many French civilians. And next day too, when, at intervals, the two torpedoes fired by MTB 74 went off by the Old Lock they again lost their composure.

> The English attack . . . is a first-class example of a well-planned undertaking thought out to the last detail and executed with great courage. But equally it is an example of half-measures. . . . Men and material for the attack were not provided on a large enough scale. The too cautious attitude which had been England's since the beginning of the war, her unwillingness to sacrifice life even for a worthwhile aim, the half-heartedness of her measures were, here again, the cause of her limited success.

But, although U-boat operations from the inner harbour were not impeded, the Normandie dock was out of action for the rest of the war. And at a time when German resources were being taxed to the limit throughout her new empire, in particular in Russia and in North Africa, the need to begin a vast programme of fortification in the West was an expensive embarrassment caused by the English.

They will carry through their attempts to make the bases for the U-boat war unserviceable by operations from the sea. . . . We shall have to reckon with attempts to block the ports, combined with surprise landings. Successful landings on a larger scale, which could affect the conduct of the war on land, may still be ruled out.

Demonstrating the myopia which was predictable from a nation whose amphibious operations in the Second World War (against Poland in 1939 and Russia in 1941) were often costly and never original in concept or execution, the Germans had nevertheless put their finger on a few fundamentals. As a result they began converting their most vulnerable coastal sectors into copies of the Siegfried and Maginot Lines. This was to have a close bearing on future Allied raiding policy, but for the British public at the time it was a moment to regret the losses and take pride in the achievement.

A week later it was for the authorities to feel disappointed that CHARIOT's running partner, MYRMIDON, did not match its predecessor's performance. The target for 1 and 6 Commandos, commanded by Col W. Glendinning, was the Bugatti works and other factories at Bayonne, along with any shipping which might be found upriver. The force was to be carried in two LSIs, partially disguised as neutrals and escorted by the destroyers *Calpe* and *Badsworth*. In outline 1 Commando was to capture the batteries at the entrance to the river and 6 Commando the industrial plant on either bank, while the destroyers moved in to deal with shipping. On board were two officers from MI9, the branch which extracted information from enemy prisoners, both of whom suffered from acute anxiety. The first spent the entire voyage under drugs because 'he was a Home Service soldier, he was too old, he had not received any training, he did not know what the operation was about before he came and if he had known would not have come'. The other spent a lot of time finding fault, with some justification, with the operational plan and its underestimation of the enemy, and making no attempt to hide his opinions in front of junior officers whose confidence he undermined. On returning home he wrote a report repeating his allegations and pointing out the reason for the failure to carry out the landing – the existence of a bar across the river's mouth which, in certain conditions of swell, was uncrossable. He indignantly wrote:

> The French Intelligence Officer and the French pilot were the only two on board in a position to gauge the initial difficulty to overcome the river bar. Neither were called upon for their advice or given any opportunity to express it. . . . The opening of the river was only made at 0230 hours, instead of the scheduled 0200 hours. For approximately thirty minutes all craft (LCAs) paraded up and down in darkness in front of the two German coastal batteries. As no shot was fired by the enemy, it can be inferred we had the advantage of surprise, or that the enemy . . . were witholding their fire until they had got us caught in the bottleneck.

This report angered Mountbatten exceedingly and he responded with a letter to MI9's masters which tells us much about his approach to operations and his use of power:

> As an example of how far wrong he was, may I say that I personally know Bayonne quite well and from the very beginning the problem of crossing the bar was the central difficulty of the plan, as it was in Wellington's attack in 1814. . . . There appears to be no way of forecasting the degree of swell. . . . In carrying out these operations I have to measure the chance of the whole show being spoiled by undesirable influences against the value of the operation. In these circumstances I am sure you will not expect me to include any further such officers.

CHAPTER 15

The American Contention

If the Germans, who underrated the British potential in their St Nazaire report, had been aware of MYRMIDON and a host of plans for large-scale attacks already under consideration they might have revised their estimate of enemy half-measures. They would also have been wiser to take into account the meaning of full American involvement. But the Germans, in their arrogance, never came to terms with reality in 1942 and had to be taught hard lessons in battle from October onwards. While it is true that the British would have liked to step up their raiding in 1942, as shipping and weapons came slowly to hand, it is equally obvious that their effort would have been weak, and that it was the stern American intent, spurred on by the ARCADIA decisions, which raised the tempo and level of aggression to a higher pitch than would have been the case if first priority had not been accorded to defeat of Germany.

ARCADIA – one wonders who allocated that singularly misleading code name to conferences which were anything but ideal or rustic – put Allied joint planning on a remarkable new footing in a way which forced a change in American practice. The creation of a Supreme Council of the military heads of the US and Britain led to the formation of the Combined Chiefs of Staff (CCS), charged with the strategic direction of the war. This was natural to the British, who already had their smoothly-working Chiefs of Staff Committee, but it was foreign to the Americans. Under the President, as C-in-C, the Navy, which had the Marine Corps under command, and the Army, which was rapidly losing its paramount control of the Army Air Corps, collaborated with bad grace. Faced with the need to present a unified view to the British, they were compelled to form their own Joint Chiefs of Staff (JCS) agency, consisting of General G. C. Marshall (Army Chief of Staff), Admiral E. J. King (Navy C-in-C and Chief Naval Operations) and Lieut-Gen H. H. Arnold (Chief of the Army Air Corps).

Nothing like CCO or a Combined Operations organization existed in the US or looked likely to do so. Outside the JCS the Army and Navy tended to go their own way; the Navy held firmly to the Marine Corps and its Commandant, Lieut-Gen T. Holcomb. For although Holcomb sat in on the ARCADIA conferences and the President, taking the Marines' part, later asked Holcomb, 'How would you like to be a member of the Joint Chiefs of Staff Committee?', Admiral King prevented this.

The Amphibious Force stood low in King's order of priorities at a time when the Allied navies had lost control of the Pacific Ocean and were hard pressed to contain the U-boats in the Atlantic. In the manner of his opposite numbers in the British Admiralty, he deprived it of adequate personnel and had no enthusiasm for an equivalent Combined Operations organization or for hit-and-run raiding. His Director of War Plans, the uncompromising Rear Admiral R. K. Turner, was more farsighted. With experience of fighting on land as a young officer, as a gunnery expert and an aviator, Turner was joint-service minded. On his recommendation the President had adopted a Joint Chiefs of Staff Committee, rather than the Super Joint General Staff put forward by Brig-Gen D. D. Eisenhower. And it was Turner who, in April, 1942, recommended that 'a joint Army, Navy and Marine Section, under a Flag Officer, be established . . . with specific responsibility to develop material and methods for amphibious forces'. When formed in June, 1942, it had been considerably whittled down by King and Marshall, and worked at too low a level to deal with a problem of enormous dimensions. But just then it was the nearest the Americans could get to a COHQ, just as Turner, as fighting admiral, thinker and organizer, was the nearest they had to a Mountbatten.* But, Turner, unlike Mountbatten, has been overshadowed in history by such men as Admirals Spruance and Halsey, and his reputation has suffered from his addiction to drink and his use of strong language, which earned him the nickname of 'Terrible Turner'.

He was aware, through the close contacts which had developed since the ABC Conferences and his meeting with Churchill during the Atlantic Conference in August, 1941, of the British system. But there is nothing to indicate any desire on his part to depart from the official doctrine which laid down that in Joint Operations the Navy was:

---

* Not until October, 1943, did King and Marshall agree to the formation of the Joint Amphibious Warfare Committee, and it was April, 1944, before it was given jurisdiction over certain amphibious projects. But a COHQ? Never!

To seize, establish, and defend until relieved by Army forces, advanced naval bases, and to conduct such limited auxiliary land operations as are essential to the prosecution of the Naval Campaign.

In other words, Turner was as enmeshed as everybody else in the traditional rivalries between Navy and Army, a schism which produced astonishing duplications of function. For example, in December, 1940, the Army's Transportation Service possessed a larger fleet of ocean-going vessels than the Navy's Amphibious Force. And, as King discovered, some senior Army officers 'regarded themselves as in the position to criticize the amphibious techniques of the far more experienced Marines', which he likened to those who could only creep instructing those who could walk when none could run.

Collaboration between the British and Americans thus posed problems of a complex though not unfamiliar nature. Allied Joint Planning for raiding started when a solitary American officer was attached to COHQ in January, 1942. But by May he had been joined by a full American Staff. They were the opposite numbers of the British Combined Operations Liaison Officer (COLO), Captain J. Knox, who arrived in Washington with his staff in April. Knox in his letters to Mountbatten gave an insight into the special difficulties underlying Joint Service work with the Americans:

You will already have tired of hearing about lack of co-operation between the Army and Navy, but still I think it worthwhile reporting that Admiral Turner . . . made the admission that the Navy Department had ordered to be built a large number of Y craft asked for by the War Department, although they (the Navy Department) considered them unsuitable for the work visualised. If this was the Army requirement it was not for the Navy to buck in on their plans. Can you beat it!

And of great significance on another occasion:

Probably Bourne has told you how the land lies here as regards the Americans setting up anything in the nature of a COHQ. Dikes has put you in the picture as to how Donovan stands. He seems to have the temperament and outlook of your predeccessor [Keyes]. As an example, I believe that having been warned off the Pacific Area (by Nimitz) he is planning raids of his own in Norway.

Colonel W. J. (Wild Bill) Donovan had something of the outlook of Mountbatten as well; as a fighting man of renown he was eager to get on with the war. A domineering member of President Roosevelt's 'kitchen cabinet', as Keyes had been of Churchill's, he visualized intensive guerrilla attacks and was working to set up what in July would become known as the Office of Special Services (OSS) which, in due course, would become the partner of SOE in Europe. Unfortunately a flurry of impracticable and bizarre projects which, as head of the Central Organization of Information (COI), he put forward to the President aroused the mistrust of the Chiefs of Staff as well as of all the other Departments dealing with intelligence and diplomacy. Some put in the shade the plans of the Directorate of Combined Operations in the early days of Keyes. There was, for example, the suggestion, in December, 1941, for a raid on Japan by 10 to 15,000 commandos supported by half the Pacific Fleet, when half the Pacific Fleet was already out of action and no American commandos yet existed.

It was hardly surprising that Nimitz and, later, General MacArthur, sheered off COI and OSS, the former giving as a reason his fear of a clash with the Marines. It was counter to common sense, when defeat loomed large, to abandon well-tried, if patently fallible, systems and replace them with a shadowy organization, totally unproven, run by a man who tended to undermine security through the generation of personal publicity. But there is evidence that Nimitz was not as hostile to raiding as postwar remarks of his suggest. When King, spurred on by Turner, was pressing him to take the limited offensive in May, 1942, Nimitz's initial idea was to raid the Japanese seaplane base at Tulagi with nearby former Marine Raiders (see below) to help hold open the vital route from the US to Australasia.

Another reason why King and Turner wanted to gain the initiative in the Pacific was steeped in Navy/Army politics. They dreaded loss of Navy prestige if, as a result of the President's and Marshall's preoccupation with Germany, they in the Pacific were deprived of adequate forces. And with reason. On 12 May, with the full concurrence of Marshall, the British Chiefs of Staff had issued a directive calling for operations in three categories: for comprehensive invasions to fulfil contingency plans, such as RANKIN; for a presence on the Continent in the most unlikely event of a crack in German morale; or GREENBACK, a sacrificial landing in the gloomily expected collapse of Russian resistance. These need not be described here and, in any case, they had a similarity in form to those in the second category, that is major raids under the heading of SESAME to take the strain off Russia. Graced by the names IMPERATOR, RANSACK, FORETOP, ROUND-UP, SLEDGEHAMMER, and JUPITER, these were raids whose invasion pretensions suffered from dubious potential for 'hit' and a good prospect of 'run' in the face of an opponent whose strength remained solid. Thirdly, a succession of smaller raids at the rate of two a month, thus doubling the ante. Outside Europe there was a peripheral project, GYMNAST, which will be heard of again.

It was the second category which caught the Americans' imagination, despite their inability to put much weight behind it until the autumn at the earliest. What few troops the army had ready were sent to Northern Ireland at once, but they amounted to little more than a token force. There was irony in Marshall's question to Mountbatten in April, 'What can I do to help?'. Try as he would to gain acceptance for a major direct assault upon the Continent that summer, he knew that it was the British who would have to provide the lion's share of assault units. And Mountbatten's reply also indicated why such an assault was impossible: 'Telegraph today to double every British order for landing ships and landing craft, (placed in January) and take over the new orders yourself. Design and produce 300 LCI(L), 150 for you and 150 for me.' He sketched out the design of Landing Craft Infantry (Large) then and there on paper: 'A craft capable of transporting 200 troops in reasonable comfort and landing them dryshod on an enemy shore'. He ensured that 1,000 of the British-designed LST 2s would be built in US shipyards. This was the 4,000-ton ship which made all the great invasions logistically possible and which Turner called 'a marvel' in its ability to change draught to suit beach gradients.

The scenario of a cross-Channel invasion at that time was sketchy and centred upon a 1940 notion of Churchill's for an irruption of ten armoured divisions working in conjunction with a swarm of guerrillas. The guerrilla swarm existed only in Churchill's and Dr Dalton's imaginations and as yet had no substance. SOE had made little headway in stirring up resistance and such guerrilla fighters as there were possessed few arms. As for armoured divisions, just five were available in Britain, and of tank landing craft only the three inadequate Maracaibos, plus a handful of LCTs whose primary task would be to ferry American equipment to England from Northern Ireland. Moreover, study after the aborted AUDACITY discouraged a major operation in Northern France because the defences were now 'far too strong'. Small raids, on the other hand, were deemed feasible and the capture of the Channel Islands seemed attractive – 'a good objective'.

With this thwarting knowledge in mind, the British Chiefs of Staff, including Mountbatten, met their American counterparts in London between 8 and 14 April to hammer out a strategy for 1942 and 1943. It was indeed fortunate for the Allies that the two Army Chiefs of Staff were men of immense stature and that Mountbatten enjoyed an excellent relationship with each. Marshall had the hardest row to hoe, for although the Americans had agreed to give priority to the overthrow of Germany, it was by no means an assured policy because it did not enjoy the support of the US Navy. Grim in council loomed the strong personality of Admiral King, who, for years had concentrated his attention on confronting the Japanese and now had a burning desire to wipe out the stain of Pearl Harbor. Inter-Service rivalries centred upon the differences between Marshall and King. In the Pacific the Navy and the Marines would dominate, in Europe the Army. Naturally Marshall strove for a leading role for the immense army he was raising in the US. So when Brooke rated Marshall's ideas for September 'fantastic', the product of a limited brain! and, with Mountbatten's support, argued strongly against a major invasion of Europe (ROUND-UP) or a prolonged occupation of the Cotentin peninsula based on Cherbourg (SLEDGEHAMMER), he was threatening the ARCADIAN priorities which favoured his own side. Brooke's unjust remarks about Marshall were, of course, reserved for the privacy of his personal diary, but there is very little doubt that, in these negotiations, Mountbatten often provided the diplomatic salve which kept things running smoothly.

In April and May, during separate conferences, Mountbatten supplied the basic data for the two most acceptable operations, of which SLEDGEHAMMER was first favourite. Shortage of landing craft of any type was the universal stumbling block. SLEDGEHAMMER was no simple infantry hit-and-run raid, over and done with in an hour or so; it was to be a prolonged effort employing six or more divisions supported by large tank and artillery arms and demanding considerable logistic support. Much shipping would be required, but King was quick to point out to Mountbatten, at a meeting in Washington on 4 June, that 'the US Navy was already fully occupied with operations in the Pacific, and that it would severely tax his resources if he was to undertake the provision, training and manning of landing ships and craft required for the European theatre.' To which Marshall had indicated that, if the Navy could not do it, the Army would. 'Whereupon Admiral King, rather than surrender the birthright of the Navy to the Army, decided the Navy would play its part.'

From its birth in 1940 politics were ever a part of Combined Operations. At no time was this more evident than when CCO and the Chiefs of Staff found themselves involved with the Americans. It is one of the hallmarks of inspired Anglo-American co-operation that Mountbatten was able to charm the Americans – Roosevelt and Marshall above all – for nobody was ever too sure if King was vulnerable to charm, so fierce was his partisanship. In a letter to Roosevelt, confirming the positions then being held by both sides with regard to operations in 1942/43, Mountbatten supported Marshall. He had a five-hour meeting with the President in which he was scarcely likely to have missed the opportunity to impress upon Roosevelt the skills of diplomacy in which he was steeped by heritage, let alone his outstanding understanding of strategy and military technique. Concessions he could not make, since he was not a plenipotentiary, but he did give an impression of British determination to do something dramatically worthwhile in the West in 1942, and helped reinforce and shape the President's resolve, as the letter shows:

> I pointed out that you stressed the great need for American soldiers to be given opportunity of fighting as soon as possible, and . . . the agreement . . . that, in the event of things going badly for the Russians this summer, a sacrifice landing would be carried out in France to assist them. I pointed out that no landing that we could carry out could draw off any troops, since there were some 25 German Divisions already in France and landing craft shortage prevented our putting ashore an adequate number. The chief German shortage lay in fighter aircraft and all our efforts were being bent towards provoking fighter battles in the West . . . I told the P.M how much you had been struck in the recent telegram by his remark: 'Do not lose sight of GYMNAST!'

Mountbatten's mission paved the way for the visit Churchill and Brooke made to Washington on 17 June, at which Churchill's dictum 'No landing with a withdrawal envisaged' was paramount, but at which positive progress was made. By then, in any case, the future had been clarified.

Russian survival seemed possible and the need for 'sacrifice' landings such as GREENBACK less likely. American victory at Midway presented the opportunity for the US Navy and the Marines to begin tentative offensive operations based on Australasia. British insistence on tackling Germany first, allied to rivalry with Marshall and the Army, provoked King to risk an invasion of Guadalcanal in August (see Chapter 18). Churchill's visit paved the way for the deferment of ROUND-UP and SLEDGEHAMMER and the adoption, in due course, of GYMNAST under another name. The strategy of bringing the German fighter force to battle and taking the strain off Russia as much as possible led to six large-scale plans: RANSACK, IMPERATOR, FORETOP, JUPITER, GABRIEL and RUTTER.

Although a lot of work was done on RANSACK – a large-scale raid of two to three days duration on Pte Ste Laire in the Pas de Calais with a view to provoking an air battle on favourable terms to the RAF – it was shelved when greater preference was given at the highest level to the other three contenders. Similarly FORETOP, a large-scale raid of invasion dimensions aimed at bases from which U-boats and raiders made their forays to fight the Battle of the Atlantic, was dismissed because it would prove too costly, particularly since it was beyond the range of fighter aircraft.

IMPERATOR was easily the most imaginative scheme ever put forward, a worthy competitor, in terms of aggression, to DUDLEY. For just as DUDLEY had aimed to raid Rome, IMPERATOR's objective was Paris, encompassing a deep penetration by two divisions, including fast, light armoured troops, and lasting three or four days. Various permutations were considered, such as basing the raid on Boulogne, where a bridgehead might be held indefinitely. First favourite was setting out from south of the River Somme and returning, via Rouen, to Dieppe where a small 'escape' bridgehead would be formed on the morning of the surviving raiders' return. Mountbatten was extremely keen on this incredible operation, and seems to have enthused the Chiefs of Staff so much with visions of light armoured troops thrashing about, while SOE arranged an uprising by the French Resistance Movement, that they recommended its approval to the Prime Minister, saying it should take place in the first week of August at the first opportunity after the completion of RUTTER, a one-day raid on Dieppe which was scheduled for the period 21–26 June.

Winston Churchill would have none of IMPERATOR, and for excellent reasons. In a long letter to the Chiefs on 8 June, he castigated it at every point:

> Certainly it would not help Russia if we launched such an enterprise, no doubt with world publicity, and came out a few days later with heavy losses. We should have thrown away valuable lives and material, and made ourselves and our capacity for making war ridiculous throughout the world. . . . The French patriots who would rise in our aid, and their families would be subjected to pitiless Hun revenge, and this would spread far and wide as a warning against similar imprudences in case of larger-scale operations.

The Prime Minister went on with unchallengeable military logic, citing among other problems the violent counterreaction to be expected at once by enemy mobile troops and the insuperable logistic task. 'We heard no more of IMPERATOR after this,' he purred. Yet he was nursing his pet extravaganza, 'my own constructive plan', namely JUPITER, which he submitted to the Chiefs of Staff on 1 May. A revision of an earlier scheme, JUPITER suffered from similar defects as FORETOP. That is, in attempting to make a lodgement in Northern Norway in conjunction with the Russians, it lacked the essential fighter support required and, moreover, would be vulnerable to interruption by major units of the German Fleet. The Chiefs of Staff would have none of it. So that left two big one-day raids, GABRIEL and RUTTER, as the only major strikes likely to take place in North-West Europe in 1942, if SLEDGEHAMMER, as military logic demanded, was deferred.

GABRIEL, a descent on the Cherbourg peninsula, remained at the paper stage. In its place stood RUTTER, a raid by infantry and armour against the strongly held enemy port of Dieppe which was conceived at the end of March and mulled over for the next six weeks before receiving Chiefs of Staff approval. It will be described in detail in its correct chronological place, after several small raids have first been dealt with. All that needs to be mentioned at this stage is the stimulating effect the debate had on American ideas about raiding and upon the future of raiding forces in general, including those of Britain. For while the Grand Design was being roughed out and put into order by President, Prime Minister and Chiefs of Staff, CCO was pushing ahead within the Combined Operation organization with a ceaseless process of reorganization and evolution.

Indeed, important as raiding was and anxious as the Americans were to get in on that part of the act, the building of a base for the enormous invasion to come was already beginning to assume first place. Of major importance was the need to restore the ports along the Channel to their original capacity in order to handle the vast quantities of stores and shipping needed when the great day for invasion dawned. Since Dunkirk they had been run down and their labour force largely dispersed. That deterioration had now to be rectified and this Mountbatten initiated in March, 1942. At the same time the expansion of COHQ went ahead fast – too fast for at least one section of the bureaucracy, the Statistical Section, which occupied accommodation in Richmond Terrace which Mountbatten urgently desired. Thwarted by civil servants, he felt compelled to write one of his irresistibly persuasive letters to Sir Edward Bridges at the Cabinet Office, asking that a Section, which tarried too long, should be shifted:

> We are working under the greatest pressure . . . and I don't honestly think we can continue like this. . . . I hate taking advantage of your kind offer (to move the Section) but war is war.

Move they did, as did everything else Mountbatten tackled. Like all great men, he knew when and how to exceed his authority.

CHAPTER 16
Canoeists, Raiders, Rangers and Marines

A good case is made out by those who argue that among the most vital functions of the Directorate of Combined Operations and the Special Operations Executive was the promotion of new ideas in the teeth of opposition from the established Service Directorates and Government Departments, an opinion with which those in America who favoured unorthodoxy would have concurred. In peacetime the regular forces contained their share of revolutionary mavericks; in wartime the number was greatly increased by bright, disrespectful, armed civilians who were eager to experiment and get on with the war. Their task in obtaining new weapons, such as Tommy-guns, sophisticated demolition devices, canoes and the like, would have been much harder had they not benefited by assistance from the new novelty organizations led and staffed by men with open minds.

If it had not been for Keyes wasting not a moment in July, 1940, to form the SBS, a valuable weapon system might have been seriously hampered, instead of being amply proven by Courtney in 1941 in the Mediterranean. As it was, work in Britain to develop the original Folbot was most fruitful. With the failure of the Folbot Company Mr Goatley of Messrs Goatley Ltd began to design and manufacture in large numbers several types of greatly improved craft, notably, in September, 1941, the two-man Cockle Mk I and in July, 1941, the eleven-man, later increased to twelve-man, Goatley collapsible assault boat.

By November, 1941, No 101 Troop, which had been formed in 6 Commando under Capt G. C. Montanaro, RE, from hand-picked men of the SS Brigade, was ready for action. On a grey November night two canoes were launched outside Calais harbour with the task of searching for and sinking an enemy ship (Operation ASTRAKHAN). It failed when one canoe, caught in rough water, capsized, the two men managing to get ashore where they were made prisoner. No 101 Troop was by now much better equipped with cockles and with improved 1¼lb limpet mines developed by SOE's experts – devices which could be attached to a ship's bottom and exploded by timed fuses.

The next attempt (Operation JV) was more precisely planned than ASTRAKHAN and was made on the night of 12 April in a canoe manned by Capt Montanaro and Tpr F. A. Preece, RAC, their target a 4,000-ton tanker anchored in Boulogne harbour. Carried to within paddling distance by ML 102, escorted by MGBs, they cautiously paddled their way into the harbour, guided by sounds from a Saturday night drinking party ashore. Groping about in the dark, they at last found the ship at 0200 hrs. Notes from the report tell of grim determination to succeed despite repeated mishaps:

> Got stuck on a concrete edge and that holed the canoe which began leaking fast. Anyway, got alongside the ship 15 minutes later with one of the paddles split. Found limpets could be got on at 0220 hours, although the ship was rather foul. Had trouble due to a large hole in the ship caused previously by a torpedo. More limpets laid along the side. Paddling out to sea and well behind time, water in the canoe was by now about four inches, we arrived at the pick-up position at 0320 hours with the canoe rapidly filling – one paddling the other bailing. Sea was rising and things looking black while we shifted stores on the canoe to assist buoyancy until, at 0400 hours, the ML appeared and took us home.

Next day the ship was seen to be low in the water with her funnel missing. The following month Courtney, who had recently returned from the Middle East, formed No 2 SBS, absorbing 101 Troop. Canoeists had won their spurs; another Private Army was in existence.

Anathema though the existence of Private Armies and Commandos may have been to inflexible traditionalists, an irrefutable need for them in specialist employment in a war unlike any other was unanswerable. They could strike accurately and reconnoitre closely where aircraft, for example, could not; they had enormous potential as the spearheads of the major invasions yet to come; and they were romantically attractive to both the public and to statesmen. Churchill's thrill in their swashbuckling exploits, when he managed to overcome his reservations, were the guarantee of their continued existence in Britain and of their emergence in the US, where he found a kindred spirit, so far as raiding went, in Roosevelt.

Raider forces in the US came about from the interweaving of several different strands of initiative. Both the Army and the Navy, with the Marine Corps, had a tradition of hit-and-run attacks dating back to the Revolution, but it was the Marines who had studied raiding in the 1930s and had formed 'Provisional Rubber Boat Companies' in February, 1941. In May, 1940, inspired by the German use of parachutists in Holland, Lieut-Gen T. Holcomb, Commandant of the Marine Corps, initiated a study of this new way of warfare and came up with a proposal for a battalion whose tasks might be reconnaissance, raiding, with a limited capability to return to the parent organization, spearhead operations to seize vital terrain and strategic installations, or as 'an independent force operating for extended periods, presumably in a guerrilla role in hostile territory'. Volunteers, of whom there was no shortage, had to be of Commando-like physique and motivation; but unlike Commandos, officers would be paid an extra $100 a month and enlisted men $50. Training of the first men began in October, 1940, but was delayed by shortages of parachutes and suitable aircraft. It was Spring, 1942, before the first battalion was ready. In 1940 the Army also formed its first parachute platoon which would act as the cadre for 501st Parachute battalion, whose role initially, like that of the Marines, would place emphasis upon sabotage missions but in 1941 would turn to large-scale operations of divisional size.

At the ARCADIA conference the criss-cross strands were woven together. Marine and Combined Operations officers talked shop and some of the discussion was of the emerging change of scene in the Pacific, where the Japanese advance bit deep among the myriad islands and coastlines, presenting opportunities which amounted to a positive necessity to raid until the tide of defeat was turned. From the President and his closest advisers, through his Chiefs of Staff, came the urge to create special Commando-type units. As already seen, Roosevelt, too, had a kitchen cabinet, notably Colonel Donovan and Major E. F. Carlson, the latter a Marine officer with a distinguished career in the 1920s who, during his third tour of duty in China (1937/38) had marched with the Communist guerrilla 8th Route March Army under Chu Teh. Resigning his commission in 1938, Carlson concentrated on the study of China and, by a stream of letters to Roosevelt, enthused the President, who welcomed novelties, with the potential of irregular, populist forces organized loosely, governed by democratic methods and proficient in hit-and-run tactics – be they against Japanese or Chinese Nationalists. But the strongest voice was Donovan's, as he endeavoured to build a raiding capacity into his own special organizations.

Threatened by the menace of wild men such as Donovan and Carlson, the latter having rejoined the Marines as a reservist in April, 1941, and by the President whose son, Major James Roosevelt, had recently been attached to the British in London and the Middle East and was strongly advocating raider operations, the Marines, on 6 January, 1942, redesignated 1st Bn, 5th Marine Regiment as 1st Separate Battalion. At once attitudes within the American hierarchy assumed a similarity to those within the British. Holcomb, while willing to permit what were soon known as 'Raider Battalions' to be 'identical to that of the Commandos', also entered the reservation that 'the training of all units in the two Marine Divisions prepares them to carry out either offensive operations on a large-scale, or small-scale amphibious raids of the type carried out by the Commandos'.

Simultaneously Holcomb sought allies who would help snuff out the suggestion from 'a very high authority' that Donovan, of whom he utterly disapproved, should be placed in command of raider operations as a brigadier general USMC, the drowning douche being thrown upon this scheme by Admiral Nimitz, who refused to have Donovan within his Pacific Area. From the Marine Commanding Generals in the Atlantic (Maj-Gen H. M. 'Howling Mad' Smith) and in the Pacific (Maj-Gen C. F. B. Price) also came standard objections to raiders. Smith said that 'All Amphibious Force Marines are considered as commandos' and that the Marine Corps, already an élite, did not require its own élite. Price worried over the manner in which a rapidly expanding Corps would be sapped of its best officers and NCOs at a time when they ought to be spread evenly and not concentrated in one place.

The Donovan threat concentrated Marine raider thinking marvellously and led to a compromise. When 1st Raider Battalion was placed under command of Lt-Col M. A. Edson, he took as second-in-command Major S. B. Griffith, who had been sent by Holcomb to England to study the Commandos. Griffith was enthused by all he saw and told Edson about Commando recruiting methods as well as tactics. Bitterly the commander of 1st Marine Division, Major-Gen A. A. Vandegrift, recalled:

'Merritt Edson, armed with appropriate orders, arrived to comb our units for officers and men deemed suitable. . . . Edson's levy against our division, coming at such a time, annoyed the devil out of me, but there wasn't one earthly thing I could do about it.' So Edson took his pick and also favoured new and exotic equipment such as riot-type shot guns, collapsible bicycles, Bangalore torpedoes and sufficient pistols to issue one per raider. Despite this, however, he retained his battalion in the form and philosphy of any other Marine battalion. But when 2nd Raider

Battalion was authorized on 4 February, it was given to Carlson, whose second-in-command was James Roosevelt. And while Edson continued to train his four-company units as a spearhead force on conventional lines, a seaborne equivalent of Marine parachutists, Carlson raised his number of companies to six, similar to six British Commando troops, and trained them with a guerrilla emphasis, Chu Teh's way. Of course, Carlson's relaxed methods appealed to the young and inexperienced among those he recruited as volunteers from West Coast Marines, but the older Leathernecks were either unsure or frankly disapproving of relaxed discipline and informal planning and 'forums', as Carlson called them, in battle. A lot of publicity would be generated by Carlson and for his warcry 'Gung ho' – a Chinese phrase which means 'Work together' but which later generations have come to regard, as one American historian says, as meaning the way 'to win the approval of higher authority by energetically doing far more than the situation realistically requires'. The hot breath of war would soon put the old and new systems to the test. In April Edson's Raiders were moved to Samoa and, in May, Carlson's to Hawaii where the C-in-C Pacific Fleet, Admiral C. W. Nimitz, found himself with a unit 'which I had not requested and which I had not planned for', or so he wrote in 1957. On 28 May, 1942, however, he proposed that Carlson's unit should raid Tulagi.

Strains of resentment permeated the American hierarchy as they had in Britain and, no doubt, were fuelled by the known advocacy of Churchill, now firmly attached to Roosevelt's kitchen cabinet, when he wrote to the President on 5 March, praising Roosevelt's intention to form Commando units on a large scale: '. . . I felt you had the key. Once several good outfits are prepared, any one of which can attack a Japanese-held base or island and beat the life out of the garrison, all their islands will become hostages to fortune', perhaps forgetting how often he had vetoed such raids himself.

In Britain the drive by the Americans for raiders came from a different direction and for different reasons. There Marines were a rarity and the Navy was dragging its feet, so the Army stepped in to fill a hole. Reflecting Roosevelt's determination to have American soldiers in action in Europe at the earliest opportunity, Marshall set in motion, through Colonel L. K. T. Truscott, the senior US Army Officer at COHQ, the formation of special units which, at the earliest possible moment, could become involved in the fighting alongside the British. In the absence of a full-blooded invasion, that could only mean hit-and-run raiding by the equivalent of Commandos or parachutists; and, since training had to be expedited, it had to be carried out by the much more experienced British.

It also made sense to ask for volunteers from the divisions of V Corps, then arriving in Northern Ireland.

Many American officers shared the British viewpoint that Commandos diverted key men from field force units, but Marshall overrode them. He desired selected American troops to acquire combat experience on a rotating basis and seems to have envisaged a US 'commandos unit' (as he referred to it) as a temporary expedient which could be disbanded once its initial purpose had been satisfied. Towards the end of May orders for what would become known as 1st Ranger Battalion were finalized and the unit began to assemble at Carrickfergus on 9 June, soon to be sent to Achnacarry Castle to endure the rigours of training under the redoubtable Lt-Col Vaughan. Despite a remark by Mountbatten that it was he and Marshall who settled on the name 'Ranger', it is much more plausible that Truscott originated it after hearing General Eisenhower remark: 'I hope that you will find some other name than "Commandos", for the glamor of that name will always remain – and properly so – British.'

Named after Roger's Rangers, a group which carried out hit-and-run raids against the French and Indians in pre-Revolutionary days, 1st Ranger Battalion was commanded by Major W. C. Darby, a West Pointer and artilleryman, and its men were all volunteers, 60% from 34th Infantry Division, 30% from 1st Armored Division and 10% from the Engineers, Signal and Quartermaster corps. The questions put by Darby at interviews surpassed those of Carlson. While the latter might ask, 'Could you cut a man's throat?' Darby might demand, 'Did you ever kill a man?' This was a question not normally put to British Commandos, but in every other department the Rangers had to be equal to their trainer's requirements. Many were mid-Westerners and included a lion-tamer and a Sioux Indian. They were a big hit with British landladies, one of whose daughters called them 'Texas Rangers' and herself later became engaged to a full Choctaw Indian who was killed in action.

'To give them the full benefit of the course,' said Vaughan, 'they were made to eat British food, which caused howls of anguish.' They were put through the hoop by men who had fought at Vaagso and on several smaller raids.

'Those bastards tried to kill us, or so we thought,' said one Ranger. 'We always manoeuvred under live fire. They used snipers dressed as Germans who fired just to miss. We learnt fast!'

Organized into six fighting companies like a British Commando, they retained their American characteristics and equipment. It was a partnership which worked well, both in training and in battle.

By default, the Armies of both America and Britain had usurped the role of Marines in amphibious warfare. But in Britain it was now time for Royal Marines to halt the slide, in effect to become Commandos even though their ranks were not wholly filled by volunteers, and therefore did not tally with the Army Commando in method of recruitment. A very high standard they nevertheless maintained, and were experts in amphibious techniques. Due to their prominent part in MENACE, PILGRIM, IRONCLAD and an uncountable number of training exercises and trials, they were second to none. Following the dispersal of the three Commandos sent to the Middle East in 1941, Churchill was insistent that they should be reformed. But his wishes were denied, leaving only eight standard Commandos and 10 (Inter-Allied) Commando for employment in 1942. Moreover, No 5 was absent from Europe taking part in Operation IRONCLAD and destined never to return to the UK during the war. Expeditiously the Royal Marines stepped in to fill the breach from their existing battalions. First to be converted was the all-volunteer 40th (RM) Commando, in February, 1942, as trail-blazers in the re-assertion of the Royal Marine domination of amphibious warfare at the expense of the Army Commandos. Typical of the Mountbatten method, this process was actuated by degrees and only much later, in 1943, codified by an official re-definition of the Royal Marines' function, making them responsible for providing:

'Units to undertake amphibious operations. Units for the rapid establishment and temporary defence of Naval and Fleet Air Arm bases'.

That this drift in favour of the Marines was used by some to pave the way to eradication of the Army Commandos is beyond doubt. Churchill hinted at it in a letter to the Secretary of State for War on 30 August:

It is natural that there should be some resentment in the Army at the undue emphasis laid upon the work of the Commandos by the Press . . . At the same time it must be most clearly understood that the policy of His Majesty's Government is to maintain and develop the Commando organization with the utmost energy and to make sure that the wastage and losses are replaced with good quality men. There can be no question of going back on the decisions taken in favour of the Commando system for a portion of our troops.

A suspicion that the standard of recruit reaching the Commandos towards the end of 1942 was declining provoked the VCCO, Maj-Gen Haydon, into drafting a letter of complaint in February, 1943. Up to then magnificent material had been received, including in 1942 a wonderful draft of policemen called up direct into the Commandos instead of passing through the regiments. Haydon wrote that he appreciated the difficulty of allocating men of quality – everybody had the same sort of problem – but he did feel time was being wasted:

> For example, quite a lot of those being eliminated were not just flat-footed or suffering from other physical ailments, but actually in some cases just about blind or very badly cross-eyed. I cannot understand any Commanding Officer, bearing in mind all that has been written in ACIs, daring to send men of this type. . . . The number of bad crime sheets is legion. On the other hand I quote for your information a sergeant of the Queen's Cameron Highlanders who volunteered three or four times with a very good recommendation and was not allowed to join.

As a sailor, Mountbatten probably favoured the Royal Marines, but there is no evidence that he opposed Army Commandos – quite the opposite, in fact. As CCO he was far more intent on drawing attention to the Combined Operations organization as a whole and it was this which prompted him early in 1942 to put forward a proposal for a distinctive arm badge to be worn by everybody, regardless of Arm or Service, within the organization. He ran a competition for the best design and from Lieut D. A. Grant, RNVR, of HMS *Tormentor*, chose the winning design of anchor, Tommy gun and eagle. This was officially adopted in September after the file on the subject had grown thick in the wrangle over who should or should not be entitled to wear it. Mountbatten also suggested on 1 May, 1942, the head-dress which was to become the most prized possession of everybody in the raiding business – the Green Beret which Commandos wear to the present day, and which was adopted at about the same time as the Parachute Regiment took to wearing the famous Red Beret.

Also towards the end of 1942 Mountbatten fought a prolonged battle to obtain permission for the Commandos to retain an unofficial shoulder flash they had worn since 1940, the struggle being waged at the highest level, as extracts from a draft letter to Lieut-Gen Sir Ronald Adam, the Adjutant General, goes to show:

> I feel I should tell you in confidence that the whole question of the Combined Operations badge and flash which the Commandos now wear came up for discussion many months ago in the course of ordinary conversation when I was with the King.
> H.M took the liveliest interest in the whole idea of the badge and

himself suggested that the various multi-coloured Commando flashes then in existence should be changed to a single one, red lettering on a blue background, to conform with the Combined Operations badge, which is red on blue.

As the King himself had selected the colours and the general layout for the flash (and I am sure H.M will remember the incident, although it was some while ago, because he took so much interest in it) I feel it would be wrong not to let you know about this, since from the wording of your letter – 'the whole matter is under discussion at a very high level' – it is clear that you are going to refer the matter back to His Majesty.

Finally may I assure you that I am not trying in any way to prevent this matter being referred to the King; on the contrary I entirely concur that this is the right course.

The letter was never sent. Perhaps Mountbatten thought that he was laying it on a bit thick! In due course he would have his way, although by discussion and with a subtler approach through regular channels, but not until April, 1943.

CHAPTER 17

Frustration

No stretch of the English Channel attracted such a weight of shot, bomb and shell as did the narrows between Dover and Calais – Hell Fire Corner as it liked to be known with grim pride. Since June, 1940, it had been the exception to a rule when some sort of aggression did not occur. Long before Spring, 1942, the towns and villages overlooking the Straits bore lurid scars of battle and had been considerably depopulated of civilians by casualties and evacuation. Fighting men were now the dominant occupants where commerce with Europe once thrived. Convoys still sailed under heavy escort, hugging the coastline. Long-range guns lobbed shells over as the occasion demanded. Aircraft tangled in combat overhead while bombers provided the most frequent form of hit-and-run raid hereabouts. The sea bed, a graveyard over the centuries for the wreckage of war, regularly received a fresh quota of ships, aircraft and their crews. Here neither side could ever afford to relax its guard. Even if the Germans had failed to put a single raider ashore by boat in 1940, that was no reason to dismiss the possibility of it still happening. And with every moonless period that elapsed the Germans were made forcibly aware that their turn to receive assailants was greater. Nightly, while the French civilians who remained took shelter, German small ships put to sea and their gunners and infantry went on stand-by, tensely watching and listening for enemy ships and craft.

Ten days after the damaged tanker at Boulogne blew up as a result of Operation JV, the alert was sounded again. Operation ABERCROMBIE should have hit the beach on the night 19/20 April, but the sea, that incorrigible wrecker of the best laid raiding plans, took its toll. Outward bound, the MGBs and LCAs were unexpectedly pummelled by a high wind which whipped up waves, one of which suddenly broke over an LCA's bows, swamping her, with the loss of two men, and causing the

MGB captain to cut the tow and abandon the sinking craft. Two days later, after a period in close confinement for security reasons, the same 100 men of 4 Commando, under command of Major Lord Lovat, set off again on what was intended as a reconnaissance but which the men eagerly hoped would lead to a fight. On board was the Exchange Telegraph Company's special correspondent whose task was almost as important as that of the fighting men – to bring back useful propaganda for world-wide consumption as proof of British intentions to strike hard in compliance with the mounting chorus demanding a Second Front. On St George's Day, when the story broke, most of the papers would focus upon the heroic and colourful 30-year-old Lord Lovat, a leader of charisma, skill and gallantry. The report in *The Times*, if more prosaic, was closer to accuracy than some of its competitors, guarded as it had to be to meet the censor's requirements:

> Fifty-three regiments were represented. All the men had blacked their faces and all wore gym shoes for silence, with the exception of one officer, a former police inspector in the East End of London, who wore carpet slippers kept on by elastic. . . . Veiled in light mist, the landing craft had crept silently inshore, and the Commandos had dropped swiftly and quietly into the shallows through which they had to wade to the beach. Searchlights began to flicker. Whistles were sounded. They could be heard by the advancing troops. . . . But the Commandos had swept across the sand and were at the beach wire before they met machine-gunfire. 'We were lucky,' said Lord Lovat.

His remark concealed the immense difficulty his men had in cutting a lane through thick barbed wire entanglements. Several things went wrong, such as the memory of a patrol leader who failed to give the correct password and might have been shot by his own side had not a Bren gun become clogged by sand. The correspondent continues:

> The Germans fired a shower of Verey lights. The first German encountered was a one-man patrol who, swinging a torch, shouted *Halten*. Tommy guns were fired at him, the torch went out, and no more was heard. British patrols went out [to a depth of 800 yards] and contacted enemy strongpoints . . . One patrol leader said, 'The pill-boxes had no idea where we were and what we were doing.' After spending two hours on enemy-occupied territory every man was withdrawn with his weapons. The Navy encountered stiff opposition

... For many minutes the sky was lit by the fierce exchange of
fire between the escort craft and the attacking German *flak*
ships and smaller craft. One of the *flak* ships made off, apparently on
fire.

It was a drawn encounter, although claimed as a victory by both sides.
The German account of the raid boasted, 'British shock troops and
equipment covered the shore'. It was also a warning to both sides – to the
British that the defences were a lot tougher than two years ago when
COLLAR landed at the same spot: to the Germans as notice of future
determined enemy intent. Nevertheless ABERCROMBIE did make an
impression, which was more than could be said for its immediate
successors. Next on the list and scheduled for May was Operation
BLAZING, the resurrection of an old ambition of Churchill's, an attempt
to capture and hold Alderney rather in the manner of the unlamented
TOMATO which had been turned down in the summer of 1940. Nothing
could have been more damning than the Chiefs of Staff's reasons in their
letter of rejection to the Prime Minister, who seems once more to have
been behind this scheme:

> The essence of the plan is to soften the defences by a terrific
> preliminary air bombardment. To be effective this must continue until
> the last moment before assault on the analogy of a barrage. For
> navigational reasons the landing cannot take place in darkness. This
> means the bombers will be exposed to attack by fighters during daylight
> and are likely to incur heavy casualties. The air defences on the island
> are exceptionally strong. Fighter Command cannot promise to provide
> fighter cover. Our fighters would only have about 20 minutes over the
> target. There would be gaps.
>   If the operation looked like paying a really worthwhile dividend it
> would be worth doing, but it would not draw off troops from Russia and
> the Chiefs of Staff do not consider the killing or capture of 2,000
> Germans worth the candle.

To what extent the islanders might have been affected seems not to
have been considered, but Churchill made no protest, so they went on to
consider another rather similar operation called AIMWELL and rejected
that also, for the same reasons. Time was wasted in setting up Aunt Sallys
for the pleasure of knocking them down when so much else was consum-
ing the Staffs' time. Yet certain important points affecting strategy and the
general conduct of amphibious warfare were exposed. Note the way the

Chiefs used Churchill's original reasons for vetoing BARBARIC, by deftly questioning the profitability of such a limited objective. Observe, too, the rubbing-in of the need for air cover which, quite clearly, Churchill had yet to understand. See, also, how the Planners were now interested in supporting a daylight landing with massive bombardment and thus turning aside from the method of attacking weak spots at night which they had pressed upon the US Marines the previous summer and towards the system preferred by their American colleagues. Yet BLAZING was small beer compared with another even larger and more risky project under consideration in June for possible execution in August.

Operational NATIONAL, quite frankly described as 'a re-planning of MYRMIDON', was conceived as a landing at St Jean de Luz by two Commandos followed up by one and a half Royal Marine Battalions, an armoured regiment and a motor battalion. The 3000 marching infantry having got ashore and formed a beachhead, the mobile troops (about forty-eight tanks and eighty other vehicles) were to move swiftly southwards to the Spanish frontier and northwards to Biarritz and Bayonne. It would have been a trial outing for the three Maracaibos, and probably their last. For even if they had put their cargoes safely ashore, it is unimaginable that massive German reaction would have been long delayed or that a force without even minimal air cover could have survived. Without convincing resistance from the planners, and bearing in mind that RUTTER or JUBILEE were already in the offing, this large-scale raid vanished.

May, therefore, drew a blank for raiding and June got off to a bad start. Operation FOXROCK – a raid against St Valery-sur-Somme by 100 members of 12 Commando with the object of destroying lock gates, railway bridges and rolling stock on the night of 1/2 June – looked set to reach its objectives when, at 2200 hours on the 1st, it found it was being shadowed by an enemy aeroplane. For the time being the navigating ML, six Eurekas under their own power and four MGBs kept going, backed up by a destroyer. But when, at 2345 hours, the Y Service, which monitored enemy radio transmissions, reported an intercept revealing that the raiding force had been spotted, the Force Commander decided to cancel, a very wise decision since fourteen minutes later the force was challenged by a German surface force.

The next intended raid was LANCING, which consisted of two coinciding raids between Boulogne and Le Touquet – DEARBORN to the north, which was dropped, and BRISTLE to the south, centred upon Plage St Cecile. As a glorified BITING, its aim the removal or destruction radar apparatus so as to create a gap in the German coverage, BRISTLE did at least have the virtue of attacking a target related to the main prop of Allied offensive pretensions in North-West Europe – the air battle which, the Chiefs of Staff were led to believe, might be of most assistance to the Russians at that moment. Had the Russians been witnesses, they could have been impressed only by British determination and courage, for nothing went to plan once the LCAs had been lowered from their LSI nine miles from the beach.

For a start the eight MGBs and navigating ML lost contact with the LCAs, even though conditions were good. Compelled to carry out a sweep in search of one MGB with a faulty engine silencer, they may well have alerted the enemy. Therefore the 250 men of 6 Commando had to navigate for themselves, unescorted and in the presence of light enemy naval forces, their course determined by the flashes from Le Touquet lighthouse and periodic disclosures by a searchlight known to be situated at Hardelot. The Force Commander, in discussion with the senior Naval Officer with the LCAs, had a tricky decision to take:

> As the moon rose the coastline became clearer and the hills inland made a good silhouette. . . . We decided that we were still 2000 yards to the north and the exact place appeared to be in front of a saddle in the hills. The searchlight to the north swept over us, but apparently did not pick us up. At about 0240 hours, [nearly an hour behind schedule] the whole flotilla did a left turn and went towards the beach – they were very strung out. Just as some of the craft grounded, the searchlights from the north were turned full on. It was found necessary to wade from between 40 and 80 yards.
>
> The troops were off the beach and into the sand dunes rapidly . . . by the time the northern enemy M.G. opened fire. . . . A white flare was put up just as we were disembarking. . . . The right-hand enemy MGs opened up shortly after the left-hand MGs. The shooting appeared very high and a considerable amount of tracer was used. A number of bullets struck the landing craft. On reaching the beach . . . I ordered the plan NOT to be undertaken but instead a large bridgehead to be formed.

Confusion, typical of any infantry battle when communications are at a premium, was now rife. For most it was each man for himself. Troop Commanders who tried to reply to the enemy fire got the range wrong. Tracer criss-crossed overhead. Fire coming from seaward indicated the presence of enemy warships.

Bearing in mind the difficulty we should have in re-embarking under fire and in deep water, I gave the signal to re-embark by wireless and by bugle.

It was essential to do this because the RAF was due to start bombing to cover the retreat at 0400 hrs, and it took a considerable time since the LCAs stayed well out. Now the moon, augmented by searchlights, flares and approaching dawn, made it easy to see, and warranted the landing craft putting down smoke screens while their gunners tried to suppress the enemy fire. From the noise, flash and smoke a terrific battle seemed to be in progress, though few were hurt and only two of 6 Commando were taken prisoner. Meanwhile, out at sea in an MGB, Major Williams-Thompson, from COHQ, experienced his first naval battle:

We sighted two enemy patrol boats and the officer in charge decided to attack them. This ended, after a thrilling engagement, with the sinking of one and the damaging of another. . . . After this engagement we were fired on by a coast defence battery, which we evaded by a smoke trail. The exposing of the searchlights about this time disclosed empty LCAs off the beach. . . . This was the first we saw of the LCAs after their dropping from the *Prince Albert*.

As the withdrawal went on, the air battle started, RAF aircraft coming in low to batter the shore defences as a fighter screen orbited the landing craft, which were reinforced by three SGBs and a couple of MLs. Again Williams-Thompson:

At this time the fighter cover had apparently been withdrawn. The planes that had been guarding us formed up together and flew away. It was about twenty minutes more before we received further fighter protection. During this interlude . . . the rear party was attacked by German fighters and bombers which caused four naval and two army casualties. They sent out an S.O.S to Dover and in due course our fighters arrived.

Williams-Thompson considered this to be masterly timing by the Germans and saw it as proof of how good the German radar system was, but it was probably a fluke. Anyway, the enemy tried later and had to be driven off, demonstrating that, although the *Luftwaffe* was content to ignore 'sweeps' by RAF fighters, it could be lured into action when RAF bombers were out or vulnerable surface targets were presented. But Williams-Thompson also voiced an old complaint that the MGBs employed, coming as they did from a flotilla not accustomed to working with Combined Operations, had fallen below the desired standard of expertise. In other words, amphibious raiding remained within the province of specialization and the universal high standards needed to support a major invasion or very large raid, such as RUTTER, were still wanting.

BRISTLE had included and used almost every weapon in the hit-and-run armoury, but this feat of intricate co-ordination had produced little or no return on outlay. The objective was not reached, the object unattained, no prisoners taken, eight casualties suffered, a couple of fighters lost, besides superficial damage to craft and, most telling of all, forfeiture of prestige – of which the Propaganda Ministry of Dr Goebbels was quick to take advantage in its English-language programmes by making the enforced British retreat seem a rout and pouring scorn upon the Commandos.

> Isn't Commando just another name for poor bloody infantry? Germany does not find it necessary to carry out tip-and-run raids on the English coast. The reputation of the German infantryman has become almost legendary by itself, without any artificial plugging. . . . But what is more important is whether Britain needs Commandos.

This was a question that Captain Maund has posed in a different context back in 1940.

In the occupied countries the German propagandists adopted the wedge-driving technique, endeavouring to exploit French sensitivity and anti-British feeling. A commentator on Radio Paris entitled his piece 'The Commando Raid on Dunkirk Anniversary', remarking:

> The British could hardly have celebrated the occasion except with a military display. So far the military demonstrations of British friendship have been attacks on our Colonies, and the assassination of Frenchmen desirous of living without the British.

And over Free India Radio, which broadcast in English for India and Indians, who, at that moment were threatened with a Japanese invasion which some India nationalists would have welcomed:

> Practically all their weapons were abandoned. This theatrical show indicates growing nervousness in Great Britain. Moreoever the

Russian reverses compel the British Government to stage farcical comedies to cheer up the British public. But in reality every attempt to land on the French coast brings home to every man in England that the way to Europe is barred to them for ever.

In Britain those at COHQ were intrigued that the German propagandists gave BRISTLE such prominence although they let it be known that it was only a small raid, suggesting 'the sensitivity of the Axis to this type of operation'. This was, in fact, all too true, and emanated from Hitler himself, who, in the aftermath of the winter reverses in Russia and the attacks against Vaagso and St Nazaire, spent an increasingly disproportionate time each day discussing raids with his military advisors.

One wonders what might have happened if the pressure had been kept up, but once more there was a lull; with three propositions in train or under consideration for July, not one left port. RUTTER, a large scale raid by Canadian troops against Dieppe, was scheduled for early July but, for reasons which will be described later, was postponed and then cancelled. FORETOP, an all-embracing operation somewhere between a raid and an invasion in support of the Battle of the Atlantic against the U-boat ports of Bordeaux, St Nazaire, La Pallice and Lorient, was dropped (probably correctly) because it was considered too costly. ARMSTRONG, a trend-setting scheme to tackle a four-gun battery south-west of Cayeux by a co-ordinated attack of Commandos from the sea and a company of parachutists or glider troops from the air, was set aside despite keen interest by General Eisenhower, the newly appointed American Commanding General, European Theatre of Operations.

Similarly SYNCOPATION, a small raid against the Ile Bréhat to capture prisoners, was 'cancelled at the C-in-C's wishes for fear of drawing unwanted attention to the location' (SLEDGEHAMMER loomed ahead); ACROSTIC, a raid on Belgian defences at Knaben, was abandoned because mines were found in the difficult sea approaches; and PIPELINE, a small reconnaissance in MLs and canoes by six members of a new private army called the Small Scale Raiding Force (SSRF) of a landing ground near Fécamp, was not proceeded with. There emerged at this time a mood of worried frustration on the part of the Prime Minister and those at COHQ. Despite the bold talk and aggressive posturing of the winter and early spring, summer raiding was negligible, the results poor and the political pressure to help Russia unassuaged. Tempers were rising, impatient men turning to desperate measures. It is arguable that the revival of Operation RUTTER under the name of JUBILEE was one such, but a fascinating two-man raid put forward by Capt P. Pinckney could certainly be classified as being within the realms of Missions Impossible.

Forgiven for his indiscretion the previous December of throwing film into the sea after Operation ANKLET, Pinckney made a hand-written submission to his Commanding Officer on 23 June asking permission to 'snatch' a specimen of a Focke Wulf 190, the latest German fighter, of which little was known:

> I further propose that the pilot to accompany me should be Geoffrey (sic) Quill who is a close friend of mine and, as a well-known test pilot of fighter aircraft, is well qualified to bring back the plane. He is also young, active, a yachtsman, and a man in every way suitable to carry out the preliminary approach by land and sea.

In outline the detailed scheme put forward by Pinckney envisaged transport by MGB to within one or two miles of the French coast, going ashore in a Folbot and hiding up, with the boat, throughout the next day. By stages the two men would then head for the airfield, penetrate its defences and conceal themselves near the selected aircraft.

> At the start of nautical twilight on D.4, when the aircraft are warmed up by ground mechanics, the two officers will take the first opportunity to shoot the ground mechanics of the selected plane as soon as it has been started up. [The need for the engine to be running was paramount; starting an unfamiliar, cold engine would have been impossible]. The pilot officer will take off in the machine and return to England. The Commando officer will first ensure the safe departure of the aircraft and will then withdraw to a previously reconnoitered hide-up.

Thereafter home by foot, Folbot and MGB, the Focke Wulf having long ago evaded shooting down by British fighters on its way to a new home and close investigation.

Operation AIRTHIEF, as Pinckney's plan was named, was given immediate attention, followed by approval. But, by a happy coincidence, as final preparations were being made, the pilot of an FW 190 became disorientated when engaged in aerial combat over England and put down on an airfield in South Wales in broad daylight, presenting the RAF with a completely serviceable specimen. AIRTHIEF, to the fury of Pinckney and the relief of Quill, was called off. Yet it presaged a new style of raiding about to be launched by SSRF by underlining the feasibility of a small party achieving results undetected, while large bodies were shown to draw unwanted attention to themselves. AIRTHIEF might well have succeeded out of surprise even if Pinckney did sacrifice himself in the attempt.

CHAPTER 18

Muddle at Makin

On or about 17 June, at the tail of the letter Mountbatten sent to Roosevelt, which was referred to in Chapter 15, he touched also upon the dramatic change in Allied fortunes in the Pacific:

> As the result of the recent losses inflicted by the US Fleet on the Japanese Fleet, particularly their aircraft carriers, there was a general desire to take the offensive from Australia, using the existing US Marine forces and combat shipping.
>
> General Marshall had suggested going for Timor and General MacArthur [C-in-C South West Pacific Area] had telegraphed on his own suggesting making for Rabaul. I said that you and General Marshall were anxious that two British aircraft carriers with their destroyer screen should join the American forces in Australia to support these operations, and that there had also been a suggestion that the amphibious force which had assaulted Madagascar should be used for operations against the Japanese.

This was one offspring of Rear Admiral Turner's operational concept in April: 'Available air, amphibious and naval forces will make minor offensive actions against enemy advanced positions and against exposed naval forces for purposes of attrition' – a halfway approach to large-scale raiding. Known as Operation WATCHTOWER, the landings on Tulagi and Guadalcanal in the Solomon Islands marked the end of eight months' Japanese expansion. On 25 June, a week after Churchill and Brooke arrived in Washington for renewed discussions about, among other pressing matters, a Second Front in Europe in 1942, orders for WATCHTOWER were issued by Admiral King to Nimitz. The reaction of the latter was sceptical concerning what he referred to as Operation

Shoestring. Evolving, as is usually the way with risky schemes, through a series of fits, starts and amendments, the plan was finally settled in Nimitz's Pacific Ocean Area under Vice Admiral R. L. Ghormley's strategic direction. The Amphibious Force would operate under the recently appointed Turner, with the British Rear Admiral V. A. C. Crutchley VC as his second-in-command. Consisting of five US cruisers and fifteen destroyers, three Australian cruisers and the 1st Marine Division (Maj-Gen A. A. Vandegrift), this was predominantly an American expedition, the proposal to incorporate British aircraft carriers and 5 Commando having to be dropped since the capture of Madagascar was incomplete. Air power was therefore also an American responsibility. The initial assault was to be covered by 250 aircraft from three USN aircraft carriers under Rear Admiral L. Noyes, backed up 261 USN, Marine and Army aircraft, plus thirty Royal New Zealand Air Force machines. But as none of the latter 291 possessed the range to operate over the Sealark Channel, the main prerequisite of WATCHTOWER was the immediate seizure of an airfield, Henderson Field, on Guadalcanal. If that was not achieved quickly there was every likelihood that the invasion would rapidly be converted into hit-and-run, with emphasis on the latter.

Since Operation WATCHTOWER achieved a strong lodgement ashore, it escaped becoming a hit-and-run operation and so also evades description in detail here, except in so far as it strongly influenced the American raiding forces' future. At Tulagi, Lt-Col Edson's 1st Raider Bn and the follow-up waves provided by Major R. M. Williams's 1st Parachute Bn, deprived of their ordained means of arrival because no transport aircraft were available and the ground was unsuitable for dropping, acted as spearhead troops, in the manner of conventional light infantry. But the fact that they attacked with the élan expected of an élite could not disguise the defects of their techniques. Like Commandos in Europe, the 1st Raiders, suffering from inadequate intelligence of enemy and shore line, became hung-up on undetected reefs and might have been destroyed had not the Japanese been taken completely by surprise by Turner's overall plan. As it was, the Raiders and Parachutists did well at Tulagi and later on Guadalcanal, sufficiently well to lay substantial claim to a permanent place in the Marine order of battle.

For 2nd Raider Bn it was different. Once WATCHTOWER obviated Admiral Nimitz's scheme of 28 May to raid Tulagi, a new task had to be found for Carlson's men, ostensibly as a trial for very long-range hit-and-run attacks. He plumped for the idea of using the two submarines *Nautilus* and *Argonaut* to carry the Raiders to the Japanese-held island

of Makin in the Gilbert Islands. The stated aim was five-fold –
seek intelligence, destroy enemy installations, distract attention from
Guadalcanal, test raider techniques and boost morale back in the
States.

Under Carlson's enthusiastic direction, they set sail on what was to
prove a most uncomfortable and cramped eight-day voyage of 2,500 miles
from Hawaii, arriving off Butaritari Island on 16 August in the entirely
false expectations of finding the lagoon entrance covered by an enemy
battery and the island garrisoned by about 250 men. That being so,
Carlson planned, early on the 17th, to land 222 men in rubber inflatable
boats through the surf on the seaward side of the island. But confusion
when launching from the submarines, and the failure of several outboard
motors, brought a change of mind and a last-minute change of plans. Now
it was to be 'follow me' to a single landing place, instead of two as
previously intended. Unfortunately one platoon leader, Lieut O. F.
Peatross, did not hear the change of plan through the noise of the sea
during launching from *Nautilus*, and went ashore where first intended,
over a mile from Carlson and the other fifteen boatloads.

The local natives, who gave immense help all along, later suggested
that the forty-three Japanese Marines under Chief Warrant Officer
Kanemitsu, were forewarned. If this is so, their defences were ill-
prepared and they were completely taken by surprise. Both Carlson's
and Peatross's parties got ashore unseen – and might well have remained
undetected until ready to attack had not one Raider accidentally loosed off
his rifle while forming up to advance towards the suspected enemy main
position. As a result they encountered stiff opposition, became involved in
a fire fight and lost momentum. At this point Sgt C. Thomason took
charge, winning a Congressional Medal of Honor by his example. On one
occasion 'he dauntlessly walked up to a house which concealed an enemy
sniper, forced in the door and shot the man before he could resist'. Later
he led the assault which cost him his life, but in so doing broke the back of
Japanese resistance at the lagoon side, though in the confusion this was
not realized by Carlson. Meanwhile Peatross had advanced in accordance
with his original orders and arrived unopposed with eleven Raiders at a
rendezvous where nobody else was waiting, in the enemy rear. His bold
attack on the lagoon sector also made progress and several enemy were
killed, but at loss to himself and without making contact with Carlson. So
he crossed to the sea sector and, as one account says:

> Puzzled, Peatross and his remaining seven men (several of them
> wounded) repaired to their boats and returned to *Nautilus*.

Meanwhile Kanemitsu had sent a radio message warning his superiors. Soon help was on the way. As Carlson's fight for the main enemy position was rising to its climax, two small Japanese ships, later said to contain sixty reinforcements, entered the lagoon and were sunk by sixty-five rounds of 6-inch shells from *Nautilus* which picked up Carlson's radio call for help but thereafter had to conduct an incredible unobserved shoot because Carlson's radio broke down. Next came the bombing, successive missions by bombers and flying boats, none of which inflicted casualties because the Raiders simply took cover. But the two flying boats which landed in the lagoon did manage to put thirty-five men ashore before being destroyed.

Towards the end of a day which Carlson sensed had gone wrong, he decided to withdraw to the submarines, an hour or so ahead of the original schedule, in the belief that the enemy, who were counter-attacking vigorously, and who had sent a message boasting 'We are dying in battle', were unbroken. Once more the surf and outboard-engine failure wrecked his plan; men and boats were flung back on the beach because paddles could not match the power of the sea. Only seventy men reached the submarines; some were drowned and the remaining 100, most of their weapons lost, soaked by heavy rain and fearing the arrival of strong Japanese reinforcements, stayed ashore in despair. At midnight Carlson called a forum, not to give orders, but, according to his creed, to ask the others their opinion and let them do as they chose – surrender or try to escape. Sgt Herrero and five men elected to try again and made it to the submarines that night, as did Major Roosevelt and fifteen more at dawn. The rest opted to surrender. Carlson sent out emissaries who discovered, to their astonishment, that apart from a few stragglers, who were shot, the enemy were all dead. Moreover, no battery guarded the lagoon entrance, so it was a simple matter to bring in the submarine to pick up the survivors in calm water. Yet confusion reigned supreme to the end. Nobody really knew who was dead and who had escaped. Everybody was anxious to be off, the next scheme – to raid Little Makin – being sensibly abandoned. Unhappily an inaccurate count left nine marines still ashore and they, in due course, were captured and ceremonially beheaded.

Carlson claimed a victory. At a cost of thirty men and large quantities of equipment, much heavier losses had been inflicted upon the Japanese. The Press let themselves go, extolling the exploit, describing the Raiders as 'experts in death, demolition and destruction', and printing their battle song (sung to the tune of 'Ivan Skavinsky, Skavar') with generous references to Carlson and 'Gung Ho'. The Marine hierarchy and the Navy were content to let it go at that. They suspected then, what later was written in the official Marine History, that the Makin raid's 'military significance was negligible' – an account which left unrecorded the fiasco of the surrender attempt and the sad story of the nine men left behind.*

Of greater direct help in the grim, main battle of Guadalcanal was a dawn raid on 8 September by elements of 1st Parachute and 1st Raider Battalions, under Edson's command, against the enemy supply base at Tasimboko village. Coming ashore as flank protection, the parachutists held off intruders while the Raiders rushed the village, supported by heavy fire. Staunchly the Japanese fought back, but surprise and superior firepower put them to flight. Triumphantly, and with few casualties, the Raiders set the supply dumps alight and withdrew, unmolested, at nightfall. This was copy-book hit-and-run raiding in the best Marine tradition, which, for the time being, guaranteed the Raiding Forces' future. Edson's exploits at Tulagi and Tasimboko, added to the public acclaim for Carlson's escapades at Makin, impressed middle-ranking Marines and, of vital significance, Rear Admiral Turner. Intent on getting at small enemy detachments scattered about the Solomons, he wrote to Ghormley on 29 August:

> In many circumstances in the future amphibious warfare in the South Pacific it is believed that a Marine Regiment, or part of a Marine Regiment, or two Marine Regiments, will be the size of force appropriate for offensive and defensive amphibious operations. The employment of a division as a landing unit seems less likely. In some cases, night landings by small units will be useful for preparing bridgeheads for the main landing next day. . . . The previous concept that Raider and Parachute Battalions are always division or corps troops is no longer agreed to.

Let it be noted that Turner was not, as some critics have since asserted, demanding the abolition of amphibious operations by large formations. He was merely saying that, at that stage of the war, it was less likely to be that way and that there was a need for more raiding units which could be introduced more flexibly into battle on what came to be known as the 'brick' system.

---

* Long after the war the Makin raid was blamed for alerting the Japanese to the threat to the Gilbert and Marshall islands, causing them to strengthen the defences. The same critics did not mention the valuable lessons concerning the impracticability of paddling rubber boats in island surf nor that Amtracks (LVT) would be needed to cross the reefs! Nor did they examine the Japanese records which showed how weak the defences were and why. In fact they did not reinforce the islands substantially until a year later and only then because they wanted to buy time in order to complete their newly designated main defences in the Kuriles, Marianas and Carolines.

Authorized in writing by the Joint Chiefs of Staff to be 'in command of the naval, ground and air units assigned to the amphibious forces in the South Pacific area', and never challenged at the time by Marine commanders, Turner went on to declare that, 'unless directed to the contrary', he would proceed with the organization of Provisional Raider Battalions in the 2nd, 7th and 8th Marines. Turner's real offence, as picked on at the time by Nimitz, Ghormley and senior Marines, was failure to consult General Vandegrift before sending the letter, and for ordering the 'idle' 2nd Marines to form a Provisional battalion at once. The order was cancelled at once from on high and Carlson's established 2nd Raider Bn sent to Guadalcanal. But despite ruffled feathers, the Marines Commandant, General Holcomb, felt bound to concede that 'the commanders in the field seemed, however, to favor the formation of more raider units and that he would interpose no objection'.

Turner was marked black for ever in the eyes of proud Marines who 'regretted' that he seemed to claim 'possession' of Marines. Ever since, they have rarely passed up an opportunity in the writing of history to warp the record by omitting mention of Turner's legitimate reasons for acting as he did. The Rear Admiral, of course, was a lot too clever and outspoken for some; highly respected, often feared, loved only by those who knew him well, he was the last person on earth to court popularity.

Despite the 'possession' row, the 3rd Raider Battalion, formed from volunteers, was activated at Samoa, and the 4th raised in California a month later and used as a cadre for the Raider Training Center in February, 1943. And on Guadalcanal the Raider and Parachute battalions continued to enhance their reputation as fine go-ahead troops – but mainly for orthodox flank landings, as at Tasimboko, of the sort Admiral King, as well as Turner, envisaged. Meanwhile the Marine enemies of élite Raiders bided their time and the Japanese gave careful consideration to the lessons of Makin as a taste of what lay over the horizon.

And back in Europe, the Germans too were worrying along somewhat similar lines.

CHAPTER 19

Dieppe – the Essential Experiment

On 24 July, 1942, after four months' searching, but never acrimonious, debate, the British and Americans reached agreement over the rejection of SLEDGEHAMMER and the adoption of a modified GYMNAST named TORCH. The objective would be French North-West Africa – another peripheral target outside the reach of rapid and strong Axis intervention. But because it fell short of an impressive, directly aimed Second Front of popular and Russian expectation, Churchill was faced with the unenviable task of visiting Premier Stalin in Moscow to explain the climb-down.

Stalin had grounds for complaint. He could claim that, whereas not a single American soldier had yet shed his blood in combat in Europe, and that the British had been thrown back once more in defeat in Egypt and had managed only two insignificant forays into France since March, the Russians were doing all the fighting and suffering grievous losses in face of the latest furious German onslaught in the direction of the Caucasus and Stalingrad. It was perhaps with Stalin's anger in mind, allied to a sense of failure, that Operation JUBILEE (RUTTER renamed) was conceived.

Operation RUTTER, a large-scale descent on Dieppe, was one of several projects put forward as a result of a request in October, 1941, by General Brooke, then C-in-C Home Forces, for raids on occupied France and the Low Countries to provide his troops, meaning units other than Commandos, with real battle experience to consolidate the lessons learnt on exercises and to do something to prevent boredom setting in. A practical experiment into the tactics for seizing a defended enemy port was also called for, since the possession of one was deemed essential to ensure adequate logistical support when the day for a major invasion arrived. Early in 1942 studies at COHQ had centred upon ways and means, and this led, in April, to a firm proposal to attack Dieppe with forces in excess of a division. On 14 April members of the General Staff, Home Forces, moved in with Mountbatten's planners and soon were joined by the GOC-in-C South-Eastern Command, Lieut-Gen B. L. Montgomery, who was thereafter closely associated with developments.

True to their contention that Maginot-type defences should not be attacked frontally in daylight, COHQ wanted to seize commanding enemy coastal batteries on the flanks of Dieppe, using infantry supported by tanks, and then pinch out Dieppe without resort to a frontal assault. Montgomery and Home Forces favoured a daylight frontal assault heavily supported by air bombardment, *after* airborne troops (glider-borne and parachutists) had seized the batteries in darkness. Strong arguments favouring the Home Forces' plan included an insistence that the town was held by a low-category enemy battalion, that artillery was thin on the ground, that reinforcements would be too slow arriving and that the tanks landing at Quiberville, six miles west of Dieppe, would have to cross two rivers on their way to the port and might easily be held up. Despite strong objections by Mountbatten, who deprecated a frontal attack, the contrary view prevailed. Unfortunately Intelligence was faulty and the plan amended until, in its final form, the air bombardment was cancelled, (much to the relief of Churchill whose embargo on blind area bombing of French towns had to be specially lifted to cover the occasion) because it was feared damage to buildings and fires would impede the tanks. Montgomery, in his *Memoirs*, washes his hands of responsibility for cancelling the air bombardment, suggesting that this was done after he had ceased to have responsibility for the operation. The fact remains that the bombing was abandoned at a meeting chaired by him on 5 June, at the request of the Military Commander, Maj-Gen J. H. Roberts and with the concurrence of the Air Force Commander, Air Vice-Marshal Leigh Mallory.

On 1 June the concentration of shipping, including eight LSIs and twenty-four LCTs, was complete and on the 13th a rehearsal (YUKON I) staged at West Bay, Dorset. It was found that the formation-keeping and timing of the landing-craft flotillas was ragged and unacceptable to the Military Commander. Consequently CCO ordered a repeat (YUKON II) on 23 June and attended it in person before permitting orders to be given to raid on the first suitable date after the 24th. After that the weather closed in, leading to repeated postponements and finally to cancellation on 7 July at the same moment as two of the LSIs were damaged by bombing. The airborne troops stood down; the Canadian infantry and tanks detailed to land from the sea disembarked with a deep feeling of let-down, and Mountbatten set about saving something from the wreckage.

The pressures which forced the revival of RUTTER, as a fundamentally modified raid under the name of JUBILEE, were irresistible. Churchill, for compelling political reasons, felt bound to demonstrate British willingness to take the offensive and satisfy a public craving which demanded Russia should be helped. Brooke, to quote the internal History of the Combined Operations Organization, was emphatic that the planning for the main invasion could not proceed until an operation of that scale had taken place. The Canadians, who had trained ceaselessly for nearly two years, were thirsting for battle, some of their commanding officers tossing up to see whose battalion should take part. Mountbatten was extremely worried by the succession of misfires, rejections, failures and cancellations since CHARIOT, which were 'virtually defeat, all this work and nothing to show for it; it was bad for morale'.

On 27 July JUBILEE was approved, but now 3 & 4 Commandos would land on the flanks to do the job originally allocated to airborne troops. Intelligence of the enemy was as imprecise as ever, but the Germans knew even less of British arrangements. Security, particularly in the light of the previous preparations which were by now compromised, was stringent. It is untrue, as had been claimed, that 'nothing was put in writing'. A typed operation order, for example, was issued on 31 July with its Object stated as:

> A raid on Jubilee with limited air and military objectives, the destruction of local defences and power stations etc in Jubilee. Capture of prisoners, the destruction of aerodromes and installations near the town, capture and removal of German invasion barges and any other craft in Jubilee harbour.

There were many other documents as well, but no evidence whatsoever in support of post-JUBILEE accusations that the enemy knew. Yet the troops, by signs of activity and repeated alerts and stand-downs, transmitted their suspicions of impending action to those among whom they dwelt. And the latter, used to the calls to 'Keep Mum (like Dad)', mostly kept their mouths shut. A barmaid recalled the atmosphere at the Gloucester Hotel in Weymouth, which was frequented by 4 Commando:

> You could sense when something big was happening, but nothing was ever said. I knew the lot that went to Bruneval. Later on I got to know the crowd that went to Dieppe. There was something going on

the Sunday night. They were really drinking up. They must have left that night. On the Wednesday morning Lord Lovat's batman sat on the stool in the bar. He said very little, but still there was that sense of knowing. He had come to fetch some of his boss's things.

The 252 landing craft and supporting ships which sailed on the night of 18 August arrived undetected within eight miles of Dieppe in the waning minutes of darkness on the 19th. But not entirely unexpected, since for many months the Germans had been in the habit of manning their defences at dawn whenever tidal and lunar conditions were most suitable for landings. Nor undetected when, without warning, the landing craft carrying 3 Commando (Lt-Col J. F. Durnford-Slater) were fired upon by five patrolling enemy armed trawlers. This was simply the first of many surprises which were about to be unveiled as the result of inadequate Intelligence.

This is not intended as a blow-by-blow description of the landing at Dieppe, for that demands a book on its own and has frequently been dealt with in detail. Rather more to the point, in the context of hit-and-run raiding, it is meant to convey an impression, along with an analysis of what went right, what wrong – and why. The gathering and transmission of Intelligence was crucial; it was upon this as much as anything else that success or failure hinged. The failure of 3 Commando, to which was attached thirty US Rangers from Darby's 1st Bn, to reach its objective in strength on the left flank was largely due to the unexpected encounter with some trawlers whose presence might have been revealed if relevant Intelligence had not been ignored. Hinsley, in a special Appendix to Volume 2 of the *Official History of Intelligence*, gives precise reasons for concluding that 'failures in communications . . . greatly reduced the value of the current intelligence that was available'. It also reduced what was intended as a landing by a complete Commando into a presence the size of a small raiding force, consisting of a single Eureka of twenty men, led by Major P. Young. The other twenty Eurekas were still at sea, having dispersed in accordance with orders to do so if intercepted. Their navigating SGB 5 was reduced to a shambles when, with nothing larger than a 20 mm gun, she had endeavoured to fight off the trawlers. Moving inland to see what he could do to silence the battery, which was emplaced in concrete, Young soon abandoned the idea of assailing it and instead attempted neutralization through long-range small arms fire. As he reported, 'It was harassing fire, more or less controlled. . . . The Germans fired back and it was presently discovered that about fifteen feet of standing corn successfully stopped a bullet.' Fire though the German guns did, their rate was considerably slowed. Bold as Young was, he still managed to return to the beach and bring his men off in the Eureka, whose skipper, Lieut H. T. Buckee, had been as resolute in staying close by as he had been in pressing on to the initial landing.

Far less fortunate, although equal to Buckee and Young in their resolution, were the men of 3 Commando in six other Eurekas who, after dispersal, made again for the beaches where, 25 minutes late and in broad daylight, they were greeted by a fully alerted enemy who sank or severely damaged several craft with devastating fire, and continued to shoot up those Commandos who got ashore and, against all the odds, tried to reach their objective. One man, seriously wounded, managed to get well inland before he was killed. The rest were killed or wounded either on the beaches, entangled in wire, or on the cliff top, under a deluge of machine-gun and mortar fire. Among those who fell was Lieut Loustalot, one of the thirty members of 1st US Rangers who had been attached to 3 Commando for the operation and one of the first of many US soldiers to be killed in combat in Europe. Most of the survivors were then taken prisoner.

Six members of 1st Rangers were also attached to 4 Commando and were among the minority of raiders who tasted success this day. The objective was the battery at Varengeville; the method, a landing in two parties, one close to the battery to give covering fire, the other wide to a flank under the CO, Lord Lovat, with the intention of making an indirect approach from inland. As it happened, the fire support party, under Major D. Mills-Roberts, achieved 4 Commando's objective simply by bringing the battery under fire and hitting an ammunition dump with mortar fire 'after which the battery never fired again'. With German attention focused upon Mills-Roberts, he and his men also managed to make contact with a French farmer 'who was inclined to become indignant as more and more of his cabbages were trampled upon, but presently disappeared within and returned anon resplendent in a short black coat . . . and offered a glass of wine.'

Ironically Lovat's main party benefited but little from Mills-Roberts's diversion. Coming ashore safely in the dark, they were pestered at once by wire and German fire and had to fight their way inland to their assault position. Casualties mounted as the enemy, whom Intelligence sources reckoned to be low-grade, fought with skill and ferocity. Major P. A. Porteous won a VC in hand-to-hand combat and, at the same point of contact, Cpl F. Coons of 1st Rangers achieved the distinction of being the first American soldier to kill a German in action and was later presented by Mountbatten with the Military Medal for his sniping activities while the assault formed up. In the heat of action Coons was less appreciative of the efforts of some RAF Spitfires who accidentally struck the house he was occupying with cannon fire while engaged in shooting up the enemy battery. Such accidents are commonplace in battle and on this occasion stopped nobody in 4 Commando from completing the assault on the guns, destroying them with charges, wiping out the Germans in merciless fighting at close range and retiring successfully to be picked up, at 0730 hours, on schedule, on the beaches. This was a classic hit-and-run action carried out with dash and precision. There are few better examples of the art on this scale on record.

Unfortunately it was the only Allied success of the day, for the disaster which struck 3 Commando was repeated when 2nd Canadian Division landed in daylight frontally and on both flanks of Dieppe itself. Nobody at any time during the planning had doubted that this would be a tough assignment. The Intelligence, partially based upon SIS reports (which were severely restricted by a German security drive) but far more upon photo-reconnaissance, was, in the main, accurate, although deficient in certain vital aspects. As the post-action Combined Report remarked:

These photographs confirmed the suspected presence in the Eastern cliff of pill-boxes and also revealed a tank encased by a concrete wall at the end of the Western breakwater. They did not, however, disclose the type or calibre of the guns in the Eastern headland, nor did they show ... that there were similar pill-boxes built in the cliffs on the Western headland. ... Though the air photographs revealed the presence of eight road blocks ... they could not show that behind some of these anti-tank guns were mounted, for the reason that ... the guns were always removed just before daylight and put back into position just after dark.

The storm of shot and shell which greeted the Canadian soldiers as they landed was thus far heavier than expected and an awful shock for troops in their first action. The attackers, not the defenders, were surprised. Not only were the German gunners forewarned by the pre-dawn commando attacks to the flanks and by the flare-up at sea, they were, in the absence of air attack and adequate suppressive fire from the ships, virtually unshaken. As COHQ afterwards admitted, 'No standard naval vessel or craft had the necessary qualities or equipment to provide sufficient inshore support'. Though that is not to say that ships and craft did not, at appalling risk, steer to close with the enemy over open sights. Nor did smoke screens laid by low-flying Blenheim bombers help all that much; indeed the thick pall was often a handicap since it prevented officers and men finding their way, picking targets or assessing the situation, as well as silhouetting the attackers to the Germans.

In summary, the Royal Regiment of Canada, on the left, after confusion during launching from their LSI, were late touching down and almost annihilated, along with the Black Watch, at Puys, beneath the German Rommel Battery. On the right, at Pourville, the South Saskatchewan Regiment, followed by the Queen's Own Cameron Highlanders, got ashore in good order and pressed inland to within striking distance of their objective, the Hindenberg battery – a determined effort which won a VC for the CO, Lt-Col C. Merritt. Thus the Essex Scottish and the Royal Hamilton Light Infantry (RHLI), supported by Churchill tanks of 14th Canadian Army Tank Battalion (The Calgary Regiment), had their flanks in the air as they landed on Red and White Beaches, facing the heavily defended Promenade and Casino, overlooked by the cliff pill-boxes. By concentrating on the experiences of individuals the terrible scene is laid bare.

Approaching the beach at 0445 hours, men saw 'Hotels and buildings along the esplanade, clear against the red glow of the sun as it rose to the east of the town. Tracers arched across the sky, lacing intricate patterns about the landing craft, and shells and mortar bombs began to raise spouts of water.' According to Lt F. Woodcock of RHLI:

> Then, just before we landed, the guns from the destroyers switched from the Casino to the headland. It was timed perfectly, and then the Hurricanes came in and plastered hell out of everything. Then we were hit. The Bangalore torpedoes exploded . . . I only remember the sound, because I was blinded. The boat filled with water and I was soon up to my neck.

Out of seventeen men in that LCA, only two survived, of whom one, Woodcock, was blind for life.

A short distance to the left of Woodcock, Pte J. T. Fleming, Essex Scottish, was landing in the first wave.*

> I saw the attack delivered by cannon fighters. . . . The first mortar bomb burst when the LCA was perhaps 100 yards from shore.

---

* This account, like that of Major Page below, is edited into the first person from a statement made in 1943 to the Canadian Historical Officer after Fleming and Page had been repatriated as Prisoners of War.

Machine-gun fire opened as soon as the troops landed. I reached the Esplanade wall and fired at a pill-box for 3 or 4 minutes, during which heavy mortar fire was coming down. I saw no organized attack across the wall. . . . I think about 9 men rushed forward at this time, but seven were hit while crossing the Promenade.

Fleming was joined by a handful of lucky and determined survivors who began to hunt snipers with Bren and Tommy-gun fire, but he was wounded in the arm and sent back to the beach. Meanwhile Major C. E. Page of 14th Canadian Army Tank Battalion was coming ashore a few minutes late from an LCT in his Churchill tank among the Essex Scottish:

I moved across the beach but found progress obstructed by a tank trap consisting of a trench dug along the front of the Esplanade wall. . . . I swung to the right to avoid the trench and was almost immediately stopped by a shell hit which broke one track and destroyed all the tank's communications. . . . The second tank on LCT 4 turned as it came off the craft to avoid my tank and got ten yards past it when it too was stopped by a hit on the track. The third tank did not get as far as either of the other two before it was stopped in the same manner. Although I confirm that some tanks were certainly knocked out on the central part of the beach . . . while moving laterally and searching for a way across the wall, I am quite certain that from 12 to 15 tanks crossed the wall in the end sectors where it was low. The majority of these tanks had returned to the beach by about 0900 hrs. The reason for this return was the fact that the tanks could get some cover there from the guns sited in the East cliff while, moreover, they could get better shooting from there.

Before the battle Intelligence had based their estimates of the beach gradients and nature upon Admiralty charts which were copies of French charts drawn from soundings made in 1830, and upon a single pre-war photograph of a family group picnicking against a breakwater. After it, criticism was made that the beach was unsuitable. Page's account demonstrates, as many German photographs tend to confirm, that it was gunfire and the wall, not the beach gradient, which stopped the Churchills, which were excellent climbers. Indeed it was no mean feat that, out of twenty-eight which landed, over half left the beach, and hardly the fault of the crews that they were unable to help much in the town when the infantry, for the most part, were prevented from working with them.

On HMS *Calpe*, which did duty as an improvised Headquarters Ship, the signals centre was overloaded by messages, thus depriving General Roberts of adequate information. Those scraps of news which did reach him unfortunately gave the impression that the Essex Scottish had penetrated into the town in strength. Upon this information Roberts based his decision to commit his floating reserve – Les Fusiliers Mont-Royal and 40th Royal Marine Commando – to exploit what he deduced might be success but which proved to be failure. Through the smoke he could detect nothing ashore. Emerging from that smoke, the Fusiliers were too far to the right and beached among the RHLI, under the West Headland, to be shot down as they set foot ashore. They simply added to the piles of dead and wounded already lying there or staining the water with their blood. Those who survived joined the others trying to swim to the LCAs out at sea. Meanwhile the Marines' CO, Lt-Col J. P. Phillips, seeing the wall of fire into which his leading company was sailing, put on his white gloves and stood up in the bows of his craft to give the signal for the rest to turn and retire. He was killed almost on the instant, but several craft did manage to escape otherwise certain annihilation. Similarly a flotilla of Fighting French *chasseurs*, whose mission it was to enter the harbour and bring out enemy landing craft, were faced with an impossible task before which they wilted.

Some select French members of SOE and ten from 10 (Inter Allied) Commando did manage to get ashore in the hope of making contact with the local populace or of carrying out special demolition tasks. Few made it, although there was ample evidence of interest by the civilians, a percentage of whom left cover to greet the invaders or take part in the fighting. Men of the RHLI, who infiltrated a short way among sea-front buildings, met some French people who 'were friendly and warned us of patrols and I even saw one woman walk down the street, buy a loaf of bread and return to her home! Some acted as guides while the men in the local theatre box office went on counting the take from the previous evening'.

Another recalled:

Machine-gun fire was heavy and I even saw the tracers passing in front of us. We went through the Hotel to the cinema, and then up a narrow street. The sniping was bad. . . . Some women waved to us as we went by and one civilian was waving with one hand with a pistol in the other. We killed him with rifle fire.

Soon a drift back to the beach of wounded and survivors began (where Padre J. Foote won a VC tending them) and at 0930 hours evacuation was authorized by an order from *Calpe*, the timing later deferred to 1030, in order to suit the tide, and later still to 1100, to enable the RAF to lay more smoke in time. The task of the smoke-laying aircraft was extremely perilous because the Luftwaffe, having been astonishingly slow to react to the raid, entered the battle at about the time evacuation was ordered. Thereafter twenty or thirty German fighters were overhead at any one time, although bombing missions did not take effect until 1000 hours and were rarely pressed home, which is hardly surprising in the face of the 2339 RAF and 123 US Air Force sorties flown by fifty-two Spitfire and Hurricane squadrons which maintained continuous cover from dawn to dusk against a total of only about 600 German fighter sorties. The air battles which erupted and swamped the control centres in Britain immensely satisfied those who wanted the Luftwaffe to be brought to battle in a big way. German fighters, brought in from all over Western Europe, struck hard in defence of their ground forces. Along with their own anti-aircraft guns, and with the help of British Navy and Army gunners who paid scant attention to aircraft recognition and shot at almost everything which flew within their sights, they shot down eighty-eight RAF fighters, eight American Spitfires, ten Army co-operation and tactical reconnaissance machines and eight bombers. In return, the RAF and the Navy claimed nearly 200 enemy aircraft destroyed as against actual German losses of only forty-eight with twenty-four damaged. In other words, the Germans won as decisive a victory in the air as they did on the surface.

Soldiers crawled to the water's edge and began to swim in hundreds, like lemmings, to reach drifting landing craft or those which courageously headed in to pick them up. Lt-Col R. R. Labatt, CO of RHLI, sat in a disabled LCS and saw an LCT half a mile distant.

> I went overboard and struck out for the LTC. Hundreds of men were swimming around, some heading out to sea, others towards the shore. I tried to keep clear of groups as they presented tempting targets and the sea about them was lashed into foam by machine-guns, mortars and artillery. As I neared the LTC I realized that it was being shelled and when I was about 200 yards from it, it received two direct hits in the engine room and began to settle by the stern.

Rescue operations proved terribly costly. The wounded Pte Fleming, sheltering on the Promenade waiting the time for embarkation,

> saw an LCT coming in and went to the beach in the hope of getting aboard. The LCT, however, blew up and sank; there appeared to be an

explosion in the centre of it. I was wounded again, this time in the leg, and the Germans over-ran the beach some minutes later.

Those shattered survivors from JUBILEE who returned to port in their savagely depleted flotillas had thoughts of Gallipoli on their minds. In the days to come the extent of the disaster gradually leaked out, although the falsity of the principal claim that victory had at least been won in the air remained unrevealed and unknown until after the war. The ambitions attending this, the biggest hit-and-run raid of all, were wrecked by the known losses. A destroyer, seventeen LCAs, five LCTs and eleven lesser landing craft failed to return, along with vast quantities of Army equipment, including twenty-eight Churchill tanks, 308 Bren guns, 256 Tommy-guns and twenty-seven 3-inch mortars. Naval casualties amounted to 550; those of 2nd Canadian Division 3,403 (69.6% of those engaged); Commandos 247 (22.9%) US Rangers 13 (26%) and RAF 153 (13%). Among the Germans and the French bystanders casualties were extremely light. The Germans, who fought mainly from behind cover, did not even have to commit their local reserves to combat, let alone 10th Panzer Division from its assembly area near Amiens. In victory the Germans comported themselves with humanity towards their wounded prisoners, while recognizing that, misdirected as the Dieppe attack appeared to be, it was probably but a taste of what was to come.

Indeed, it is worth noting that, without the smaller raids which preceded it, JUBILEE might have been an even more expensive disaster. Having said that, let it be added that from bitter ashes there emerged a lengthy Combined Operations report which Mountbatten was to circulate among all invasion commanders of all nations, setting out the vital lessons learnt. Hardly a detail was omitted. Above all the truth that a frontal assault upon a defended port was impracticable was rubbed in by Mountbatten, who could have remarked that Montgomery and those in Home Forces, with experience during the First World War of hitting their heads against brick walls, should not have needed so expensive a trial to demonstrate it. Montgomery's hindsighted criticism that 'there were far too many authorities with a hand in it; there was no one single operational commander who was solely responsible for the operation from start to finish, a Task Force Commander in fact', did, however contain substance in so far as it was directed at a failure to implement genuine joint command at critical points in the chain of command. But it is debatable if, as he suggests, the information and experience could have been gained in any other way in the time remaining before TORCH.

Each weakness did require demonstration, notably the incapability of

Naval inshore fire support as yet totally to neutralize, let alone destroy, enemy defences or to react swiftly to sudden changes of demand by craft and troops. Improved weapons, including multiple rocket projectors, to saturate enemy defences, more sophisticated communication systems and better integrated methods of command and control would evolve from the intensive studies set in motion. Likewise the admission that pre-raid examination of beach profiles and an over-reliance on air photography was insufficient promoted the pursuit of far more thorough information gathering. The need for examination of potential landing sites by highly trained and well equipped men employing the techniques inherent in small hit-and-run raids was acknowledged. In addition to these quite fundamental lessons there were matters of detail to settle – the need for closer inter-Service and inter-Arm co-operation from the planning stage onwards; the necessity for more exact navigation and identification of beaches and stricter traffic control across them and the demand for ways and means to help tanks and other vehicles negotiate the variety of obstacles which could be expected at most landing sites.

Few of these requirements would have been identified and understood without JUBILEE. Each and all of these lessons would have to be absorbed, implemented and, above all, practiced before Operation TORCH took place in November and the all-out invasion of Europe begun sometime in 1943. Meanwhile the whole policy of raiding, perhaps to Mountbatten's astonishment, was called into question and dispute.

CHAPTER 20

Small Raiding Intensified

Among Admirals, Sir Bertram Ramsay was probably best versed at this time, by operational experience, in getting craft and men on and off beaches. The evacuation from Dunkirk had been his masterpiece of improvisation. Since then he had had a finger in several small raids across the Channel and also been privy to plans which had been stillborn. When SLEDGEHAMMER was mooted, it was Ramsay the Allies appointed as Naval Commander, mainly on the advice of Mountbatten to the First Sea Lord. And when TORCH replaced SLEDGEHAMMER as the main Allied effort for 1942, Ramsay again took the top naval job.

In this capacity, in the aftermath of JUBILEE, Ramsay wrote to Mountbatten expressing concern about raiding:

My dear Dickie,
Raids on the occupied coastline have not done very well in the last 12 months. The Germans no doubt welcome these raids for nothing shows more clearly the weakness of defences than an attack with a very limited objective. Every time we find a weak spot on the enemy's coast we point out its weakness, and there is ample evidence that he is taking full advantage of this information to increase the strength of his defences both at sea and on land. If it is our intention at some future date to make an attack in force upon the enemy's coast, we are now doing, or proposing to do, our best to make that attack less likely to achieve success.

This, of course, ran counter to the spirit of the Chiefs of Staff directive of 12 May which had called for substantial air and coastal raiding, culminating in the capture of the Cotentin peninsula followed by ROUND-UP – a large-scale descent on Western Europe in the Spring of

1. King George VI and Sir Roger Keyes (right) watching soldiers assembling an assault boat during the fateful Operation LEAPFROG, August, 1941. A Commando with a Folbot canoe can be seen in the background.

2. Lord Louis Mountbatten welcomes Commandos home from the raid on Vaagso, December, 1941.

3. The perils and problems of beach operations by assault craft as discovered by A. J. Higgins.

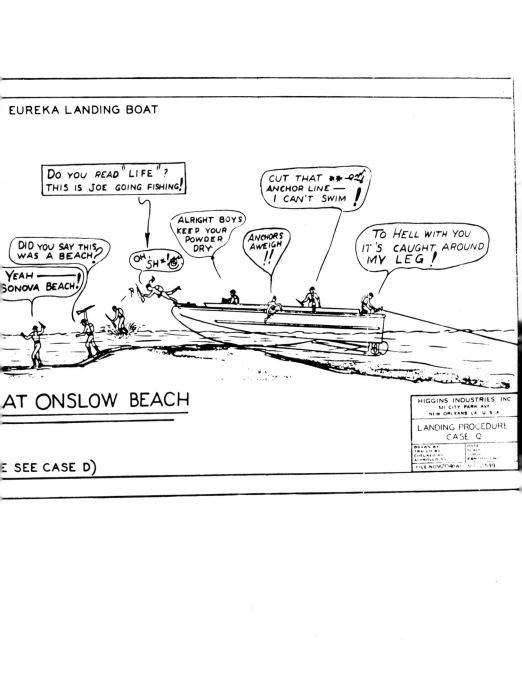

4. An ML ready to navigate for LCPs (Higgins Eurekas) before going ashore at Dieppe.

5. Commandos and sailors with a captured German after Dieppe.

6. LCAs being launched from LSIs.

7. Assorted landing craft under tow by an ML.

8. Rear Admiral Kelly Turner and Major-General Alexander Vandegrift planning the assault on Guadalcanal.

9. US Marines landing from a large, ramped Higgins boat.

10. US Marines very much on the alert in the jungle.

11. Operation TORCH – follow-up landing by LCM from LSIs by British and American troops. The LCA right foreground seems to be in temporary difficulty, broached to, after the initial landings.

12. Meeting at Casablanca between, left to right in foreground, General Dwight Eisenhower, Air Marshal Sir Arthur Tedder, General George Marshall, Winston Churchill, General Sir Alan Brooke and Lieutenant-General Bernard Montgomery.

13. US Marine Tommy-gunner hunting a Japanese sniper on Torokina.

a) Folbot canoe.

14. INSTRUMENTS OF PILOTAGE AND SURVEY

b) LCP(N) developed from Higgins Eureka. Note the QH receiver aerial for Gee.

c) X Craft.

d) Folbots, inflatable rubber boats and stores being loaded on to a coastal craft in the Mediterranean theatre.

15. Sweating it out on the beach at Koiari, hoping that the pick-up will take place before they are overrun by the Japanese nearby.

16. The pay-off from raiding. A British flail tank wades ashore from an LCT during the invasion of Walcheren, November, 1944.

1943. Mountbatten's response, reminiscent of Keyes only a year previously, was to attack obstruction at source. A Memorandum from his
Headquarters stated:

'It appears that our small raids are frequently cancelled by the Naval
C-in-C concerned on the grounds that the value of the objective does not
warrant the risk of the Naval covering force', and went on to show ways of
overcoming such obstruction. Mountbatten declared that, if small raiding
ceased, the enemy's suspicions might be aroused as he came to analyse the
large shipping movements associated with the mounting of Operation
TORCH. Insisting that raids must continue, Mountbatten did all in his
very considerable power to step up their frequency and improve their
effectiveness.

To defeat half-heartedness, Mountbatten succeeded in getting the
Navy fully involved in Combined Operations in order to eliminate a
professional tendency to regard them as a spare-time occupation. The
craft which had taken part in JUBILEE and which were unsuitable, due to
their short range, for inclusion in TORCH, were kept together under
Captain J. Hughes Hallett RN in the Solent, which was an ideal training
area for landing techniques. Force J, as this command was called, was
intended, as Mountbatten wrote on 2 October, to be 'reasonably self-
contained as a potential raiding force', including specially trained coastal
craft, needed as leaders, and a permanent Headquarters ship. Unless this
was done, Mountbatten foresaw 'a miniature upheaval in the naval
Command' whenever an expedition was to sail. As he pointed out, 'While
the Army and RAF are so organized that they can employ formed and
trained units for any operation . . . in the case of the Navy the landing craft
and small craft have to be specially collected together and organized as an
ad hoc force.'

Mountbatten sought to regularize organization and procedures under
'Fighting Instructions' which would simplify and shorten the mounting of
future amphibious operations, and would be adopted by the US Navy in
the Pacific. He also insisted upon the need for Force J to operate against
the enemy:

> Unless this is done I regard it as certain that there will be a
> progressive decline in its discipline and morale . . . the craft which will
> comprise the proposed raiding force are, in their nature, only suitable
> for offensive operations. If such operations are not undertaken, there-
> fore, the personnel . . . are bound to feel that their services are being
> wholly wasted. . . . From this point of view, it is largely immaterial
> whether raiding operations achieve complete success or not, since the

essential thing is to give as many of our fighting forces as possible a periodical battle.

This somewhat spine-chilling lapse into a blood-letting First World War attitude was not in accord with the views of senior officers who rejected, from bitter experience, the pointless inculcation of offensive spirit by trench raiding. At times Mountbatten may have taken his brief to attack a little too single-mindedly. Imbued with enthusiasm and a sense of urgency, he could be compared to a man with both hands on the engine telegraphs, demanding full-speed, but in need of somebody to help steer the ship. Fortunately both Churchill, in the case of IMPERATOR, and the Chiefs of Staff, on various occasions, deftly took the tiller. For example, Mountbatten's support for Operation AFLAME, a spoof demonstration to draw the Luftwaffe into battle in October by deploying a large naval force off the French coast and dropping dummy parachutists near Berck, south of Boulogne, led to nothing because the Navy said it had its hands full. Excuses were subtler than blank refusals, it was sometimes felt, when dealing with the eager CCO.

Yet Admiralty unwillingness to collaborate was brought about in some part by a disinclination to surrender their traditional right to rule the waves, but also by unservicability of landing craft caused, as Mountbatten was quick to tell his own Service, by loss of Naval control under the extreme pressures of mounting Operation TORCH in addition to its other vital tasks. Dissatisfaction with his own Service is as plain in Mountbatten's letters as it had often been in those of his predecessor. Casting about for allies, he joined hands with SOE, an organization which not only shared his enthusiasm for coastal raiding but had been denied the right to do so by the Chiefs of Staff Directive of 12 May which instructed it to 'conform to the general plan by organizing and co-ordinating action by patriots in the occupied countries', and yet deliberately excluded raiding. The relationship between Combined Operations and SOE, although theoretically natural, had its difficulties, as Foot describes:

> The nature of the clandestine weapon was ill understood by most of Mountbatten's staff who sometimes asked SOE to do the impossible. . . . On another and less vital naval front, CD (the executive director of SOE) and the CCO were more easily able to work together. The CCO (because of his key seat among the Chiefs of Staff) had little difficulty in mounting operations when and where he wanted, and by a series of personal accidents SOE could provide a small force of highly skilled and intelligent toughs of several nationalities . . . who were looking for targets.

This reference is to the Small Scale Raiding Force, assembled within SOE by ex-commando Major G. H. March-Phillipps (who refused to blacken his face for night operations because 'I'll die looking like an Englishman and not like a damned nigger') and including Appleyard (who wrote 'every time you get that tight feeling round your heart and the empty feeling in your tummy, you are mentally and nervously tougher than the time before, and so are better fitted for real military action') and Pinckney (who was inspired to propose AIRTHIEF and volunteered to sacrifice his life to ensure its accomplishment in the stealing of an FW 190). Under the name 62 Commando, it was lodged at the beautiful, secluded Anderson Manor in Dorset, administered by SOE but loaned to CCO for such raids as he wished to make. In effect it was SOE's disciplined striking arm for tasks which irregular, often undisciplined, indigenous guerrillas were neither willing nor able to attempt. Already SSRF had undertaken a number of daring ventures, including the cutting out from port at Fernando Po of a German liner (Operation POSTMASTER). Appleyard concurred with what Mountbatten had in mind when he wrote, for propaganda purposes, about the need for a vast number of small raids every night (possibly several a night), involving only a few British troops, and all over the whole length of the occupied coast, forcing the enemy to strengthen his coastal defences and make substantial alterations in the disposition of his forces in Europe.

In striving to loosen the departmental bonds hindering raiding, particularly those of the kind with limited objectives, Mountbatten managed to establish with the COS Committee, on 27 July, the principle of Force Commanders whose task it would be to process, under CCO's responsibility and with the C-in-C's approval, the detailed planning, operations orders, preparation, training and launching of intensified small raids.

By also obtaining the exclusive use of MTB 344, CCO was able to put his and SSRF's theories into practice, and, in opposition to Admiralty wishes, launch a private offensive which was to revolutionize small raiding and, incidentally, trigger Ramsay's protest already referred to. Four nights prior to JUBILEE, March-Phillipps with ten companions, armed to the teeth, crept ashore, paddling four abreast, in a new collapsible Goatley dory, three miles north of St Vaast. Launching from MTB 344 had been well rehearsed, and the navigation accurate—by a soldier (Appleyard), just to underline the competence and degree of inter-service collaboration established. Operation BARRICADE's aim, like that of almost all those to follow in quick succession during the coming months, was the acquisition of information, allied to the capture or killing of enemy soldiers. On this occasion they ran up against a familiar barrier—wire which had to be cut before reaching their objective which turned out to be a camouflaged Freya radar station, alongside a largish enemy camp. Mildly daunted, but fortuitously assisted by the enemy, who began to stalk them, the raiders found themselves close enough to throw three plastic bombs among the enemy, followed by generous squirts of Tommy-gun fire. 'Altogether,' wrote March-Phillipps, 'some 5 lbs of explosive went off within three feet of the enemy and nothing was heard afterwards except a few strangled coughs.' After that it was a comparatively simple matter to hose the camp with machine-gun fire and retreat in good order to the boat, disturbed only by a few Verey lights in the sky from a shaken enemy.

Often MTB 344 would be at sea night after night waiting for clear weather to enable a landing. Operation DRYAD was attempted several times before 2/3 September when twelve men landed on the Casquets rock and stealthily climbed the eighty steps leading to the lighthouse. As Appleyard said, 'I have never seen men look so amazed and terrified at the same time . . . Three (wearing hair nets and taken for women) were in bed (it was 1.00 in the morning), two who had just come off watch were turning in, and the two on watch were doing odd jobs . . . Not a shot was fired and no violence had to be used.' The haul comprised a collection of weapons (dumped into the sea); communications equipment (destroyed); documents and codes plus seven prisoners who, back in England 'are talking quite well'. Meanwhile the Germans spent all the next day calling up the Casquets by radio and getting no reply.

Operation BRANFORD, carried out on 7/8 September, was simply a reconnaissance of the island of Burhou to see if it would be suitable as a battery position to support an attack upon Alderney, and was uneventful. But Operation AQUATINT, five nights later to the north of St Honorine, near Port-en-Bessin, was quite another matter. As at St Vaast, March-Phillipps, caution tempering his daring, thought the objective was too strong and decided to retreat. Also as at St Vaast, the enemy obliged by following, to be ambushed at short range, losing seven men. But this was not an end to the incident. The Germans pursued them to the shore-line, put up a flare when the Goatley was still only 100 yards out to sea and raked the craft with devastating fire. March-Phillipps and three others were killed at once, the Goatley sunk and the rest, over a period of days, captured on foot. One French member did manage to escape to Spain where he was incarcerated by the authorities before escaping again to England and returned later to France as an agent. Another managed to swim to within fifty yards of MTB before Appleyard, who, as usual, was navigating and had not gone ashore because of a fractured leg sustained on DRYAD, had to haul off under heavy coastal battery fire which hit the MTB and put one engine out of action.*

As the autumn nights lengthened, attention could again be paid to Norway where some very special targets demanded destruction. On the night 15/16 September Operation MUSKETOON got under way as Capt G. G. Black, South Lancashire Regiment, nine other members of 2 Commando and two Norwegian corporals specially employed by the War Office, stepped ashore from a Free French submarine at Bajaering Fjord and trekked across the formidable Swartisen glacier to their objective, the Glomfjord hydro-electric power station. It was a singular feat to cross the glacier undetected in a single day's march, even though it has to be noted that local security was lax. 'There was no proper blackout at the power station; several lights were showing, door was wide open,' says the report. The three Norwegian guards did nothing to interfere after one of the German guards had been shot and the other had escaped into a tunnel which the raiders at once filled with smoke. Dividing into two, Black's party laid charges against two of the three turbines, while the others, 100 yards up the penstock path, tackled the pipeline. Shortage of time made it impossible to do more. The explosions were expertly laid. Immense damage was done to the machinery, and a landslide of sand and stone, brought down by an onrush of water, buried the third turbine.

Then things began to go wrong. Unnecessarily delayed in making off in the direction of Sweden, Black's men ran into a German patrol which killed a Norwegian and a British soldier. Six men, including Black, were captured, put in chains and taken to Oslo. Four got away, the first to arrive in Sweden being the Norwegian, Cpl Christiansen, followed on 27 September by Guardsman Fairclough and Pte Twigg and on 3 October by Sgt O'Brien. Their endurance through harrowing journeys, with enough adventure to fill a book, were epics in themselves. Speedily and informally repatriated to England by the Swedes ('who did not ask too many questions and whose press gave out a highly inaccurate account of what had happened'), they brought with them a vast amount of extremely valuable information.

MUSKETOON produced solid results by using a simple formula with a low outlay, and it hit the Germans at a critical moment in the war's development. The drive on the Suez Canal had been decisively broken at Alam Halfa. Crushing defeat at El Alamein was a month distant; the armada carrying TORCH to North Africa was assembling; the struggle in

---

* M. R. D. Foot is mistaken in *SOE in France* when he says that 'SSRF never recovered from the death of March-Phillipps'. As will be seen, it went from strength to strength.

Russia had yet to grind to a halt before Stalingrad and in the Caucasus; the U boats were still winning the Battle of the Atlantic. Yet those in the know in Berlin already sensed that the days of runaway victories were over. In the immediate aftermath of victory at Dieppe and the almost total repulse of a series of badly co-ordinated raids against supply ports in North Africa, Hitler became even more sensitive. He had been considerably angered by a paragraph in the orders for Operation JUBILEE which laid down: 'Whenever possible, prisoners' hands will be tied to prevent destruction of their documents'. A denial by the War Office on 2 September that hands had been bound was followed by a naïve instruction that 'any such order, if it was issued, will be cancelled'. Already Hitler was threatening to chain prisoners' hands as a reprisal.

In this state of mind he came to hear about Operation BASALT, the next and certainly the most momentous of all raids carried out by SSRF. With Appleyard in command and Sark the objective, detailed information about the defences was the aim. Landing on a deserted part of the islands, Appleyard was astonished to meet, in an apparently empty cottage, 'an old lady fast asleep in bed! On being awakened she was naturally terrified to find her room full of tough-looking men with knives and pistols. . . . It transpired that she was English but had lived on the island from child-hood. . . . For about two hours she described in detail every German strongpoint on the island. . . . Other useful evidence obtained was copies of the island newspaper and also some proclamations issued by the Germans giving details of the proposed deportation of the Channel Islanders.'

This final item of news was of great interest, confirming that the forced labour programme initiated by the Germans in the previous March was now widespread. Proof, too, of the extent to which the German economy was under strain as those in charge endeavoured to cope with the stupendous demand for armaments, and to build up the Atlantic Wall which, in the aftermath of St Nazaire and Dieppe, was making vast calls upon labour and material. This was what Churchill, Keyes and Mount-batten had hoped for, yet even they probably did not envisage the degree of hatred which this programme would create. As people were taken to work and die far from home, the collaboration or placid acquiescence to German occupation which until recently had prevailed, was replaced by passive resistance, or even by active strife, by those dedicated few to whom death was preferable to slavery.

With the information obtained from the English woman Appleyard might have been satisfied. But his patriotic fervour was stronger than March-Phillipps' prudence. Impulsively extending the duration of the raid by two hours, and thus risking being left ashore if a message, asking MTB 344 to wait beyond the agreed time failed to reach the captain, he began hunting for a prisoner to provide corroboration of the old lady's story. Breaking into a nearby camp and seizing five sleepy German soldiers proved easy; leading them away when one of them kicked up a fuss and attracted the attention of an enemy patrol was quite another matter. In the confusion Appleyard tied the prisoners' hands and then shot three of them on the way to the boat when the recalcitrant one continued to make a noise. Meanwhile the skipper of MTB 344, even though the message to wait had not reached him, hung on until dawn because he could not believe Appleyard would not make it. They were lucky to do so, but thrilled by the extent of their success. Most of all, Appleyard was delighted by their surviving captive who 'proved a winner', the most useful prisoner obtained by anyone to date: 'He has proved very chatty and nothing is too much trouble for him'. Extremely useful, too, was the news of the deportations which British propagandists instantly turned against the Germans.

Almost as damaging in reverse was the use the Germans could make of Allied treatment of prisoners of war. Reporting the discovery of soldiers' bodies which proved that the British *did* tie prisoners' hands and that the declarations of 2 September were worthless, they announced what became infamous as 'The Hitler Commando Order':

> From October 8 at 12 noon all British officers and men captured at Dieppe will be put in chains. . . . In future, all sabotage and terror tactics by the British and their accomplices, who behave like bandits rather than soldiers, will be treated as such by German troops and will be ruthlessly exterminated wherever they appear.

The timing was wrong, a typical battlefield error in the heat of the moment. The Hitler Order was the expression of a man who rated himself above existing Conventions dealing with prisoners, and of a military caste which, since it had elevated its code of military conduct to what it considered a higher plane than that of guerrilla warfare, rejected all such irregular acts as breaches of honour and decency. There were those among the German military hierarchy who avoided obediance to the Order and those who denounced it after the war. But few protested at the time and many implemented it on the spot. Moreover, it was applied retrospectively. Soon those captured on MUSKETOON would be executed under its terms. Instantly the British and Canadian response to manacling of prisoners was tit for tat; Mountbatten at once obtained from

Churchill permission to chain 100 Germans. Inevitably this figure was raised as if at auction until, for example, 1376 Germans had been manacled in Canada—and without the slightest deterrence to either side. The war was whirling inextricably into a vortex of bitterness and cruelty, and to no positive advantage. For although the Swiss Government was able to negotiate an end to manacling, ultimate reprisals against raiders, partisans and anybody thought to have associated with them continued unabated. Few commandos, who put their lives on the line the day they volunteered for the job, were deterred, estimating execution by firing squad as just another hazard in an already dangerous occupation.

The adventures of SSRF in MTB 344 might have provided valuable propaganda material for the uplift of British morale at a time when the war seemed to be going badly and the likelihood of a Second Front delayed indefinitely. But when radio intercepts indicated how puzzled the Germans were about the way the raids were being carried out, it was decided, for the time being, to maintain silence. Instead, Mountbatten exploited the positive results obtained from BASALT as a pretext for persuading the Prime Minister and Chiefs of Staff to intensify small scale raiding. On 13 October he introduced Appleyard to Churchill, Eden, the Chiefs of Staff and other senior officers and allowed this remarkable officer's enthusiasm to infect them. On the spot, it seems, CCO was given the green light to expand SSRF (eventually to about 60 men) and instruct his Search Committee to widen its enquiries among various departments and come up with all manner of economic and military targets for attack.

Meanwhile Appleyard carried on where BASALT left off, although there are indications that the manacling business upset him and that, subsequently, his cavalier approach to raiding lost its edge. Operation FACSIMILE, scheduled for 16 October against Morlaix airfield in Brittany, was called off due to 'insoluble weather'; and a few days later INHABIT, against Cap Levy, Cherbourg Peninsula, came to nothing because the force 'could not make the correct landfall'. On 11 November, however, FAHRENHEIT, under Appleyard's direction but executed by 12 Commando in the style of March-Phillipps, was carried out.

Again the objective was in Brittany, this time the Semaphore Station at Pointe de Plouézec. The post-action report is unusually vivid:

The party went ashore under command Capt P. Kent, Intelligence Corps. At once they found mines across the path leading to the Semaphore Station. They carefully took their time getting through these, cut the telephone cables from a pill box to the Station, reconnoitred round about and placed guards before advancing in three groups. The night was uncannily still, the slightest sound being audible. The two leading groups managed to crawl within ten paces of the sentries, who were very alert, trip wires alongside the path being noticed. It was not possible to get any closer. After lying still for 16 minutes, Capt P. Rooney unscrewed the top of a No 6P grenade. The sound attracted the attention of the sentries who stopped talking and listened carefully. As soon as they recommenced talking, Capt Rooney threw the grenade. There was a blinding flash and a shattering explosion followed by cries from the sentries. Capt Rooney's party were first over the wire followed by Capt Kent's party and the third group. A dog was seen to scuttle round the corner of the guard house. The sentries were on the ground, one silent and covering his face with his hands, the other crying '*Nicht Gut*; *Nicht Gut, Kamerad*,' all the time. Both the sentries were finished off with Tommy-gun fire. . . . A man was seen to leave the Station house and come down the path towards the wire. He whistled, at which the party opened fire, Sgt Barry bringing him to his knees, continued firing until he was brought to the ground and silenced. Men started to come out of the door, leaving the light on inside, and on this magnificent target Sgt Brodeson opened up with two bursts of silent Sten. A man fell on his face and Cpl Howell put in about ten rounds of Tommy-gun fire. After this it seemed reasonable to retire. No losses were suffered by the landing party.

The epitome of hit-and-run raiding and a very satisfactory night's work, it could be claimed – of a sort which inspired Churchill to exult about 'a hand of steel which plucks the German sentries from their posts'. But fatigue and adverse winter weather were beginning to tell on Appleyard and the men of MTB 344. Four days later when, once more, he, two officers from SSRF and an officer and seven men from 12 Commando approached the Cherbourg Peninsula conditions again procluded action. The report on Operation BATMAN explaining its abandonment on the grounds that there was a 'sea running' and 'a lot of rocks', has an air of weary resignation about it, almost of relief. The original SSRF men and, perhaps above all, the crew of MTB 344 who can have had very little rest during three months' of persistent danger, had probably moved into reverse from the point at which, according to Appleyard, 'a fighting man got nervously tougher than the time before'. In due course he and a few select colleagues would be transferred to North Africa.

CHAPTER 21

Mediterranean Turning Point

Events in the Mediterranean during the first half of 1942 had been as unkind to Combined Operations as to the whole British cause. Indeed, the rout of Eighth Army in June and the retreat to El Alamein presented conditions which were ideal for raiding. The long Axis lines of communication, stretching back along the coast to Tripoli and across the sea to Europe, invited interdiction by raiding parties of all kinds.

The discontinuation of large-scale amphibious operations throughout Middle East Command did, however, allow techniques to fall behind those being developed elsewhere. Skills were outdated; training lapsed. When G (Plans) at GHQ in Cairo dreamed up an operation sometimes known as ROSEMARY they were under command of Lt-Gen H. G. Alexander, whose only previous venture into Combined Operations had been the disastrous Exercise LEAPFROG which had brought down Keyes. Employing the survivors of Laycock's Commandos, plus 11th Bn Royal Marines (organized as a Commando) and a handful of ordinary gunners and infantry, it was conceived by Lt-Col J. Haselden. Haselden was one of the cut-and-thrust types from whom the early Commandos drew inspiration, but lacking, perhaps, that gift for precise planning and execution which motivated specialists in the latest Private Armies, such as SSRF. He has been depicted describing ROSEMARY 'lit up with the thought of some trickery. He was delighted with the whole project which he was bursting to explain to me . . . [A plan] whose chances of success lay in complete surprise and a very great measure of luck.'

ROSEMARY aimed to strike at the principal Axis points of entry into Cyrenaica along with a simultaneous inland raid by the Sudan Defence Force against Jalo oasis (Operation NICETY). Benghazi would be the target for the SAS (Operation BIGAMY); Barce (Operation CARAVAN) for the Long Range Desert Group; and Tobruk (Operation AGREE-

MENT) by a mixed force, mainly brought in from the sea. It is the latter, with its amphibious element, with which we are concerned here, but let it be said that, from the outset, ROSEMARY breached nearly every rule in the Combined Operations book. Setting aside the dangers of chronic over-complication, its involvement of so many diverse elements inevitably menaced security. Plans were discussed openly in L Section, which was a civilian establishment, spread throughout Cairo, that city of hot-bed rumour, and soon reached Axis ears. Likewise, intelligence about the enemy, although it may at first have been correct in stating that defence of the objectives was meagre, at once was out-dated when the enemy reacted to this revealed threat. A hot reception met the raiders at Benghazi, Jalo and Tobruk. Barce was the only place where things went well because the local commander had ignored the warnings.

Tobruk was to be attacked from the desert by the so-called Middle East Commando (Force B) under Haselden, while Force A, consisting of 400 Marines under Lt-Col Unwin, landed north of the harbour from two destroyers. Thereupon Force C, an all-arms force of artillery, line infantry and medium machine-gunners, would be brought ashore in sixteen MTBs and MLs which had sailed along the coast from Alexandria. It was the intention to hold the port for twelve hours and destroy the installations, fuel, ammunition and stores before withdrawing by sea, covered by Force D which consisted of two cruisers and thirteen destroyers. A large force of this size was bound to arouse suspicion even if news of its intentions had not already leaked out. Surprise, upon which everything depended, was never achieved. A fiasco was assured.

To begin with, the destroyers *Sikh* and *Zulu* of Force A were a totally inadequate substitute for LSIs. They restricted the size of assault craft and lighters which were to carry the Marines ashore and were inadequate launching platforms, thus complicating lowering when undertaken, as it was, in a heavy swell. This, as Capt C. N. P. Powell of the Marines pointed out, 'had the effect of pushing the craft forward, when the power boats (for towing, which was in itself an out-moded method) took the strain, of jerking the lighters so that the stem of at least one gave way.' Tow ropes began to part and wind round propellers; the assault formation was disrupted at the crucial moment when the enemy, already aware of the approach by Force B inland, illuminated the destroyers with searchlights and opened fire with artillery.

Suddenly [wrote Powell] the warm sea was spurting with tracer shells, and mortar bombs resounded against the wooden hulls like depth charges. The lighters rose up and dumped their contents out on the rocks instead of good beach. Men were crushed between the bows of their craft and the rocks. One or two craft received direct hits and from others the heavily equipped men leapt out into water above their heads.

Force C had an even unhappier experience. Only two of the MTBs found their destination. Arriving late, one was holed on the rocks. The others never landed at all and, in due course, two of the MLs and four MTBs would be attacked and sunk by aircraft, all the rest suffering damage. This was a disaster shared in full by Force A, which lost both destroyers, and Force D, which lost the cruiser *Coventry*.

Through no fault of the Navy, a handful of survivors were marooned ashore, surrounded by a triumphant enemy whose only complaint seems to have been that the invaders arrived two hours later than expected. Despite a hopeless situation, they fought on into the afternoon, struggling with weapons clogged by sand. This was little more than a stubborn gesture of pride in the Commando tradition. For the main body was easily located by the enemy, and of those who tried to escape across 400 miles of desert to Egypt, less than a score made it. Only ninety Marines who had sailed in the destroyers were saved after the ships were sunk. The Axis claimed a triumph against raiders to be set alongside the recent victory at Dieppe. Operation AGREEMENT simply rubbed in the lesson that, even if forfeiture of surprise might *just* make it feasible to throw a large body of troops ashore against opposition, men caught in the act of re-embarkation against an alerted enemy were doomed. Re-embarkation, difficult under almost any conditions, under fire invariably led to heavy losses of men and equipment. In others word, large bodies, once put ashore, had to be in strength enough to remain there; hit-and-run attacks were suitable only for small parties.

Nevertheless, the impact of AGREEMENT bore out Mountbatten's conviction of the long-term value of raiding, regardless of cost. Henceforward Axis Commanders in the Western Desert were perpetually looking over their shoulders, fearing amphibious attacks against their over-extended communications. When Montgomery struck at El Alamein on 23 October, considerably more than a division was held back by the Axis as a coastal guard, and remained so while the defences at the front crumbled into ruin. Likewise, throughout the so-called Fortress Europe, Axis equanimity was disturbed. Allied intent was revealed two weeks later by Operation TORCH.

The invaders of TORCH came to stay just as those of WATCH-TOWER had come to stay in August at Guadalcanal. Both operations would lead to a reassessment of raiding policy. Neither could have been launched with assurance had not the incentive and practice of raiding strengthened existing amphibious techniques, laid deep roots in realistic training and created specialist élite forces to show the way. Infirm, patchy and sometimes non-existent as French resistance was against the landings at Casablanca, Oran and Algiers on 8 November, they could not have been undertaken at all if those in the Admiralty, such as Captain Maund, had managed to prevent the formation at an early date in 1940 of Commandos and associated amphibious forces. TORCH was a rebuttal of those who had resisted raiding.

Yet the spectre of Maund-like sceptisicm of Combined Operations' Private Armies loomed overall. In August, as a result of a bitter lesson from Dieppe, 'Party Inhuman' was formed to exploit the pioneering work in March, 1941, of Clogstoun-Willmott and Courtney by surveying, and later marking, landing places as 'human buoys'. Recruited from the SBS and the highly expert Admiralty Hydrographic Branch, Party Inhuman's role was to make up for two deficiencies in the composition of the enormously expanding amphibious forces – the lack of adequate charts wherever landings were proposed and the acute shortage of top-grade navigators. It was a cause of deep concern that few landing-craft navigators, British or American, were capable of anything more than coastal work pure and simple.

After only one week's training at the SBS Depot at Hayling Island, Party Inhuman was rushed out to Gibraltar where, almost immediately, the Naval C-in-C prohibited their employment inshore in canoes for the good reason that their detection or capture would compromise the entire Operation TORCH. In addition the OSS had managed to acquire up-to-date hydrographic material from a Frenchman. As a result this forerunner of what would become known to the British as Combined Operations Pilotage Parties (COPP) and to the Americans as 'Beach Jumpers' or 'Amphibious Recon Patrols', were restricted to making daylight surveys from submarines' periscopes. Only once before D-Day was a canoe used, and that time for a celebrated mission in which a canoe from a submarine secretly carried General Mark Clark ashore to contact French Army officers, friendly to the Allied cause, and arrange their collaboration.

Not until the night of 7 November, as the invasion fleet drew near, were the canoeists allowed to do the task they were trained for. Launched offshore from submarines eleven miles out to sea it was the canoeists' job to creep inshore, avoiding the local fishing fleets as they put to sea, and position themselves where their infra-red lights and, if required, flashing beacons, could be seen by the navigators of the waves of landing craft approaching the shore. So it was that at Algiers British commandos were helped by men from Party Inhuman and at Oran Darby's 1st Ranger Bn was delivered intact to its destination.

A splendid example of raiding carried out by Allies in unison was provided on 8 November at Arzew Bay by Darby's 1st Rangers. Their task was to secure US 1st Infantry Division's right flank by capturing two French batteries overlooking Z Beach before the infantry came ashore. The plan was similar to that so successfully put into practice by 4 Commando at Varengeville – a surprise landing at a distance from the objective, exploited by rapid marches inland by two separate yet mutually supporting groups. The main improvement on the Dieppe method was the addition of a Party Inhuman canoe to guide the assault accurately. Split up among three LSIs, the Rangers were fortunate, along with the rest of the TORCH armada, to reach the launching area undetected and to land unopposed on time at precisely the right place. Dammer Force, named after the Major commanding, wasted not a minute; its two companies found their way unerringly into the battery without a shot being fired. It needed only fifteen minutes to bring about the surrender of sixty Frenchmen and their Adjutant's wife.

Darby Force of four companies, led by the CO, had a longer approach march of two miles along the coast and a more difficult task. Spotted before they reached the battery, they came under machine-gun fire as they attempted to breach the outer wire barrier. But there, with what might have been a costly fight on their hands, the irresolution of the French became plain. No sooner did the Rangers bring down mortar fire than the French machine-gun fire was turned off, 'as if someone had pulled a switch'. Darby wrote:

Needing no orders, several Rangers rushed the big guns, thrusting Bangalore torpedoes – four sections of steel piping crammed with explosives – into the muzzles. At the same moment, a larger party of Rangers slammed through the main entrance of Batterie du Nord, shooting enemy sentries barring their path. The battle was practically over. The French soldiers had barricaded themselves in a powder magazine underground thinking the mortar shells were aerial bombs. They did not answer the call in French that they give themselves up. Grenades were pushed down the ventilators along with a Bangalore torpedo. The French came out with their hands in the air, sixty prisoners in all.

The Rangers had pulled off a classic 'hit' mission with precision. It was thus a strange irony that their British mentors, who landed at Algiers dressed in American uniform in the hope that the anti-British French would take more kindly to them, were lucky to survive after suffering from indifferent seamanship and navigation, such as had upset the assault at Dieppe. Faulty lowering of craft in a swell, plus failure of the lead MLs to make contact, delayed 6 Commando by over two hours, scattered its elements and landed some of them opposite the most heavily fortified French defences instead of on an undefended sector where Frenchmen loyal to the Allied cause had neutralized the defences. Noise from the engines alerted the enemy and drew fire. When at last 6 Commando did manage to concentrate and advance, its objective, Fort Duperre, was already engaging the ships. Furthermore, it was unable to overcome the defenders because 'the light weapons which were all the Commandos possessed could make little or no impression on the strength of the fort'. Eventually dive-bombing persuaded the garrison to surrender. As a result, Commandos soon took steps to copy their American comrades and acquire mortars and other heavy weapons to enable them to fight as normal infantry in the months to come. It was fortunate, indeed, that Fort Duperre was almost alone in offering serious resistance. 1 Commando, in fact, came ashore unopposed.

Totally unpublicized, and for excellent reasons, were the activities of 30 Commando sometimes known as the Special Engineering Unit and later as 30 Assault Unit, which consisted of specially selected members of the Royal Navy and Royal Marines and worked for the Director of Naval Intelligence. It was their task to land ahead of the assault and make for specific targets where it was expected that highly secret information might be found. At Algiers a small party under Lt-Cdr D. M. C. Curtis managed to apprehend the members of the German and Italian Armistice Commission complete with their documents and wireless codes – a rich haul. The surviving documents concerning this highly secret organization make entertaining reading if only because those who sponsored it in Combined Operations knew so little about what it got up to!

Unknown to the Rangers and the Commandos, the days of hit-and-run raiding in North Africa were over for them. In the invasions to come their role would be that of infantry, albeit of the 'shock' kind, demanding skill, dash and amphibious expertise. To begin with, the seizure of Bone by 1st Rangers and 6 Commando on 11 November, to link up with 3rd Bn Parachute Regiment as it landed at the airfield, provided a classic example of the spearhead technique of the future. Paradoxically, the successful execution of TORCH in North Africa and WATCHTOWER at Guadalcanal, which represented large dividends for the capital invested over the past two years in raiding and amphibious techniques, sparked off a radically new look at the philosophy and nature of striking at enemy coastal targets.

In the immediate aftermath of TORCH, nobody of importance in London or Washington seems to have realized that a time of change had arrived. The booming determination of Roosevelt, Churchill and Mountbatten to adhere to the existing larger and smaller scale raiding policy was unchallenged. In the Pacific, however, Admiral Nimitz and the US Navy were steering raiders into orthodox channels, though without totally outlawing raiding as a way of supporting conventional amphibious assaults. It was, of course, easier for Nimitz in Hawaii and King and Marshall in Washington than for the British Chiefs of Staff and C-in-Cs in Britain. Nimitz and Turner saw eye-to-eye on most matters and Turner was strictly subordinated as a Force Commander. Unlike General Brooke and the British Chiefs of Staff in London, they did not have to deal with an *enfant terrible* like Mountbatten whose dynamic style could sometimes ruffle his colleagues as they endeavoured to formulate Allied Grand Strategy in an orthodox manner. Perhaps because Brooke, as Chairman, tended to leave the development of organization, methods and tactics to subordinates, Mountbatten was free to provide a dynamic drive which, as time went by, exceeded his terms of reference in a way which also drove the British into a lead over the Americans in the prosecution not only of amphibious operations but much else besides.

Raiding, so far as Mountbatten was concerned, needed to increase in frequency and expand in effort. But the dividing line between invading and raiding was sometimes indistinct. Maybe Mountbatten held back a little when Churchill, on 16 September, returned to JUPITER and the seizure of North Norway, claiming, 'I have no doubt we could have a couple of Arctic-trained American Divisions, and with the Canadian Corps, and also several Russian divisions, apart from the Russian offensive, we could get quite enough forces to conquer the "Jupiter" area', without explaining how they would be moved there, supplied or protected from the air.

Churchill's mind was fixed on an invasion in Western Europe in 1943 – Operation ROUND-UP – the Chiefs of Staff upon an exploitation of TORCH in the Mediterranean in which, it was hoped, the Americans would participate. The occupation of Sardinia or Sicily, to be known respectively as Operations BRIMSTONE and HUSKY, were favourites. BRIMSTONE was preferred by the Joint Planning Staff and liked by Mountbatten and Portal, the Chief of Air Staff. Churchill and Brooke

wanted HUSKY, while General Eisenhower at Allied Forces HQ dis-
liked COHQ's BRIMSTONE plan. At this stage it becomes plain from
the minutes, and from the remarks of Brooke's biographer, that Mountbatten's relationship with the CIGS was becoming strained. As Chairman, Brooke felt that CCO's voice 'should properly be confined to
amphibious matters. Yet the choice between Sardinia and Sicily would
certainly be such, and Mountbatten had a right to have his say.'

Influential and fecund of ideas as CCO and his staff were, a firm curb
was already being placed upon them as 'invading' took precedence over
'raiding', and this applied to the Pacific as well as to Europe. Once the
German and Japanese were thrown back on the defensive and started
their long retreats, the original *raison d'être* for raiding forces came up for
re-assessment, albeit in an atmosphere of hope and expansion.

CHAPTER 22
By Horsa and Cockle

Although SOE had been forbidden to indulge in amphibious operations and COHQ had confined its raiding to the coastal regions, there were occasions when the latter staged operations inland without use of sea transport. Operation COLOSSUS, in February, 1941, had partially set a precedent when the raiders landed by parachute, although the intended and thwarted escape route was by sea. BITING was a similar example. It is not entirely clear, however, why Operation FRESHMAN, an attack upon the hydro-electric plant at Rjukan in Norway, became a COHQ responsibility in October, 1942, since, in this case, delivery of the raiders was to be made by air and escape overland. Of course raiding had been excluded from the directive to SOE in the Spring of 1942, and the reputation of SOE had fallen to a very low ebb as the year went by, due to internal squabbles, rows with the Foreign Office and other departments, plus a shortage of measurable success. No doubt the high regard in which Mountbatten and COHQ were held in Whitehall had something to do with the choice. The fact remains that Sir John Anderson, the Lord President of the Council, with full Cabinet backing, endorsed the order with the highest priority because the SIS had unearthed sufficient evidence to suggest that the Germans might be working on the design of an atomic bomb and that the heavy water manufactured at Rjukan could be essential to its production.

The plan by COHQ did, however, involve SOE, one of whose parties set up a camp thirty miles from Rjukan on 18 October upon which the raiders were to be based. It was intended that thirty-four Royal Engineers belonging to Airborne Forces should be carried in two Horsa gliders, each towed by a four-engined Halifax bomber, to land on a glacier five or six miles from the target. Then, assisted by information from a previous employee at the plant, they were to move in, blow it up along with the stocks of heavy water, and escape across the mountains to Sweden. The risks were considerable, along with the knowledge that MUSKETOON, in September, had alerted the Germans to the threat. The aircraft took off on 19 November, got lost over Norway and, weighed down by heavy icing, had insufficient fuel remaining to tow the Horsas home. Casting off at between 11,000 and 12,000 feet in the belief that they were over the sea, the gliders spiralled down rapidly into cloud, one pilot ordering 'ditching stations'. A few minutes later both crashed into the mountains, one near Egersund, the other close by Stavanger. At the same time one of the Halifaxes also crashed, killing all the crew. Of those in the gliders who were not killed, most were injured and all badly shaken. Understandably their first reaction was to seek help and abandon their orders, which stated:

'Whatever happens, someone must arrive at the objective to do the job.'

Shortly, at their own request, the survivors were transferred to German custody. The party at Egersund were apparently taken out almost at once and shot by the roadside in compliance with the Commando Order. The men at Stavanger were also executed after interrogation, under which they resolutely refused to give information. Nevertheless the Germans were fully informed of the target from a marked map and from remarks the soldiers had made to the Norwegians who found them.

On 12 December those in London who waited anxiously for news were sufficiently informed by SIS and the Norwegian authorities of what had taken place. In the Swedish press the men had been described as 'Armed Civilians'. After interrogation the Norwegian interpreter had been told:

They could not be considered as prisoners of war because their action was not in connection with a Military operation. Nor had they been taken during armed resistance. They wore, moreover, black underclothes beneath their uniforms that could be used as civilian disguise for escape into Sweden. All were supplied with a few Norwegian kroner. So, they would be treated as guerrillas.

Rjukan and other power stations were at once substantially reinforced. In due course it fell to the Norwegian Army, working with SOE, to show that difficult inland targets were better left to specialists working in their own element. Far better suited to Combined Operations' aptitude was another important industrial target at Bordeaux.

In July, 1942, in conformity with the policy of increasing Royal Marine involvement, the RM Boom Patrol Detachment (RMBPD) was formed, additional to the Small Boat Section, for the purpose of reconnaissance and raiding, under Mountbatten's control, equipped with Mr Goatley's latest two-man Cockle Mk II canoes. The previous February Lord Selborne had taken over from Dr Dalton as Minister of Economic Warfare, and with it the responsibility for SOE. He now asked Combined Operations to tackle enemy blockade runners which sheltered in Bordeaux harbour between their secret voyages with vital cargoes to and from the Far East. For some indistinct reason he also asked SOE to take on the same task. So as CCO was preparing No 1 Section RMBPD, under Major H. G. Hasler, for Operation FRANKTON, an SOE Circuit called SCIENTIST was also being briefed to undertake the same work.

After two months' work, modifying the cockle to enable it to be hoisted out of a submarine fully loaded and crewed, six crews sailed in the submarine *Tuna* for the mouth of the River Gironde. On the night of 7 December, five were successfully launched and began the difficult paddle inshore. Lashed by chilling spray and buffeted by the tide race, the weaker crews began to fail. *Coalfish* disappeared in the dark waters. A second, *Conger*, overturned, could not be righted and eventually, to the distress of Hasler, had to be left behind. Cpl Sheard, its commander, said bravely, 'That's alright, sir. I understand. Thanks for bringing us so far.' Their bodies were later washed ashore. The next setback took place in the narrows at the mouth of the Gironde where, as they passed unseen between the shore and some destroyers, *Cuttlefish* lost touch and was never seen again by Hasler whose force was now reduced by two-thirds. In fact *Cuttlefish* continued independently but was later wrecked near Bordeaux and the crew captured as they tried to escape overland. At dawn Hasler, accompanied by Marine Sparks in *Catfish* and Cpl Laver and Marine Mills in *Crayfish*, were safe, on course and hidden up at Pointe aux Oiseaux just inside the river estuary.

Ahead lay sixty miles of river to be paddled at flood tide on two successive nights. Attendant by day was the danger of discovery by the Germans, or French who might betray them. They were, indeed, found on the 8th by fishermen who seemed disinclined to believe they were not Germans, but eventually Hasler managed to persuade their unwelcome visitors to keep silent. He also declined offers of hospitality. Two nights later they were hidden up within striking distance of the target, ready to lay alongside and attach limpets to their chosen victims, seven one side of the river, two the other, on the night 11/12 December.

Searching the east bank on the flood tide, Laver managed to place limpets on a large cargo ship and a small liner without being observed. Pressed for time to deal with so many targets, Hasler on the west bank had to take serious risks, abandoning the rule of silence in order to tackle the maximum number of ships before the tide began to ebb and he had to make for safety downstream. He managed to attach limpets to four ships, last of all to a light naval type called 'Sperrbrecher'. Then a sentry on deck spotted the cockle. Hasler reported:

> Fortunately we were able to get back close to the ship's side and drift along with the tide without making any movement. The sentry followed us along the deck, shining his torch down on us at intervals, but was evidently unable to make up his mind as to what we actually were, owing to the efficiency of the camouflage scheme. We were able to get into a position under the bow of the ship where he could no longer see us, and after waiting there for about five minutes, everything seemed quiet, so we resumed our course downstream.

They paddled openly and fast in midstream with the intention of putting as much distance as possible between the targets and their next lying-up place before the limpets began exploding at 0700 hrs on the 12th. Near the village of Blaye they separated and set off overland for Spain and thence home.

So it was that the astounded Germans, the people of Bordeaux and the somewhat scandalized members of SCIENTIST were disturbed the next morning by the sight and sound of ships blowing up for no apparent reason. Gradually came news of the extent of success – one cargo ship completely destroyed, four others seriously damaged. Also came news of the missing marines. Four had died in the approach to the target, four were later captured and executed. Only two – Hasler and Sparks – got back to tell the tale and receive their awards.

The Germans were rattled by this demonstration of their opponents' ability to penetrate harbours so easily without detection and to come and go along the coast much as they pleased. In the months to come considerable information reached London revealing from German sources the strain being placed by raiding from the sea and by SOE who, under new management and with increasing collaboration from the people of the occupied countries, were causing serious damage and disruption. In a signal on 23 March, Admiral Dönitz warned the Navy's coastal defenders that an invasion might soon take place. This most certainly was the wish of the Americans as they contemplated winding up the campaign in Tunisia and returning to England prior to invading France in 1943. Yet, as 1942 drew to an end there came an unexpected check to Mountbatten's ambition.

CHAPTER 23

Setting a New Course

Loyalty, above all loyalty to traditional values and organizations, is a watchword among members of Armed Services throughout the world. It was loyalty to the existing order which had been behind the resistance to COHQ and SOE, as well as to the creation of Raiders within the US Marines in 1942. Regardless of initial successes, which enabled Forces of the New Order to obtain authority for a considerable expansion in 1943, the upholders of the Old Order prevailed in the resistance to changes which they instinctively regarded as pernicious, as Mountbatten found out when C (the symbol for Maj-Gen Sir Stewart Menzies, the Director of the SIS) made known his latest objection to small-scale raids.

The SIS had undergone a most deflating experience since 1940 when its principal espionage agents in Germany had been eliminated and its contacts throughout Europe disrupted by German occupation. The dissatisfaction of its principal customers – the Foreign Office, Armed Services and Ministry of Economic Warfare – was justified, at least until the end of 1942 when discontent within the occupied territories began to generate sufficient dissidence to produce a renewed flow of information. Only then did C feel strong enough to call for special favours from old friends to ease the movement of new agents he was recruiting in and out of Fortress Europe. There was general agreement within COHQ, SOE and SIS that, so difficult was it now to land on the Dutch and Belgian coasts and so strongly guarded was the coast of Northern France, that only Norway and Brittany were relatively easy to penetrate. C complained that raids stirred up these safer havens and hazarded the insertion or extraction of agents.

The matter was thrashed out on 4 January, 1943, by the Vice-Chiefs at the Chiefs of Staff Committee. The VCNS explained the difficulty of adjudicating between the conflicting interests of SOE, SIS and COHQ, and proposed a formula which allowed the Admiralty to arbitrate when there was a clash of interests. The Army and the RAF, abetted by the Navy, felt that information provided by C should have priority over small raids. At this point Mountbatten entered the meeting, briefed to be sympathetic to SIS but to resist his veto as far as possible, on the lines that small-scale raids, by forcing the enemy to strengthen key points along his coast, were likely to compel a reduction in the standard of coast-watching generally. But in emphasizing that it was the Prime Minister's decision to intensify small raiding, Mountbatten drew from the VCIGS, Lt-Gen A. E. Nye, the retort that, in giving effect to the Prime Minister's instructions, other interests, such as C's, must not unduly suffer. Mountbatten's tacit acceptance of what amounted to a *fait accompli* by the Vice-Chiefs provides yet another example of his realistic approach to obstructions which would have driven Keyes to distraction and been followed by an impassioned appeal to Churchill. Moreover, the formula suggested by the Admiralty, although it restored a strong measure of control to the Navy, was by no means totally prohibitive or inflexible. For although the Admiralty was granted the role of arbiter in settling who raided, where and when, and gave priority to SIS over SOE, it also reserved to the Chiefs of Staff the power to intervene, thus guaranteeing Mountbatten a strong voice of appeal in case the Navy placed too heavy a hand upon his activities, as C-in-C Plymouth was already proposing to do by adopting the Ramsay line that 'raiding was forcing the enemy to improve his defences'.

In practice the new policy proved totally prohibitive only to SOE. A specially appointed Admiralty Deputy Director, Operations Division (Irregular), who proved, as Foot says, 'no friend of SOE', stated imperiously: 'In home water clandestine operations are controlled by the Admiralty'. This confrontation merely went to show that, beneath the surface, the Admiralty retained its entrenched sectional interest and that if Churchill had not formed a Directorate of Combined Operations in 1940 and placed men of drive and character in charge, amphibious operations would have remained seriously retarded and the return to the Continent delayed longer than it was. The existence of collusion between the SIS, the Admiralty and the Chiefs of Staff in provoking a crisis which would trim Mountbatten's influence cannot be entirely ruled out, but is unlikely. SIS, instinctively guarding its authority and genuinely fearing the intrusion of additional agencies to the clandestine field, had resisted SOE from the start and successfully blocked efforts by America's OSS to act independently of SOE in 1942. In the short run, Mountbatten's comprehensive raiding programme had to be curtailed and SOE's amphibious activities limited to unobtrusive missions to ferry in agents and supplies on suitable occasions and to the annoyance of DDOD(I) who favoured a complete ban on SOE. As Foot wrote: 'SOE was seldom contented to let well alone, or to be satisfied with an inch when an ell seemed there for the taking.'

A redefinition of priorities was overdue in the raiding field and departmental overlapping was rife. If SOE tended to encroach on SIS and COHQ ground, the same could also be said of COHQ in reverse. It could be claimed that FRESHMAN in November had been a genuine SOE task, as was proved in February, 1943, when a party of Norwegian soldiers under SOE direction in a brilliant action (Operation GUNNERSIDE) wrecked the Rjukan plant without loss, putting it out of action until August. It was therefore logical that the 'inland' projects CCO's Search Committee had laid claim to should not be proceeded with. Such were:

CORNET, an attack by commandos flown in by flying boats upon the Mohne Dam in Germany, scheduled for February/March and eventually carried out with celebrated success by RAF Bomber Command, using a 'bouncing' bomb.

COMATOSE, a sort of AIRTHIEF to steal an aeroplane.

COGNAC, a parachute attack on power stations at Milan.

In other words, SOE and Combined Operations would become complementary rather than competitors.

Most of the SSRF raids projected for Brittany, as well as some by 14 Commando to Norway, were also cancelled, eight of them falling foul of SIS objections – the so-called C ban. However, the Admiralty placed nothing in the way of small raids againt targets which identified with Admiralty interest, especially operations such as PETRIFY/WITTICISM, which was intended as a joint SSRF/MGB raid against shipping in St Peter Port, Guernsey; or PUSSYFOOT, another landing on Herm. Fog stopped both of these, winter weather accounting for far more last-minute cancellations than the enemy. Only BACKCHAT, a typical SSRF reconnaissance from MTB 344 of the beach at Anse de St Martin, had to be cancelled because of a chance encounter with two enemy patrol vessels.

With typical prescience, allied to faith in Churchill's and Brooke's abilities to weld the Americans to British strategic intentions, Mountbatten at a second meeting on 4 January, explained to his newly formed Military and Air Committee the deep effect of the North African campaign on Combined Operations policy. The Americans were intent upon ROUND-UP in 1943 – intended as a heavy blow to the enemy heart, as opposed to the British leaning towards pinpricks against extremities.

The British were against it because they were convinced that re-entry into Europe by way of strongly-defended coasts was impossible until the enemy had been further worn down and their own forces and techniques improved and built up. The Americans wanted to complete the conquest of Tunisia and close down major operations in the Mediterranean. But Mountbatten confidently told his staff that ROUND-UP would have second priority and ten days later he was proved right during Conference SYMBOL at Casablanca where he helped Churchill, Roosevelt and the Chiefs of Staff hammer out the strategy which would win the war.

Germany would remain the prime target but sufficient resources would be allocated to the Pacific to enable the commanders there to mount a sustained offensive against Japan. The massive strategic bombing offensive which would be launched against the Axis might shorten the war; but the policy of Unconditional Surrender would embitter and, arguably, prolong rather than hasten the end of the struggle. ROUND-UP would be deferred and the North African campaign extended beyond Tunisia into Southern Europe via Sicily (Operation HUSKY). The effect upon COHQ, as Mountbatten had envisaged, was profound. Automatically the debate between Eisenhower and Mountbatten over Sardinia was snuffed out when HUSKY superceded BRIMSTONE. By focusing on the Mediterranean there occurred a large-scale subtraction of resources from British waters. Many vessels were taken from Force J, notably LCTs, of which, at this crucial moment, the latest Mark IV version was found to have a structural weakness demanding instant modification. The immediate re-deployment of CCO's best planning staff from London to Algiers to advise Allied Forces HQ (AFHQ) on HUSKY distracted attention from a series of larger-scale raids already in preparation against France and Norway. To begin with, and working on the assumption that Operation BUNBURY would be linked to ROUND-UP, General Paget, the GOC-in-C Home Forces, had 'strongly opposed' it on the grounds that it would draw attention to the Cotentin Peninsula and lead the enemy to strengthen their defences in an area which was likely to be included in any major operation on the Continent. For BUNBURY aimed to destroy the garrison on Sark in May and would comprise an attack by 120–240 parachutists against Big Sark and a troop of sixty men from 4 Commando, carried in two LCIs to Little Sark, plus assistance from twenty to thirty men of SSRF placed ashore from an MGB and an MTB. It was inevitable, once HUSKY was decided upon, that larger scale raids should be struck from the list, such as:

HADRIAN, the capture of Cherbourg

ARABIAN (later LETHAL), an attempt to seize the submarine bases in Brittany, and thus related to other operations in the spring such as:

CONTOUR, a naval and airborne landing on Brittany.

COUGHDROP, a parachute attack on Lorient in company with heavy bombing in June, rejected by Brigadier Laycock as 'a bad one'.

KLEPTOMANIA, a very large raid against Ushant which was deemed impracticable at any time in any circumstances.

AUDACITY, a revival of the cancelled 1942 raid against Norway referred to above.

Nevertheless, the Admiralty nurtured distinctly aggressive designs against Norway, despite SIS objections and the deep concern of the C-in-C Norwegian Forces in London, who feared a recent German proclamation imposing the death penalty on any Norwegians who might discover, and not report, the existence of raiding parties. There were valuable prizes to be won from raiding Norway, which, the Chiefs of Staff implied by their acquiescence, on 4 January, to a raid upon pyrites mines, out-weighed all other considerations. These prizes included the interruption of a vital enemy supply line, the damaging of warships threatening the convoy route to Russia, the smashing of the heavy water plant at Rjukan and, of indirect but immense importance, the known German fear of invasion and the diversion of forces from more threatened areas as a result of expensive fears implanted at low cost in Hitler's mind.

SYMBOL also marked, if indistinctly, a change to the purposes of small-scale raiding in all theatres of war. In addition to establishing a clearer demarcation line between work by clandestine parties of SOE nature and by uniformed raiders, there was of necessity an abandonment of 'periodical battles', as Mountbatten phrased it, or 'raiding for raiding's sake' as others said. The heavy fighting in Tunisia, the prospective invasion of Sicily and the greatly enhanced opportunities of striking at the Japanese in Burma and throughout the Pacific, made battles easier, if not all too easy for some, to come by. And linked inextricably with each invasion were the vital pre-attack phases of reconnaissance and softening-up of the enemy which so often fell to execution by raiders of one sort or another.

For example, the decision at SYMBOL to provide sufficient support to allow Nimitz and MacArthur to continue an offensive in the South-West Pacific, which coincided with the admission by the Japanese of defeat at Guadalcanal, led to a thorough reappraisal by the Americans of their amphibious techniques and an expansion of their raiding forces. The outstanding combat abilities of Darby's 1st Ranger Bn in North Africa led to multiplication of the number of Army Ranger battalions by four prior to HUSKY. 2nd Battalion formed in the US in April, 1943, made up of 500 out of 2,000 eager volunteers from many units. 3rd and 4th formed in North Africa, based on cadres from 1st Bn. In September, 5th Bn took shape in the USA, and finally the 6th in the Pacific in August, 1944, formed from the 98th Field Artillery Bn. It must be made plain that small-scale raiding was not the purpose of these new Ranger units; with campaigns based on opposed landings ahead, it was deemed essential for standard combat formations to be spearheaded ashore by specialist units who could storm the beaches and take out particularly tough defences which might prove beyond the capabilities of tyros in amphibious assault.

Likewise the expansion of Marine Raider and Parachute units in the Pacific had 'spearheading' largely in mind, although there would be occasions when they did raid. 3rd and 4th Marine Raider Bns had been formed, respectively, in September, 1942 – the former in Samoa, the latter in the US. Opposition from the Commandant of the Marine Corps was now quelled because he was in no position to stand up to the combined weight of his President, some among his own senior officers, including General Vandegrift, commander of the 1st Marine Division, Rear Admiral Turner (who successfully promoted Raider battalions as being far more effective tactical 'bricks' in island warfare than larger formations) and popular support in the Press, whipped up by Carlson. The creation of 1st Raider Regiment in March, 1943, appears, however, to have been an administrative and training concept in support of the four existing battalions. For although the Regiment would soon assume an operational role, it never operationally commanded all its Raider battalions together since, usually, they were detached to separate tasks.

The Marine Parachute Battalion underwent a similar experience, 1st Marine Parachute Regiment being formed on 1 April, 1943, to take charge of the existing 1st Bn (formed 1941), 2nd Bn also (formed 1941) and 3rd Bn (formed Steptember, 1942), with 4th Bn joining later after its formation in the US on 2 April, 1943.

Never would a Marine parachute unit make an operational jump. Infrequently would they, or the Raiders, raid in the British manner. Preference for concentrated blows no doubt had a bearing upon it, along with Service rivalries – quite apart from the problems of fighting an island war over a vast expanse of ocean. Yet it remains a misconception in the writing of popular American history that hit-and-run raiding came to an abrupt end after Makin in 1942. For the nature of island topography and deficiencies of information alone made it essential that these techniques should be used for survey, for pilotage and obstacle clearing, slow as Turner was to recognize it.

In the aftermath of WATCHTOWER, as preparations were being made to reconquer the Solomons, the Gilberts and the Marshall Islands, an intensive study was made of the known amphibious shortcomings. High on the list was the need for pre-attack survey of the invasion area to fill gaps left by inferior maps and the inability of aerial photography to penetrate the jungle canopy. Through the intermingled staff communication systems linking London and Washington to Theatre Headquarters, similar lessons were already being disseminated as a result of JUBILEE and TORCH. Thus knowledge of British reconnaissance parties in Europe was available to Nimitz and Turner in the Pacific. In addition, the Americans held in high respect the Australian Coast-Watchers Organization which had been raised prior to the war by the Director of Naval Intelligence (DNI). This consisted of unpaid volunteers drawn from the native islanders, led by Administrative Officers, traders and others with the task of reporting by radio the movements of hostile craft. In due course they were joined by men of the Australian Independent Companies (recruited in 1940 as the equivalent of British Commandos), also by several New Zealanders and Americans. Engaged initially for a passive role, and told officially to disband once the enemy had arrived and been reported, many, using their knowledge of jungle survival, withdrew inland to continue reporting. Gradually they assumed military status and, despite heavy losses, fought on as guerrillas, joined in April, 1942, by the New Zealand 'Southern Independent Commando Company'. Later what became known as the South Pacific Scouts, comprised mostly of Fijians, began to arrive on Guadalcanal towards the end of WATCHTOWER and shortly after this the Americans started to employ them to work with their amphibious Reconnaissance Patrols.

Guadalcanal became the home of a Combat Reconnaissance School at which experienced Marine Raiders and Coastwatchers instructed small élite teams, recruited initially from the Raider units, to probe ahead of every subsequent Allied landing. Carried to their destination in MTBs, submarines or PBY flying boats, they would travel either in rubber boats or in native war canoes. Theirs were the tactics of caution in arrival, stealth in investigation, commonsense use of local knowledge and diplomacy for survival, and shrewd, timely withdrawal with the requisite information before detection. They were similar in many respects to the COPP which, raised in December, 1942, from survivors of the Party Inhuman, were starting in January their examination of

Sicily's beaches. Like their opposite numbers in Europe they could not count on a friendly welcome from the natives. Many islanders were pro-Japanese.

British raiding forces were expanding as fast as those of America, and, in some respects, in a more diverse manner. As early as September, 1942, when the ships and craft for TORCH and Force J were assembling and at a time when new craft were coming in quantity from the British and, above all, American shipyards, the First Sea Lord concluded that the task of running this enormous Assault Fleet was getting beyond COHQ and ought to be taken over by the Admiralty. At the same time CCO reported the very great difficulties being experienced in the maintenance of craft and the provision of sufficient crews. As a result of instructions from the Chiefs of Staff to solve the problem quickly, a large-scale change in responsibilities took place in 1943. The Admiralty took over the running of the Assault Fleet at about the same time as the Royal Marines underwent a radical alteration of role linked to reorganization. At a stroke the existing Royal Marine Division was disbanded and its battalions converted to Commandos (under a new Commando Group Headquarters) with 43, 44, 45 46 and 47 (RM) Commandos coming into being to join 40, 41 and 42 already in existence. No doubt Admiral Turner would have approved, for this tallied with his ideas. At the same time the Army, the RAF and the Marines were to 'join' the Navy by providing crews for landing craft of all sizes up to LCT, introducing a major departure from past practice by authorizing Marine officers to skipper craft. Consideration was also given to inviting American participation, but was rejected on the grounds of administrative and disciplinary difficulty, and a prevalent nationalistic prejudice that this would add to the danger of the Americans claiming the whole subsequent victory for themselves.

Inevitably, Joint Service workings created an intricate jumble of overlapping functions and associations which could never be tidily resolved by those at COHQ or anywhere else. It was a very complicated war in which no single plan or activity could be viewed in isolation since all plans interacted upon each other with knock-on effects which were incalculable. By this time it was almost a miracle if any of the small raiding groups consisted neatly of one nationality, let alone a single service or regiment. For example, 14 Commando, which was formed towards the end of 1942 to specialize in raiding Norway in kayaks, incorporated British, Canadians and Red Indians, plus the Norwegians who had to be attached for local expertise. A COPP team usually consisted of four Naval and one RE officer, four Naval ratings and three Sappers and was commanded by an experienced Navigator or Hydrographic officer, since it was essential that the evidence they were seeking should not only be quickly and accurately found but also be reliable.

Like the American Amphibious Recon Patrol, COPPs were taken to their working areas in submarines, MLs or aircraft. The submarine was the favourite since it could make an unobserved daylight reconnaissance through its periscope before putting the party ashore at night. The technique developed will be described below. Here it is only intended to mention the evolution of a new kind of carrier, the midget submarine, which also demanded specially trained men to operate it. The first of the type was, in fact, a British invention of the First World War, but it was the Italians and Japanese who developed and first used them to sink ships in harbour. Using what were really manned torpedoes, the Italians had sunk many British ships in Gibraltar Bay when operating from hulks in neutral waters and laying their charges beneath their targets at night. On 18 December, 1941, three of these 'slow-speed torpedoes', each manned by two rubber-suited frogmen, had slipped into Alexandria harbour and severely damaged two battleships, a destroyer and a tanker. For their part, the Japanese had developed larger, two-man submarines which could be carried to their destination by ocean-going submarines. These failed at Pearl Harbor but one managed to sink a British battleship in Diego Suarez Harbour on 30 May, 1942, and others penetrated Sydney Harbour a day later.

Operations by midget submarines, being of a naval character, will be excluded from this work, except in so far as they impinge upon amphibious operations. The British developed three types – the two-man Chariot, similar to the Italian design, the four-man X-type, similar to the Japanese and a one-man craft called the Welman. Mainly the crews were sailors, although the first, abortive Chariot operation (TITLE) against the German battleship *Tirpitz* in October, 1942, in a fjord near Trondheim was crewed by Norwegian sailors and Sgt D. Craig, a Royal Engineer belonging to the Commandos. Bad weather, which sank the two Chariots close to the objective, accounted for the failure of the operation.

Less familiar is the story of the Welman one-man submarine which was intended by SOE to land supplies on the enemy coast for partisans. An initial order in December, 1942, for twenty was later increased to 150, of which eighty would belong to SOE as freighters, forty to CCO for survey and raiding and eight to the Navy, the latter preferring Chariot and X-Craft. Nobody thought much of the Welman. Lack of a periscope was one severe handicap during inshore reconnaissance, while its frail construction provoked an angry and frightened trials officer to complain that a nearby grenade going off would cripple it and that it was only suitable for its original SOE role. Mountbatten, too, experienced one of its weaknesses when the vision block cracked during a dive. A claim that the Welman was a superior substitute to the canoe in inshore operations was rejected. Manned by men from the SBS in 62 Commando, four were used in November, 1943, to attack shipping in Bergen harbour, but failed to penetrate the defences and were lost.

It was apparent to those involved with raiding in Europe that the time had come to put their house in order and control the spread of Private Armies which COHQ, SOE and OSS so diligently encouraged. A start had been made by Mountbatten when, in accordance with the COS decision of 27 July, he formed North Force on 6 October, 1942. Sometimes called Fynn Force after its leader Major F. W. Fynn, Gordon Highlanders, it consisting of men from the Royal Navy and from 10, 12 and 14 Commandos. North Force was tasked to tackle targets in Norway, using 14 Commando for attacks on shipping. It consisted of British, Canadians, Red Indians, Norwegians and US Army Rangers and specialized in the use of Canadian kayaks, which they preferred to Cockles.*

In due course all would come under the control of the special Small Raids Planning Syndicate set up by Mountbatten in November. Increasingly, too, raiding forces were being brought under strict control by Theatre Commanders who simply could not afford to have plans of enormous moment spoiled by the wild depredations of a handful of adventurers to whom the war was something of a game. It was bad enough when a recognized Private Army did something eccentric, but quite unacceptable when two bored dental orderlies stole a boat and carried out a personal foray to France in 1942, a breach of discipline which earned them due punishment and posting to the Commandos after they returned home. In the Middle East, on 28 September, 1942, 1st SAS was formally established under the command of Lt-Col A. D. Stirling and tasked to dovetail its raiding in jeeps and trucks with LRDG in the forthcoming offensive by Eighth Army. There were to be no more AGREEMENT fiascos. The indiscretions of amateurs had to give way to precise execution by professionals.

---

* The Rangers concerned were from 29th Ranger Bn which was formed from volunteers from the National Guard 29th Infantry Division and activated on 20 December, 1942. Known by the British as 2nd Ranger Bn and sometimes by the Americans as 2nd Provisional Ranger Bn, its identity always caused confusion, particularly since North Force operation orders sometimes name it 2nd and at other times 29th!

CHAPTER 24

The Hornet's Nest

Almost at once the SYMBOL Conference stirred up a veritable hornet's nest for the Axis. Having called for world-wide offensive action, the Combined Chiefs of Staff gave the green light to Theatre Commanders to initiate the probes and raids without which no major attack could be contemplated. Not long after the Conference COPP would begin their investigation of Sicily's beaches in preparation for HUSKY. And at about the same time another new raiding force would be created to complement the COPP's work.

During SYMBOL a proposal had been put by Mountbatten to Generals Eisenhower and Alexander at AFHQ for a raiding force to strike at the enemy rear in Tunisia. Both men had jumped at the idea. In a rapid exchange of signals and letters with London it was agreed that a force of fifty men (not 200 as originally suggested) should be formed, assisted by two or three members of 1st SAS. It was specifically laid down that the force would be separate from Commandos. Initially Lord Lovat was proposed for command but later dropped because it was thought he did not 'always see eye to eye' with his cousin, the CO of 1st SAS, Lt-Col David Stirling. It was also proposed that the Americans should send Rangers to the UK for training prior to joining the force, although this does not seem to have taken place.

In the end an independent force, at first called Detachment 62 Commando and sometimes SSRF North Africa or No 1 SSRF, was sent out in February under Lt-Col William Stirling, including in its ranks several of Appleyard's SSRF, among them Capt Pinckney.

Meanwhile, in the South-West Pacific, a new form of raiding had already started. No sooner had the Japanese come to recognize that the loss of Guadalcanal was the prelude to events of more serious consequence than they became aware of a ripple in the tide of enemy aggression, with Coast-watchers, whom they had previously regarded as stay-behind guerrillas, now taking the offensive. Towards the end of February, 1943, news filtered in of a staff officer and six Marines who 'prowled Roviana Lagoon and the Munda area [in New Georgia] . . . contacting coastwatchers, scouting and mapping trails and selecting possible landing beaches'. Like all pioneers, the Amphibious Recon Patrols used impro-vised equipment and tentative methods. As the Marine Corps History so aptly phrases it: 'Travelling by night and observing during daylight hours, the patrols checked travel time from point to point, took bearings on channels, scouted enemy disposition and sketched crude maps to help fill in the scanty information already available'.

Without this dangerous exploration across shark-infested waters in rubber inflatable boats and uncomfortable, unwieldy native canoes, no subsequent step forward among the islands could have been safely undertaken. Not until Capt C. A. Boyd, the patrol leader at Munda, had reported could Vice Admiral W. F. Halsey pronounce with confident assurance, 'Well gentlemen, we're going to hit that place'. The Americans called on air forces to do most destruction by raiding and depended largely upon surface patrols for information which was otherwise un-obtainable. Yet they took note that such rudimentary methods could not guarantee perfect results.

Pacific raiding, compared with its European counterpart, may have been, as yet, unsophisticated, but it took place, after all, in an undeveloped quarter of the globe, populated extensively by primitive people, some of whom were still head hunters and habitual raiders themselves. Moreover, the war in the Pacific had been in progress less than a third as long as that in Europe, and European 'civilization' tended to impose humanitarian restraints in order to avoid disturbing political sensitivities or upsetting general principles. Call it primitive or civilized, raiding had become an integral component of modern war. In the aftermath of the destruction of Japan's carrier-borne air force, their loss of Guadalcanal, the setbacks in North Africa and something akin to rout in Russia, a few pinpricks implied nothing important until simultaneous irruptions made Axis defences look like a pin-cushion. Nobody was more susceptible to this sort of pressure than Adolf Hitler.

The SIS embargo ('C' ban as it was called) by no means crippled raiding. The Admiralty cheerfully encouraged it in Norway; there was no ban on activity by guerrillas within France, and AFHQ was eager to stir up what trouble it could for the enemy in numerous vulnerable spots throughout the Mediterranean.

As an example of Admiralty determination to raid, and their willingness to co-operate with COHQ when it suited, the activity of its Norwegian flotillas in collaboration with North Force may be quoted. VP operations aimed at German shipping within the Inner Leads of Norway, using MTBs and MGBs, were proposed in October, 1943, and almost at once seized upon by Mountbatten. He not only envisaged them as carriers for the raiders of North Force but feared that, for lack of a central co-ordinating authority, duplication and clashes of activities would result, as already had occurred elsewhere. Departmental confusion there still would be, but the feasibility of having MTBs and commandos 'lying up' among the islands and fjords while striking at the enemy during the dark winter months was demonstrated in November by a trial VP operation in MTBs accompanied by Major Fynn, the commander of North Force. Already his men were assembling and undergoing rigorous sub-Arctic survival training with Canadian kayaks. Serious proceedings began on the night 23/24 January with Operation CARTOON, an attack by fifty-three men from 12 and 10 (IA) Commando, carried in four MTBs, on the iron pyrites mines at Lillebo and Silo on Stord island. Destruction of the mine workings was enough to deprive the Germans of a year's production of 160,000 tons of specialized ore. Opposition by the garrison was negligible. The four defending guns were unmanned and the garrison of about twenty quickly rounded up. Casualties to both sides were light. The seven Norwegian MTBs involved managed to bag a 2,000-ton enemy ship and a JU 88 bomber. And, as a final reminder to spare the local populace from reprisals, a note was pinned to a door: 'Achtung! Commandos! Auf Wiedersehen!'

Throughout February the daily reports placed before Hitler informed him of mounting trouble from plain-clothes guerrillas as well as uniformed intruders. Attacks against industrial and communications targets by SOE Circuits, of which twenty-four alone were intermittently active in France at this time, were frequent; a new one called FARMER, for example, announced its presence by wrecking a train between Lens and Bethune, destroying forty wagons. SOE had endured more than its share of disasters, many caused by mismanagement and inexperience, but at last it was beginning to function as originally intended.

Never did a dark night pass but that the North Sea, the Channel and the Mediterranean were infested by small craft going about their errands, MTBs, MGBs, MLs, fishing smacks and feluccas putting ashore and taking off SIS and SOE agents and stores. Foot quotes one agent's impression: 'At a point fifteen miles from the enemy coast, main engines were cut and we went forward on auxiliaries in complete silence, at a maximum speed of approximately 6 knots.' Inshore contact would be made by S-phone or signal light, always with the fear that German radar had spotted them or the plan been compromised. Movement between boat and shore would be by dinghy hauled by grass rope. Elaborate precautions were taken to hasten and conceal the mission.

Nearby, Combined Operations parties would also be busy. For example, at the beginning of the moonless period on 21/22 February, two MGBs equipped with QH receivers went to the area of Roches Douvres (Operation HJA) to plot the accuracy of, and discover any 'blank spots' in, the new Gee navigational equipment. Simultaneously, in Norway, two MTBs of 30th Flotilla under Lieut C. Herlofson, Royal Norwegian Navy, were entering the Sognefjord, carrying sixteen men from 10(IA), 12 and 14 Commando and 29th Rangers of North Force to begin an eight-day 'lying-up' operation, confusingly under the name VPK, CRACKERS or OMNIBUS 42, depending upon which department was handling the operation in London. Camouflaging their MTBs inshore during the short hours of northern twilight, this group demonstrated the possibilities of this kind of operation by putting men in kayaks ashore under Lieut K. P. H. Waggett and Sub-Lieut J. Godwin, RNVR, bombarding enemy strongpoints and laying sea mines. They might have achieved even more had not the weather turned so bad that plans to attack land targets from the kayaks had to be abandoned and, indeed, so delayed the return of the MTBs to the Shetlands that they ran out of rations and had to break open the emergency packs in the life rafts. Nevertheless, this demonstration of lying-up acted as a spur to future aggressions.

Meanwhile, on the other side of the mountains, the Norwegian Army/ SOE party of Operation GUNNERSIDE, sent by air to the Rjukan power station and heavy water plant, were, on the 28th, on the eve of making amends for FRESHMAN by blowing it up and putting it out of action until August.

These dramatic events were in stark contrast to the activities of the first COPP probes of Sicily's beaches on the night of the 26th. Taken to their cast-off points by submarines working from Malta and Algiers, they suffered, despite the inclusion of a nucleus from Party Inhuman, from deficiencies of technique and equipment. Of the seven officers who went out the only survivors, Lieut P. R. G. Smith RN and Lieut Brand, owed their lives to superb physical fitness which enabled them to paddle the seventy-five miles back to Malta, Brand wearing through part of his anatomy to the bone. Thereafter canoe parties were forbidden to venture ashore. As soon as possible, Lieut F. M. Berncastle RN, using an improved method, was brought out to complete the work in LCNs.

Already, on the night of 27/28 February, Berncastle proved to everyone's satisfaction the value in survey work of converted Eureka LCP (L)s (later known as LCNs). Escorted and towed by three MGBs, two LCNs were approaching the east coast of the Cotentin Peninsula (Operation KJD) when, just short of the Isles of St Marcouf, they bumped into an enemy convoy, were challenged, and fired upon at 4,000 yards. Evasive action carried them clear, permitting the completion of several approaches to the beaches while taking soundings by the 'taut wire' system – streaming an anchored piano wire and heading inshore, taking readings, until the prow of the LCP grounded, when they would cut the wire and retire in the hope that neither radar nor human eyes had spotted them. Indeed, on this occasion one LCP did actually touch down close under a pill-box just as the moon rose, but without attracting attention.

The work of Berncastle and his team was no less exacting than that being undertaken at the same moment on the opposite side of the peninsula. A party from SSRF, under Capt P. A. Porteous VC in MTB 344 (Lieut E. F. Vann RNVR), was paying a call upon the island of Herm (Operation HUCKABACK). Referred to as 'an artillery reconnaissance' prior to putting guns ashore two nights later in support of HUCKABACK II, a raid against nearby Guernsey, Porteous and his men were also hunting for a prisoner. But although they spent three hours ashore and guaranteed their presence would be noticed by leaving behind propaganda leaflets at a deserted house, of enemy there was no sign. Once they were alarmed when, to quote the report, 'The force was ambushed by a sheep which could be heard moving in thick undergrowth'. Later a mine went off and a man was wounded. So they withdrew, removing a few mines as specimens. In fact, had they investigated a nearby local inn they would have captured several German officers who, the landlord later reported, were incapably drunk. But, in the event, HUCKABACK II was also abortive, since, as the main raiding party approached Guernsey two nights later, it was to find a full-scale German defence exercise in progress which they felt might best be left to its own devices.

Two nights later MTB 344 was attempting to land four members of the SSRF at Anse de St Martin (Operation BACKCHAT) but this time was detected at sea, perhaps by radar, caught by a searchlight and fired at by two patrol vessels, forcing it to withdraw. The Gee survey, Operation KJA, off Pointe d'Ailly near Dieppe, on the other hand, was uneventful, yet another episode in the never-ending gathering of information which attracted little public recognition. How often, in fact, it has been that a claim has been lavished on charismatic public heroes and denied to the modest. It is perhaps worth mentioning the men of the élite Hydrographic Branch who pioneered reconnaissance and who, in proportion to num-

bers on strength, won more decorations than any other department of the
Royal Navy, and of whom the least is known. What, for example were the
thoughts of an MGB commander, whose perilous job of landing agents
was disguised under its secondary object of taking Gee bearings, when his
wife urged him 'to do something dangerous like other boys'?

Small wonder the Germans began to fear the worst and to expect
imminent invasion. Raiding had proved a worthwhile distraction to the
enemy. Later even Field-Marshal von Rundstedt, the C-in-C West, who
after the war denied being deluded by an elaborate Allied plan simulating
invasion in 1943, admitted that this period was 'a serious turning-point in
the interior situation of France. . . . The organized supply of arms from
England to France became greater every month.' He was, of course,
referring to SOE depredations, and correctly so, for on 20 March, 1943,
the British Chiefs of Staff had directed that SOE was now 'the authority
responsible for co-ordinating sabotage and other subversive activities
including the organization of Resistance Groups', these being defined as
'organized bodies operating within enemy-occupied territory or behind
enemy lines'. Maybe, as Foot points out, the Chiefs were not at this stage
strongly in favour of guerrilla activities, but SOE needed only a slight
nudge to rouse itself; and its ambitions overrode the advice given to CD to
keep in touch with CCO and hammer submarines as best he could.
Henceforward SOE would be the chief arbiter of inland hit-and-run
raiding by small forces sent in and supplied by air and sea. But it was now
under close control of the British Chiefs of Staff who laid down that future
activities by SOE must be 'related to our operational plans'. This edict
was matched by one issued at the same time by the American Chiefs to
Donovan's OSS.

Next it was COHQ's turn to be brought into line with the requirements
of the forthcoming invasion of Normandy which were under the direction
of Chief of Staff, Supreme Allied Commander (COSSAC), Lt-Gen F. E.
Morgan. He was appointed on 13 April to make detailed preparations for
what was later called OVERLORD, the greatest amphibious operation
ever. Almost immediately CCO was instructed to raid only with the
approval of COSSAC. This, in effect, abolished large-scale raiding for
ever and limited small-scale raids to reconnaissance and deception,
particularly in the strongly held Le Havre-Ostend sector, the Cherbourg
peninsula and the Channel Islands. It also coincided with German
counter-measures in those areas, such as the 25-kilometre zone of
restricted movement back from the coast along with a curfew, were being
more strictly enforced.

Mountbatten fell into line by reorganizing COHQ to suit the new conditions, a move which impelled Churchill to minute, along with his approval, 'but pray take care to maintain the position of CCO and his command intact'. Among the changes was the setting up of a special Raids and Reconnaissance Committee to co-ordinate the requirements of COSSAC as it formulated the plans of 1943 and those operations leading up to OVERLORD.

In the Mediterranean raiding was at its most virulent at that time. Here Stirling and Appleyard were making the presence of the fifty-man-strong No 1 SSRF felt – to begin with rather in the manner of 1st SAS in the Western Desert, by operating in the enemy's rear in Tunisia, but later, like the Amphibious Recon Patrols of the Pacific, in the lead-up to HUSKY. Although it was both Stirling's and Appleyard's intention to enter enemy territory by parachute instead of by sea, the first major operation involved Appleyard and a small party in a three-week submarine voyage. This included an abortive attempt to land on the island of La Galite and getting ashore successfully on the well-fortified island of Pantelleria.

By this time the authorities had decided that Appleyard was showing undeniable signs of acute stress. When it came to HUSKY they forbade his landing on Sicily. So he compromised by watching from the air a deep-penetration drop by his men to seize a bridge in the enemy rear, a mission from which he failed to return. It was tragic that he should meet the end he had always courted at a moment of triumph, for by this time No 1 SSRF had been expanded to become 2nd SAS. Within a year no less than five SAS units would be under command of Airborne Forces, poised for action, a testimonial to the original SSRF as well as David Stirling's L Section.

CHAPTER 25

Flow and Ebb in the Pacific

In the train of SYMBOL and the capture of Guadalcanal, Allied offensive activity gradually expanded in the Pacific and was spearheaded by the nearest thing to raiding the Theatre Commanders felt essential. Due to crippling losses inflicted on their Navy, the Japanese were pinned to the static defence of a sprawling perimeter of possessions and thus vulnerable to Operation ELKTON, a twin-pronged amphibious drive aimed at the harbour of Rabaul, which could pick and choose its specific objectives. For American amphibious assault methods had been modified since Marine and Navy representatives had voiced their views to Keyes in the summer of 1941. General Vandegrift stated on 21 February, 1943, that landings should avoid organized resistance if possible; and in the Mediterranean the Navy had adopted the British practice of night arrivals, changes with which Admiral Turner, for the time being, fell in line.*

Vandegrift's preferences dominated Operations ELKTON, CART-WHEEL and TOENAILS (the invasion of New Georgia) and coincided with Turner's conception of using Marine small-unit 'bricks' in the raiding role. Infiltration instead of head-on assault became the watchword. For example, when the Japanese lost patience with a particularly effective party of Coast Watchers under a New Zealander, Capt D. G. Kennedy, at Segi, and took steps to destroy it, Turner at once responded to Kennedy's call for help by sending in a rescue party of 4th Marine Raiders (Lt-Col M. S. Currin) on 21 June, nine days ahead of the planned invasion. Once the Marines were established ashore, Kennedy took this as a signal, as any respectable pioneer would when the frontier got

* It should be noted, however, that at Tarawa on 20 November, 1943, Turner, deprived of adequate reconnaissance of the beaches, reverted to the original bull-headed direct daylight assault supported by heavy bombardment against strong defences – but at a cost of 980 Marines killed out of the 5,000 put ashore.

over-crowded, to push ahead, seeking ways round enemy opposition to ease the way ahead for the Marines who would follow towards the first principal objective, Viru Harbour. This was the model for all successful operations to follow, the failures frequently being those occasions when finesse was ignored or overlooked. Extensive information gleaned by Coast-Watchers and Marine Amphibious Patrols during the previous month convinced Currin that the published plan was faulty. On his recommendation the main landing was made wide of Viru, at Regi, on 27 June. And it is a Marine's account of this stealthy landing which perfectly describes so many of similar pattern:

> It was a weird moonless night with black rubber boats on black water slipping silently through the many islands of Panga Bay. The trip was uneventful except for one scare. It came just before reaching Regi, while lying offshore waiting for word from native scouts who had gone ahead to make certain no Japanese were in the village. Due to the sudden appearance of a half moon which began to cast a sickly reflection, a small island appeared to be an enemy destroyer.

The unopposed landing at Regi was the first step towards the establishment in November, 1943, of a large beachhead at Empress Augusta Bay on Bougainville Island and prompted what were to be the final two hit-and-run amphibious raids of any consequence in the Pacific Theatre of Operations. The first was a landing on Choiseul Island (Operation BLISSFUL) on 27/28 October, timed simultaneously with seizure of the Treasury Islands as a diversion to the major invasion of Bougainville. Under orders to 'get ashore and make as big a demonstration as possible to convince the Japanese that a major landing was in progress', Lt-Col V. H. Krulak, commanding 2nd Marine Parachute Bn, landed his 650 men at Voza by night, piloted by a native scout under the command of Coast Watcher C. W. Seton. Thrusting towards Sangigai on the 30th, the Paramarines bumped into several enemy outposts, which might have been avoided if only they had been able to understand the pidgin English spoken by Seton's scouts, took the village without difficulty for the loss of only four killed against seventy-two enemy, destroyed enemy equipment and stores and then withdrew to their beachhead.

Likewise, on the 31st, a large patrol of eighty-seven men under Major W. T. Bigger struck out westward by sea from Voza to land at the village at Nukiki and hit Japanese positions along the nearby Warrior River and at Choiseul Bay. Splitting his small force, Bigger plunged amidst a nest of enemy and only gradually discovered on 1 November that it was he who was the hunted and by superior enemy units which, unlike Bigger's, knew precisely their own location and way about. Having failed to hit the enemy hard on the mainland, Bigger mortared their dumps on Guppy Island and withdrew to await pick-up by LCPs on the 2nd. Again he was late, caught this time at the water's edge by a strong forewarned enemy force. After suffering losses, he was saved by the determined work of the LCPs and the strong intervention of two MTBs (one commanded by a future President of the US, Lieut J. F. Kennedy) which came close inshore, guns blazing.

At Voza Krulak concluded that it was time to go, even though a stay of twelve days was originally intended. Seton's scouts reported nearly 1000 Japanese who, satisfied that Krulak's force was small, were on their way from Sangigai. On the night of the 3rd embarkation of all men and stores was calmly completed just as explosions ashore announced that the enemy were stepping on mines thoughtfully left behind by the raiders.

Try to convince themselves, as the Marines did, that BLISSFUL had been worthwhile, no real diversion was achieved. For the Japanese themselves were convinced that the Americans would land on Choiseul and assumed, too, that the real objective on Bougainville would be the east coast instead of Empress Augusta Bay. Like ARCHERY, the British diversionary raid in Norway in December, 1941, BLISSFUL produced disaffection among natives who, unlike many in other areas, were aggressively hostile to the Japanese. Seton reported a devastating decline in native morale and E. Feldt remarks that 'natives do not understand broad strategy; they only know what they see before them. They had seen a large body of troops land and had assumed that the days of the Japs were over; now the troops had gone and the Japs remained.'

BLISSFUL further concentrated the minds of those at the top who, since August, had been evaluating raiding in Pacific conditions and particularly the landing at Cape Torokina in Empress Augusta Bay. There amphibious reconnaissance was the sole hit-and-run contribution and it was recognized that meticulous amphibious reconnaissance was decisive in selecting the exact landing-place and shaping the entire Bougainville campaign. Two months prior to the assault by 3rd Marine Division, Recon Patrols from submarines, PBYs and MTBs searched the coastline and probed inshore by night while the submarines used their periscopes by day to verify the accuracy of the charts. Negative and positive information combined to indicate that the vicinity of Cape Torokina was not only a suitable place hydrographically but also thinly defended. It also revealed reefs where none were charted, and proved that Cape Torokina itself was seven miles displaced on the chart. Opposed though the main assault would be on 1 November, it was completely successful and at low cost.. Part of the price, however, was paid by Pfc H. Gurke of 3rd Raider Battalion who, on 9 November, found himself and another Marine in a foxhole under heavy shell and grenade fire from a Japanese counter-attack. When a grenade dropped into the hole, Gurke 'mindful that his companion manned an automatic weapon of superior fire power . . . thrust him roughly aside and flung his own body over the missile to smother the explosion'. For this he won the Congressional Medal of Honor. But bravery alone did not influence calculations of cost-effectiveness when manpower was at a premium and prejudices intruded. The Marine Raiders were under threat.

Perhaps the protagonists of the Raiders' cause hoped for a miraculous reprieve when, on 29 November, it was decided to raid an enemy supply base at Koiari, ten miles along the coast from Cape Torokina. 1st Parachute Bn (Major R. Fagan), reinforced by M Company 3rd Raider Bn, was to land on an unguarded beach to a flank, seize the base from the rear and cause maximum destruction while searching for intelligence about enemy plans. It was reasonable for Maj-Gen R. S. Geiger to order the expedition at less than a week's notice. But to neglect careful reconnaissance and depend excessively on fire support from three destroyers and a single battery of Army 155 mm guns firing at long range was risky, and potentially disastrous when the destroyers were diverted at the last moment. The raid might just have succeeded if the two reconnaissance patrols had been more careful, but there is reason to believe that they reported all clear after visiting the wrong beach. In consequence those Marines who hit the wrong beach were surprised to be greeted by an astonished Japanese officer standing there in the expectation of welcoming his own boats to the base.

Nothing went right for the Paramarines that night. Four companies, penned into a small beachhead, were rudely made aware of lively enemy interest and found too that their HQ Company and the company of Raiders had landed 100 yards away. Then, as enemy fire began to fall, and they dug frantically for safety, a sense of isolation settled upon them. Major Fagan's radio was broken and with it the means to call for help.

Good news came later with the arrival of the Raider Company and the remnants of the Paramarines, who fought their way along the beach to join the main beachhead, and then the establishment of external communications through the artillery radio which enabled defensive fire to be brought down and planning to commence. The next bad news was the repulse by Japanese artillery of two attempts to send in landing craft and the storm of fire falling among Marines with their backs to the sea, signs that the enemy were forming up for a major attack, and a dire shortage of ammunition. Nightfall saw an end to it. As the Japanese formed up to charge, the guns of three destroyers, rushed to the scene, from a few light support craft and from the Army dropped a curtain of shell fire round the perimeter as the landing craft went in for the third time. This time the Marines retired in good order, though abandoning much heavy equipment, and embarked without interruption. They had lost fifteen killed, seven missing and suffered ninety-nine wounded. The raid, to quote their own history, had been 'a dismal failure'.

Already the naval and Marine hierarchy had got to work undermining the Raiders and Paramarines. They had experimented at Makin and tried diversions at Choiseul and on Koiari. It could be pointed out that four raids in twenty-one months of existence was poor justification and that each operation was stained with defeat, no matter what the propagandists said. In a paper submitted to the Chief of Naval Operations on 3 December HQ Marine Corps concluded:

The Marine Corps has always felt that its infantry elements are essentially raiders and that Pacific conditions are different from the European which resulted in the establishment of commandos. It would like to end its raider program so as to make all infantry organizations uniform and to avoid setting up some organizations as élite or selected troops. It feels that any operation so far carried out by raiders could have been performed equally well by a standard organization specially trained for that specific operation.

Old, familiar debating points, in fact, to which a list of serious deficiences could be appended as the real reason for change. As the nation's war effort drained the manpower pool of the best leaders, those who were available had to be spread around evenly to obtain the best results. And in battle it had been found that Raiders and Paramarines had been at a disadvantage in firepower (as had commandos) from lack of heavy weapons. Incidentally, so far as the parachute units were concerned, not one had yet been called upon to make an operational drop.

At root, alongside absence of incentive and need, lay unwillingness to raid among the American commanders at sea and in the field. This led, maybe, to forgetfulness, into making raiding a spare-time occupation unrelated to essentials. Arguably there was no requirement and certainly there was far less chance of its creation in the absence of a strong belligerent central co-ordinating defence organization or an equivalent of

COHQ. Essentially the Americans lacked a dedicated personality in the right seat of power, such as Keyes or Mountbatten.

Be these things as they may, the joint Chiefs of Staff now had a firmer hold on the President and his advisors than early in 1942. Within twenty-four hours of receiving the Marine Corps' request the Chief of Naval Operations had granted it. The ground had been well prepared! At once the existing units began conversion, either into normal marine battalions or were dispersed to other units, including those committed to reconnaissance and guerrilla raiding. Objections were silenced. Suscepti-bilities among the traditionalists had been assuaged.

Amphibious hit-and-run raiding by regular forces was virtually snuffed out in the Pacific theatre except on rare occasions when some enterprising commander might take advantage to patrol aggressively, but locally, round an exposed enemy island flank. Which meant also that raiding by irregular forces was almost entirely stifled since, despite repeated requests by Colonel Donovan in 1943 and 1944, Nimitz and MacArthur steadfastly refused to allow OSS to operate within their boundaries, still on the pretext of avoiding a clash with the Marines, despite their renouncement of the practice. Brute force by massed men and material would in future dictate American operations.

If pin-prick attacks were to be inflicted upon the Japanese, they were to come from the British, the Australians and the New Zealanders whose military attitudes tended rather more in the direction of guile.

CHAPTER 26

Overtures to Invasion

With the elevation of COSSAC, in April, 1943, to a position from which he could influence raiding in North-West Europe and dovetail it to Operation OVERLORD, raiding for raiding's sake from Britain became virtually extinct. Larger-scale raids, such as COCKSURE, which was put forward as an airborne attack on Norway in August, were frowned upon. Small ones were strictly related to special events, reconnaissance and deception of the enemy. Almost the last of the old-style hit-and-run attacks were carried out along the Norwegian coast by North Force until the long nights and its luck ran out.

Some North Force raids came to nothing, such as GUNHOUSE, aimed at sending in a party in February in a Norwegian-crewed Catalina for a month's sojourn, attacking bridges and viaducts along the important Narvik railway and which was cancelled by CCO who lost faith in it. Others, like ROUNDABOUT on 23 March, produced little to their credit. Led by Capt Gilchrist of 12 Commando, the party included an officer and four GIs from 29th Ranger Bn, two soldiers from 12 Commando and five Norwegian soldiers from 10(IA) Commando. Its aim was to land at Landet, near Roydefjord, from two MTBs, and attack shipping. But as two scouts led the way inland they were fired at by Germans holding a swing bridge. The scouts retired fast. The volume of firing swelled as the main body came up and the Germans began to open the bridge. With surprise forfeited, those on the MTB decided to withdraw. A sensible decision, but one which caused a bad taste at the inquest, when outsiders criticized the attackers, notably an American officer, for abandoning the mission too soon and losing his pack. Pointing out that he had no disciplinary powers over Americans, the Force Commander asked with asperity, 'Of what value is a pack to that of a man's life?'

North Force's last act, Operation CHECKMATE, beginning on 28/29 April in the area of Haugesund, was a different sort of muddle compounded of tragic irony. An Army sergeant and five sailors, led by Sub-Lieut J. Godwin RNVR of CRACKERS fame, were put ashore in a coble with two kayaks from MTB 626, commanded by Lieut K Bøgeberg, Royal Norwegian Navy. The idea was to hide up for ten days and attack shipping with limpets, laid from the kayaks.

From the moment of their casting off from MTB 626 direct contact with Britain was lost for ever and only sporadic and sometimes incorrect reports of their fate came to hand. Not until after the war was the story pieced together. To begin with the engine of the coble broke down and they were unable to stick to the original plan. The only ship which presented itself for attack was a minesweeper tied up in Kopervik and this Godwin and three companions sank on the night of 3 May with four limpets. After that Godwin seems to have acted eccentrically, leaving the coble and three men in hiding on an island, moving about independently in the two kayaks with the rest of the party, seeking targets nearer Haugesund and failing to keep in touch with the coble before the first scheduled pick-up on 9 May. Then the weather broke and became extremely foggy, preventing the MTB getting through. Food was running short and could only be supplemented by Norwegians at the risk of being given away, as eventually occurred when a Norwegian told the Germans about the coble's whereabouts and was paid 10,000 kroner. On the 13th the coble party was picked up and, next day, Godwin and his companions, in each case without a fight.* Every attempt thereafter to obtain confirmation through neutral sources and the Red Cross of the party's whereabouts met with denials of their existence. Eventually news filtered through that they had been handed over to the Gestapo and were liable to execution in accordance with the infamous Commando Order. After the war it was ascertained that they had been treated abominably, removed to Germany and placed in one of the most notorious camps reserved for obdurate foreigners. Here, in February, 1945, like many more of their high calibre, they were taken out and shot.

Throughout 1943 and into the Spring of 1944 the gathering of information about beaches and their defences absorbed COSSAC, COHQ and, later, HQ 21st Army Group whose task it would be to carry

---

* The vast majority of the Norwegian population remained as bitterly anti-German as the day the Germans invaded in 1940, with only a handful collaborating with Quisling at any time. But fear of reprisals for failing to report knowledge of partisans or Commandos made its imprint in a region of *Festung Europa* where strong German forces were retained to deal with an expected Allied invasion.

out OVERLORD. Techniques had been refined since TORCH, HUSKY, BAYTOWN, AVALANCHE and the Anzio assault (SHINGLE) would provide ample experience in different conditions. For the most part COPP used canoes and LCNs as their means of transport after departing from the craft or aeroplane which carried them to the operating area. It was a perilous, slow and laborious business searching beaches, logging currents and taking soundings sometimes five nights in succession in moonless periods. Usually LCNs were employed using the 'taut wire' system for measuring gradients; occasionally a wader, dressed bizzarely in a swimming costume coloured by horizontal rings, was tried successfully. Beach texture samples were obtained by swimmers using a wooden prodder 18 inches long.

In the summer of 1943, while most of the offensive activity took place in the Mediterranean, the need to make the Germans expect an imminent invasion of Western Europe was considered essential. To this end elaborate operations were conceived. Operation COCKADE was a gigantic feint simulating a major invasion of France in September. Operation STARKEY was a fourteen-day series of air attacks by the RAF and the USAAF aimed at a variety of targets along the coast and inland and intended to suggest a forthcoming invasion, to bring the Luftwaffe to action and build up to a climax as surface forces gathered at British ports and airfields. Two divisions of Canadians and five Commandos were assembled (Operation HARLEQUIN) while Force J flotillas entered ports and prepared to embark them, without actually doing so. The force would set sail in daylight as if bent on landing, only turning back in mid-Channel at the last moment. Spoof radio traffic was generated and there was controlled leakage of information. Operation TINDALL was intended to suggest a thrust against Stavanger; WADHAM, a series of minor operations between Cap de la Hogue and Brest, to show an interest in that area, and FORFAR – small raids as indication of the main attack in the region of the Straits of Dover. Only a number of FORFARS were actually launched by 12 Commando and 2SBS, allocated to FORFAR FORCE, under Major Fynn, after the disbandment of North Force. It was hoped that US Rangers of the 2nd and 5th Bns could also take part, but eventually they were 'not recommended' because of 'lack of experience in this type of operation' and no training in the use of LCPs, although as individuals they did participate.

Since the FORFAR raids were mostly to be directed against what were regarded as the strongest German coastal defences, fierce opposition was expected every time. The fact that this was far from the case was the first surprise therefore. FORFAR EASY against Onival on 3/4 July spent two and a half hours ashore without making contact. Two nights later DOG got ashore at Biville, again unnoticed and was stopped only by wire at the top of the cliffs. The same night BEER at Eletot and HOW at Quend Plage were attempted but foiled, respectively, by an enemy trawler and heavy surf. Again, on the night 31 July/1 August, a repeat of BEER failed, this time due to breakdown of the dory and bad weather; while a repeat of EASY was abandoned due to uncertainty over position, and a repeat of HOW, two nights later also failed because the dory could not get through the surf. At the third attempt that night, however, BEER did get ashore and stayed there, undetected at the foot of the cliffs, for the whole of the next day before coming home, but without the prisoner they sought. In other words these FORFARS failed as a diversion because they came and went unnoticed!

Far more obvious and a lot more perilous was LOVE on the night of 3/4 August, of which it was minuted, 'no planner will steel himself that he is prepared to tackle it'. LOVE was to be a 2 SBS party by two paddle cockles manned by Capt Livingstone and Sgt Weatherall and Lt Siddles and Sgt Salisbury. The objective was Dunkirk pier; the prize, one prisoner and intelligence. Carried in MGB 116 and successfully launched, they were picked up by a searchlight when twenty-two yards short of the pier, fired on and forced to retire. Contact with the MGB by walkie-talkie radio then failed utterly. Smoke floats and Verey lights by day did no better. They had a long paddle ahead and were part-way home when spotted and rescued at midday by a Walrus amphibious flying boat under Spitfire escort.

As the culmination of the COCKADE/STARKEY feint drew near, with its attendant air attacks intensified and the assembly of shipping between Southampton and Dover nearly complete, FORFAR raids became more ambitious. A repeat performance of BEER on the night 1/2 September was both adventurous and positive. Carried in Lieut Vann's veteran MTB 344, and skilfully avoiding enemy E-boats on the way to Eletot, Major Fynn and nine others from 12 Commando spent two successive nights ashore, gathering intelligence, avoiding the enemy and having most fruitful contacts with local French fishermen. Their leader, a man with a wife and four children, took appalling risks when he and his comrades provided detailed information about German positions at a moment when considerable doubt was being thrown on the effectiveness and alertness of the enemy defences. German patrolling was virtually non-existent. What there was was noisy and lacking in fire-discipline. Commandos strolled the beaches as if on a day trip to Brighton. So low did the men of FORFAR hold the enemy in estimation that they lightheartedly contemplated ambushing Germans on their way between the 'local' and their pillbox. The trouble was that nobody knew about French licensing laws or the effect of the curfew, or, indeed, if the Germans were allowed time off for a drink.

Further insight into German apathy was gleaned from ITEM on the night 2/3 September when two sticks of parachutists from the Para Troop, 12 Commando under Capt A. Rooney were dropped in the vicinity of St Valery-en-Caux. The parties became separated but each found its way uninterrupted to the RV on the cliff top where walkie-talkie contact was made with MTB 252 (Lieut D. Rigg RNVR). A nearby searchlight position was found unoccupied and so the stiff abseil down the cliffs to the beach, where a dory was waiting, went ahead unseen. They all managed to get away safely with their parachutes, despite the breakdown of the dory and having to patch her and paddle, a delay while somebody went back to find a man who had gone back to look for the Tommy-gun he had forgotten, and breakdown of radio contact with the MTB.

If FORFARs were 'routine' small raiding of a nature which would have gladdened the hearts of the original SSRF, so too was POUND, on the night of 3/4 September, when a party from 12 Commando and 29th US Ranger Bn evaded a new German radar on Ushant to kill a German sentry and retire in safety, though fired upon. Amid general astonishment at the supine enemy performance, disappointment pervaded the councils of the COS where it was voiced that STARKEY had produced a lower reaction than JUBILEE the previous year, perhaps because the Luftwaffe was much weaker, more likely because the Germans had rumbled the feint. On the other hand it was noted that the enemy had increased minelaying at sea and inundated low ground in the Cotentin Peninsula. In fact, as von Rundstedt said after the war, they had seen through the deception and deliberately ignored it.

Talk of extending the FORFAR series into the next dark period came to nothing, partly because there was no strategic call for it, partly because COHQ had more pressing matters on hand which, temporarily, reduced the number of specialist raiders to a minimum. 14 Commando had been disbanded on 31 August and 12 Commando and 29th Rangers suffered the same fate immediately after POUND. On 20 September Mountbatten, in putting forward another reorganization of COHQ to dovetail with the rapidly changing circumstances ahead of OVERLORD in 1944, suggested that 'Raiding might now devolve on COSSAC so that it could be related to future operations', in which, incidentally, the newly created 21st Army Group would also have a say. He favoured a smaller COHQ with fewer functions, since 'the techniques and problems of combined operations were by then widely known' – one in which CCO would retain his seat on the COS Committee and report to the Minister of Defence through them. Following study by a special Committee under Air Marshal N. H. Bottomley of Mountbatten's preference for control of Combined Operations by one Head, as opposed to the abolition of COHQ and a system of control by committee within each Service Ministry, put forward by the Admiralty, Mountbatten's ideas were accepted. The old anarchy of divided councils with Ministry set against Ministry took another blow; the creation of a central Ministry of Defence had come a step nearer.

As if to place a special mark upon a development which, for the time being, had gone as far as possible but which would lead eventually to the implementation of that vital change (brought to reality in the 1960s by Mountbatten in person) he was at once sent to head the new South-East Asia Command, where his activities until the end of the war would reflect in full the experience and techniques he had acquired while CCO. Taking his place and soon to be operating the latest directive to CCO which specified, among several subjects, 'Study of tactical and technical problems of amphibious operations including small-scale raids' and 'Offering advice on all aspects of planning and training for amphibious operations', was one of the great Commando leaders, Maj-Gen R. E. Laycock.

Among the earliest of Laycock's initiatives was the resumption of raiding. He complained towards the end of October that there had been none for nearly two months. He had small raids mainly in mind, but flirted with larger ones using airborne troops. Raiding from Britain was now, however, dominated by a shortage of available raiders and the requirements of OVERLORD, above all the reconnaissance by COPPs of the designated beaches along the Calvados coast and the Cotentin Peninsula. And as COHQ began examining ways and means in November, 21st Army Group made its presence felt by submitting requests for raids, seeming to an anxious Staff at COSSAC to be 'jumping the pistol'. At once Laycock applied the classic solution to all complex raiding difficulties. He re-formed the Small Raiding Syndicate and drew up fresh Standing Orders for Military Force Commanders who were tasked to mount a considerable number of reconnaissance raids whose other purpose was to cover the survey work of COPPs.

Of several raids planned under the names MANACLES or CANDLESTICK and scheduled for the dark period 24 December to 1 January, none got ashore, although attempts to do so were made. MANACLES 8, for example, on the nights 27/28 and 28/29, had to be called off when approaching the enemy coast because phosphorescence, stirred up by the craft's wake, made them visible for up to three of four miles. And MANACLES/CANDLESTICK 5, which was to be quite a big show by five officers and seventy-five enlisted men from 2nd US Rangers, under Capt C. A. Lytle with a large pillbox near Onival as its objective, was called off because, by the time it was due to be mounted in January, circumstances had changed.

It was the eight HARDTACK operations, conducted by LAYFORCE II, under CCO's brother, Major P. Laycock, which saw most of the action. The principal purpose was to attract attention to localities away from the NEPTUNE invasion area, while No 1 and No 2 COPP explored various beaches. On 24/25 December, while No 2 COPP, assisted by No 6, began a series of LCN surveys (Operation KJH) under Lieut Berncastle, the men of HARDTACK 2 were in trouble at Gravelines. The dory, carrying two English and three French Commandos, capsized in the surf but was baled out while the patrol went ashore for three hours. But again the dory filled and a Frenchman was drowned swimming out to it. Nobody got back to the MTB and the Germans claimed next day that the patrol had been 'wiped out'. In fact two did manage to escape, but were not on hand when, the following night, the MTB returned to the scene hoping to pick them up.

The night of 26/27 December seethed with activity. Apart from the routine KJH mission, several landings were made. HARDTACK 28 went to St Peter Port, Guernsey by MGB under a French officer (Lt Hulot) who chatted to farmers who guided them to a well-protected strongpoint and came away safely, despite a British officer setting off a mine.

Again, on the night of 26/27, a force including two US Rangers, representing HARDTACK 4, landed at Ault and found notable enemy unreadiness – mines and wire defences in bad repair, strongpoint un-occupied and no sign of interest when a Schu mine was set off. At Oriel Plage, a few miles down the coast, it was different. Here the MTB was shelled while lying stopped as the force went ashore and, after climbing the cliff, found fifteen Germans at the top and decided not to tackle them. They withdrew unseen. HARDTACK 21, at Quineville, also escaped unopposed and spent three invaluable hours ashore in which they discovered a new type of obstacle called Element C which was to assume considerable importance in the months to come. Nothing, however, was uncovered at Sark where HARDTACK 7 found it impossible to scale a rocky promontory and were allowed to come and go by the Germans who preferred to engage the enemy on ground of their own choosing.

The following night the enemy held their fire as HARDTAÇK 7 was repeated, the raiders coming ashore at the spot where Appleyard had landed with BASALT in October, 1942. The German communique summed up a disaster: 'When the enemy approached the beaches, several heavy explosions were heard and fires seen, which allows the conclusion that the mines did their stuff. . . . German defences did not have to go into action.' Two dead were left behind, one the officer commanding.

Whether or not these pinprick raids were instrumental in effectively covering Operation KJH is unknown. The fact is that Berncastle operated on five nights from LCNs without undue trouble, confirming him in a strongly held opinion that this small and relatively quiet craft provided not only an undetectable means of transport but an efficient one from which swimmers could operate with reasonable ease, thus enabling far more work to be done than in canoes or the latest survey vehicle, an adapted X-craft midget submarine. With this view the original COPPist, Clogstoun-Willmott, was in dispute, although he was the first to admit that the performance of two LCNs in their vital examination on the night 31 December/1 January of the NEPTUNE beaches designated for OVERLORD was exemplary. As navigator of one of them he had watched the adroit way in which two swimmers, Major L. Scott-Bowden and Sgt B. Ogden-Smith, had gone about their work in the latest design of 'frogman' suit.

Clogstoun-Willmot was an enthusiastic advocate of the use of X-craft modified for survey by the installation of an echo sounder, a QH receiver, taut wire gear, a compass on deck, an 18-foot sounder pole and an anchor wire and winch to keep the craft bow on when beached. But when he proposed using X 20 in place of LCNs on the Neptune beaches, because he rated detection even less likely, C-in-C Portsmouth forbade it for fear of risking the submarine. By 17 January, however, the ban had been lifted and X 20 (Lieut K. Hudspeth RANVR) set out on a momentous four-day survey of beaches which one day would become famous in history as OMAHA. This was Operation POSTAGE ABLE. Also on board were Clogstoun-Willmott, as navigator, Scott-Bowden and Ogden-Smith as divers, and Sub-Lieut B. Enzer, RNVR, as engineer. Living in super-slum sanitary conditions, and stale air, they prowled offshore by day, scanning the shore-line by periscope and noting intensive fortifications in progress. When darkness came the swimmers would struggle into their suits and begin close investigations which, on occasion, took them well up the beach where mines, Element C, timber ramps and 'hedgehogs' barred the way. Meanwhile the submarine would lie off or take soundings, conned by an officer who found it desirable 'on watch on the outer casing to be able to lift his head above the water for breathing purposes. He is strapped to the induction pipes and has a bar to which he clings with fervour while floating on his front like a paper streamer on the bosom of the ocean while the rest of the craft is submerged beneath him. There is need for a merman to fill this role', so the report claimed. 'Remarkably all personnel remained reasonably fit during the operation [benzedrine and hyocine having helped in some cases].' At times tempers were strained and the worst effects were felt after return to base, but the comprehensive information obtained was invaluable, and gained without loss or compromise to OVERLORD.

The moment had arrived when, once more, raiding policy had to be reviewed in the light of familiar fears concerning security felt by COSSAC and 21st Army Group. Just suppose, it was argued, that either Clogstoun-Willmott or Scott-Boyden, with their knowledge of the OVERLORD plan, were captured. On 27 January, Maj-Gen de Guingand, 21st Army Group Chief of Staff, pronounced judgement, saying: 'Since our information is very complete both from agents and from COPP', raiding should cease, 'unless some vital piece of information could be procured by this means'. 'There was,' he added, 'always the danger that a spoof raid might not be detected while the actual raid was.' So, while COPP continued to investigate, only four more raids would be made prior to 6 June, 1944, when OVERLORD was launched.

The first of these raids, Operation PREMIUM, was a rather sinister oddity originated and run at its first abortive attempt (Operation MADONNA ABLE) on 27 October, 1943, by DDOD(I), at the request of DNI, and not COHQ. Major Porteous, with fifteen men from 4 Commando, was to be put ashore at Scheveningen in Holland, ostensibly on a reconnaissance in which enemy patrols were to be avoided; in reality as a probe to test enemy reaction and, as the order stated 'to reopen a line of sea communications with Holland'. The need was urgent. Two agents, recently escaped from Holland, had reported that the Germans had penetrated the SOE network and, for two years, had been capturing every agent sent in and secretly running the circuits to their own advantage using SOE codes. DDOD(I)'s inexperience in launching raiders as bait was evident throughout. There were technical failures due to inadequate preparation. A 'sticky' compass in Porteous's craft made it impossible to steer a correct course through thick fog to the beach and radio failure baffled subsequent attempts to regain contact with the MGBs supporting them. Firing Verey lights and 20 mm cannon also proved useless for homing. Then the craft ran out of fuel and the men had to start paddling, until picked up by a RAF Air Sea Rescue launch next morning. And when a week later they tried again there was a screen of E-Boats awaiting them and 'a nasty little action in which our escort was set on fire and sunk'.

Porteous could well have been fortunate. An alerted enemy was probably lying in ambush ashore, as was probably also the case on the night 24/25 February when a party of five Frenchmen from 10(IA) Commando, under Capt C. Treppel, attempted PREMIUM. The two Frenchmen who remained in the dory saw flashes, heard loud cries and then waited in vain for their comrades to return. It could have been mines. As likely as not it was an ambush. Not until after the war were the bodies found buried nearby.

Only a major threat to OVERLORD could persuade anybody at COHQ or in 21st Army Group to allow coastal raiding in Western Europe, and the danger of German rockets or pilotless aircraft disrupting preparations was just that. Positive intelligence concerning these weapons had been available since the summer of 1943. In August a parachute operation called COUNTERSTROKE had been considered to investigate 'new construction at Eperleques Forest for the purpose of building rocket guns', but dropped when sufficient evidence was acquired from other sources. By January, 1944, however, identification of numerous launching sites for the V1 flying bombs called for extensive measures as part of Operation CROSSBOW. Initially air attacks were considered the most likely way to achieve total destruction. At the same time CCO was asked what might be done by way of Commando raids, leading his Planners first to propose airborne attacks, but then changing their minds when it became clear there would be little chance of withdrawal. This view was shared by the Chiefs of Staff who believed from the start that so hazardous an operation was unjustifiable. They regarded with more favour, if still with reservations, CCO's February offering, Operation PAPOOSE, which postulated eight to twelve simultaneous amphibious commando raids in March, preceded, four days in advance, by a reconnaissance carried ashore by MTBs. Units were selected, special training and rehearsals begun and a detailed plan for close air support and final withdrawal prepared. Probably most fortunately for the fighting men concerned, the CROSSBOW organization concluded correctly on 23 March that heavy air attacks had already wrecked the sites. So PAPOOSE was called off. In fact the Germans had abandoned the original sites in favour of a more easily concealed launching ramp.

There remained just three final reconnaissances, called TARBRUSH, which had to be laid on in great haste by COSSAC through the Raiding Syndicate only three weeks before OVERLORD was due, in order to obtain up-to-date information about underwater obstacles, mines and booby-traps, such as now littered the Normandy beaches. It was an indication of the efficiency of the system that within forty-eight hours of the request being made by 21st Army Group, a special HILT FORCE, under Capt B. Hilton-Jones RA, had been formed, a mass of relevant intelligence collated, orders written, equipment assembled, MTBs positioned and men of 10(IA) Commando briefed and trained. Landings were made on the Pas de Calais coast as a contribution to a cover plan aimed at convincing the enemy that the main invasion would be there and not in Normandy. Between 15/16 and 17/18 May, TARBRUSHs 5, 3, 8, and 10 put eight-man parties ashore at, respectively, the old stamping grounds of Les Hemmes, Bray Dunes, Onival and Quend Plage. Some went off course; a few stumbled on the enemy and were captured; enough got there to bring back the vital information. Decorations were lavished upon the survivors, with Hilton-Jones receiving an MC for his conduct of the whole operation and his behaviour on the last night when he returned to the beach, though dawn was breaking, in the unfulfilled hope of finding two missing men.

The work of LAYFORCE, HILT FORCE and the COPP paid off on 6 June when X 20 and X 23 provided the vital navigation marks for the approaching massed flotillas of assault craft, with beach clearance parties of frogmen making excellent use of the technical information gathered to demolish the dangerous obstacles. And the highest words of praise for COHQ, the Commandos and every other amphibious unit involved in this incredibly orderly assault from a naturally hostile sea came in the signal sent to Mountbatten at SEAC from a secure Normandy beachhead by Churchill, Brooke, King, Marshall, Arnold and Smuts, ending:

We have shared all secrets in common and helped each other all we could. We wish to tell you at this moment . . . that we realize that much of this remarkable technique and therefore the success of the venture has its origin in developments effected by you and your Staff of Combined Operation.

CHAPTER 27

Mediterranean Raiders' Paradise

It was in June, 1943, a year after COI had become OSS, that W. J. Donovan at last welcomed the fulfilment of a dream to possess his own commando force when a new Operational Group Section was formed under Colonel E. Huntingdon. There had been a protracted struggle against Departmental opposition and bureaucratic obstruction, and it would take longer yet to recruit sufficient men of the right calibre from the Navy and Army for raiding and clandestine warfare. In fact, final opening of the manpower coffers was witheld until September when, in line with the approaching abandonment of the Marine Raider concept, the Army transferred many dedicated fighting men from certain élite 'ethnic' units it had tried to form. Rapidly the OGs increased from a handful in June to nearly 6,000 by the end of October, and of these over 5,000 were abroad, the major portion in the Mediterranean where the successful invasion of Sicily in July, followed by a landing in Italy on 3 September, opened up an infinite number of opportunities for action.

The contrast between the strong, fortified coastlines of Norway, Holland, Belgium and France and the extended and vulnerable 'soft underbelly of Europe', in Churchill's celebrated phrase, was absolute. The shores of Southern France, Italy, Yugoslavia and Greece, with their innumerable islands, promised to be a raiders' paradise. No sooner had Italy secretly indicated to the Allies her intention to quit the Axis than the countries under her suzerainty began to crawl with the maggots of an alien presence. Allied agents were inserted to collaborate with indigenous anti-Fascist elements who now openly combined with active partisan bands, particularly in the Balkans. Operations and supply by air and sea were controlled by the representatives of SOE, OSS (by mutual agreement) and agents of the Russian armed forces, aided by skirmishers of the conquering armies. How bare of defenders the coastlines were on the eve of the invasion of Italy's toe by the British Eighth Army (Operation BAYTOWN) was revealed on the night 25/26 August when a commando patrol under Major P. Young crossed the Straits of Messina and penetrated well inland without making contact. The thunderous bombardment which announced the arrival of the main assault on 3 September, on the heels of careful prior survey of the beaches by Berncastle and two LCNs, was thus an over-insurance, underlined when subsequent commando landings elsewhere found evidence of a speedy and orderly enemy withdrawal.

Orderliness went by the board, however, when, on the night of 8/9 September an Armistice between the Allies and Italy was announced and the Fifth US Army began landing at Salerno (Operation AVALANCHE). At once the entire Italian mainland and wherever Italian troops garrisoned the Balkans were thrown into turmoil, as partisans, anti-Fascists, Allies and Germans struggled to seize whatever arms they could from the surrendering Italian armed forces. Simultaneously the gates of prisoner-of-war camps were thrown open, releasing a horde of amazed Allied sailors, soldiers and airmen who roamed the countryside in a state of ebullient freedom without knowing how to reach safety.

To exploit opportunities in the enemy rear, a motley collection of 30 Commando, LRDG, SAS, OG and an AFHQ organization called Force A were deployed. 30 Commando was at once foraging ahead of the advancing Eighth Army, and later landing on the Island of Capri, to pluck priceless naval secrets from safes and depots. Dropping in by air or going ashore from a rapidly increasing flotilla of purloined ferry boats, MFVs, feluccas, US Navy PT boats and Italian MAS were parties of SIS, SOE and OSS agents acting as runners of guns and all manner of supplies to the partisans, particularly those in Yugoslavia, Albania and Greece.

Usually these landings were carefully planned, after-dark affairs met by clandestine reception committees. Operations by Force A's N Section, for example, required meticulous organization. Teams of two officers and a W/T operator would direct six-man parties of SAS and OG behind the enemy lines to contact known or suspected concentrations of prisoners, who sometimes were in partisan care and invariably in need of feeding, clothing and protection before being guided to safety. Occasionally the route for small groups would be overland but generally it was expedient to take larger numbers to the coast and ship them out. On 30 November, in one area of Italy alone, some 13,000 men with two Lieutenant-Generals and four Major-Generals, were estimated to be at freedom. At first a small fleet of fishing boats and fast motor boats was pressed into service, a single demand in November calling for ten sorties a week. Mostly they picked up soldiers but one US Navy officer working for an OG had the pleasure of bringing back thirteen US Army nurses who had been rescued by partisans in Albania. In due course much larger craft were used, as for example for Operation DARLINGTON II, on 24 May, 1944, near Ancona. On this occasion US Navy Beach Jumpers, guided ashore by Force A agents, found the right place and, in desperation, packed twenty-five out of a hundred PoWs in their inflatable boats because the LCI with a beachhead force from 9 Commando had gone astray. Fortunately the enemy were nowhere about and it was possible for the LCI to complete the work before dawn and save the remaining seventy-five.

More orthodox, but a complete fiasco, was Operation PIPSQUEAK on 14 June, when seventy-three men of 9 Commando again formed an unopposed bridgehead sixty miles behind the enemy lines at the mouth of the River Tenna to allow armed jeeps of Major V. Peniakoff's (Popski) Private Army to operate deep in the enemy rear as the Allied offensive began to flourish to the southwards. Waspish in his disparagement of Commandos, as was Peniakoff's way, he thought better of proceeding when it was found that the defeated and fast-retreating enemy was already pouring back and filling in strength the previously deserted terrain he intended to raid. Having wisely called off the operation, it was discovered that the LCT was immovably stranded on the beach, leaving no alternative but to wreck the jeeps and the LCT's engines prior to making an ignominious evacuation on the single escorting ML. 118 men packed into this small, wallowing craft just managed to get home in safety.

Trying to penetrate a war zone in which the enemy was constantly alive to the threat of ambush, raiders were frequently ambushed themselves and sometimes disappeared without trace. On 21 April, 1944, for example, MAS 541, attempting to land two French saboteurs ten miles from Genoa (Operation CADEX), was apparently blown up by a mine. The next night two PT boats landed fifteen uniformed members of an OG near Sestri Levante to block the Spezia to Genoa railway line by demolishing a tunnel (Operation GINNY), but were caught by the Germans at once and shot without trial two days later.

Far happier had been a raid by eight men of an OG who landed on the Yugoslav island of Korcula on the night 16 April. Met by partisans, they moved to a hide before setting out next night successfully to ambush a German road patrol. Isolated episodes such as these merely irritated the enemy. Seen as a whole, as part of a series of operations closely related in time to major partisan raids elsewhere, they had an influence, although they never achieved decisive results. Deprived though they were of freedom of movement throughout most of the hinterland, the Germans managed to retain control of vital inland communications, so that, when the time came to withdraw in the autumn of 1944, they departed in good order and to an unshaken schedule. But of course their problems and losses were much increased by constant fear of ambush, while Allied morale was strengthened and intelligence enhanced by the work of raiders who moved, barely checked, around the enemy, striking at an innumerable number of targets as opportunity permitted.

The principal restrictive influence on most Allied operations in the Mediterranean was caused by the diversion of resources once OVERLORD had been decided upon. As a result nothing like the advantage which Churchill would have liked to take of Axis weakness was possible. Particularly was this so on the Allied right flank where responsibility for the attack fell on Raiding Forces of Middle East Command and the activity was more fluid, widespread and diluted, directed as it was against Crete, the Greek Islands and the mainland of Greece itself. Here the SBS had conducted a private war of hit-and-run since 1942, merged in September, 1943, with attempts by LRDG and other forces to obtain a permanent footing on strategic islands such as Leros, Kos and Samos. But, as on the mainland, the swift German reaction to the sudden Italian *volte face* prevented a lock, stock and barrel handover of Italy's holdings in the Dodecanese and Aegean. Until the Germans were levered out by the main strategic force to the northward, Raiding Forces Middle East had to be satisfied with small raiding alone.

An outstanding example of what could be achieved fell to three patrols of an eleven-man SBS squad on the night 15/16 November, 1943, which penetrated Simi town, partially destroyed the local Headquarters, killed the OC Troops, wrecked the power station, blew up the ammunition dump and killed twenty-three of the enemy, before withdrawing without loss to themselves. But the most lucrative dividends paid by LRDG and SBS here, as elsewhere, were volumes of information which not only pointed out fresh strike targets but gave forewarning of intentions and counter-action. And, of course, they pinned down enemy troops urgently needed elsewhere.

Along the Yugoslav coast and across Axis lines of sea communication in the North Adriatic Commandos, OGs and associated elements seized a firm base on the Island of Vis as a first step to giving direct support of Marshal Tito's hard-pressed partisans on the mainland. 2 Commando, ten men from 10(IA) Commando and two OGs moved there in mid-January to form the centre of Force 133 which, in the ensuing months, would be reinforced to include 40 and 43 (RM) Commandos, 2nd Bn

Highland Light Infantry, batteries of field artillery and light anti-aircraft guns, a COPP and a few captured Italian guns to support more than a thousand partisans. Their volume of raiding expanded in ratio to the progressive arrival of fresh units and the gradually diminishing size of enemy garrisons which, to the end, remained determined and very alert. For a start three troops of 2 Commando in company with a thirty-strong OG crossed twenty miles of sea to capture four prisoners on Hvar island, the first of several such ENDOWMENT missions aimed at this objective and designed to create a sense of uncertainty among all the local enemy garrisons in the vicinity. They also interfered with coastal shipping, thereby placing a greater load on the threatened inland routes.

In return, of course, there was also a feeling of insecurity on the Allied part and the need to retain strong forces on Vis for fear of a sudden fierce enemy counter-attack, such as had been accomplished with such dash in the Aegean. Only pinpricks could be made until, on 10 March, after 43 (RM) Commando arrived, Operation DETAIN I against Solta Island was launched. This time the raiding force numbered 500, including artillery, in two LCIs supported by MGBs, MTBs and aircraft and had as its objective the town of Grohat. In the classic manner the landing was launched at a distance from the objective. Enemy outposts were overrun during the cross-country march to the objective and final assault on the town was made with full air and artillery support. Over 100 of the enemy were accounted for against only a dozen Allied casualties. Then, just to rub in its threat, Force 133 sent 43(RM) Commando to tackle Hvar again four days later (ENDOWMENT VI) and followed this up with a joint commando and partisan raid on Korcula on 23 April.

Periodically the Germans would mount heavy punitive raids against Partisans, and few caused more disruption than operation ROESSEL-SPRUNG, launched in mid-May with the aim of capturing Marshal Tito and the Allied Military Missions attached to the Partisan headquarters. It nearly succeeded and resulted in some 10,000 Partisan casualties. To help relieve the strain, Force 133 was asked to create a diversion. The result was Operation FLOUNCED. Hastily laid on and including nearly every available unit, it aimed at the island of Brac where 1,200 Germans were thought to be. Carried across forty miles of sea in an LCT, a coaster and a fleet of MFVs, MLs, LCAs and caiques, 6,000 men were put tidily ashore by night at three separate places on 1 June as a demonstration. Unfortunately that was the end of events as planned. Moving quickly inland on the 2nd, the intended attack to seize vital high ground fell apart due to a breakdown in radio communication at the crucial moment. Coming under heavy artillery and mortar fire and stumbling on a

minefield, a bayonet charge by 43(RM) Commando achieved considerable local success, but could not be sustained through lack of co-
ordination with the rest of the Force. Leaders were killed or wounded,
including Lt-Col J. Churchill, the Force Commander, who was captured.
Subsequent attacks failed to drive the Germans off and casualties
mounted as the essential factor of surprise was lost. In conditions such as
these raiding ceased to be practical, so withdrawal was carried out on 4
June without undue trouble due to exemplary work by a rearguard and by
the Navy. As at Dieppe, the weakness inherent in large-scale raiding
against emplaced defences by forces which lacked surprise and the
participation of armoured troops, in a war dominated by tanks, had been
exposed. In the crunch of a fire-fight, Commandos, for all their excellence
as shock troops, were flesh and blood like other soldiers.

The style of Mediterranean raiding after FLOUNCED represented a
continuation of the proven formula of repeated miniatures, although only
in terms of distance from base to objective was there much similarity to the
raids across the English Channel. The base camps were on foreign soil as
opposed to cheerful English seaside resorts. Life and battle took place
among a grim populace whose internecine tribal hatred – Croat against
Serb, Royalist against Communist – were every bit as ferocious as their
struggles against the German invader. Morale could be damaged; it made
a lot of difference when the destination of return from peril, death and
maiming was to the welcoming arms of landlady, publican or family as
opposed to a harsh military environment.

Among the most daring and most successful operations was SUN-
BEAM A, carried out by three canoes under Lt J. F. Richards RM of
RMBPD against Portolago Harbour on Leros to attack three German-
manned destroyers and three escort craft on 17 June. Crossing three
harbour booms was one difficulty they easily overcame; creeping un-
harmed alongside the ships to fix their limpets another. 'At one point we
were urinated upon by a sentry we had not seen or heard. We listened to
various crewmen chatting excitedly to each other.' But they fixed their
limpets to some of the targets and retired to a shore-side hide where
'through the day we listened to various explosions taking place within the
port. Some were depth charges'. Next night, after spending a day pestered
by doubts and scares, they re-entered the harbour to complete the job, but
this time were challenged three or four times. 'Cpl Horner called out
"Patrol". There then occurred what appeared to be a state of panic on the
Anita and gestures were made that Cpl Horner move alongside. He
replied xxxx! (sic) and did move alongside. Nobody on board seemed to
know what to do, so Cpl Horner moved away into the shadows.' Later he

withdrew and the whole party was picked up and taken to safety by the ML.

Simi was again the target for attack on 13/14 July, this time leading to the virtual destruction of a weak garrison and beginning a process of complete domination by which, over the ensuing months, the garrisons were worn down to the point of evacuation or surrender. Chios fell at the end of September, Samos a few days later and Lemnos in the middle of October. But, when all was said and done, the depredations by raiders, particularly those of the amphibious hit-and-run variety here, on the right flank of the Anglo-American front, were side-shows within a side-show. The fiercest action in the Balkans was of the inland, partisan kind supplied by sea and air but depending mainly on the thrust of an approaching Red Army for substantial military and political reinforcement.

In similar collaborative style, raiding forces and clandestine operators in Western Europe approached the zenith of their contribution hand-in-hand with orthodox armies, once OVERLORD had deposited its massed invaders ashore on 6 June. This was the hour of British and French SAS units, American OGs, Inter-Allied Missions and SOE Resistance Circuits, combining under such titles as Jedburghs, Suffolks and Massingham, and sent in to infest the French mainland as the Germans struggled to consolidate a crumbling front in Normandy. Now the emphasis lay preponderantly upon insertion and resupply by air. Although several units were infiltrated through the lines in Normandy and stores continued to be smuggled across the beaches of Brittany and southern France, the *raison d'être* for amphibious hit-and-run raiding had disappeared. Once airborne raiders had touched down, they tended either to be destroyed by the enemy or to maintain their presence within specified areas of responsibility. To assure survival they were compelled to convert an initial, shadowy presence into the substance of solid occupation, either by winning absolute control of ground by persuading the enemy to vacate or surrender, or, through a process of gradual attrition, by easing the way for the approaching armies. The sea was only occasionally a suitable escape route.

By mid-August everything was leading up to the final breakout from Normandy. This coincided with Operation DRAGOON, the major landing by Allied armies in southern France in the by now familiar landing pattern of initial probing and sabotage by partisans and agents, survey and pilotage by COPPs and spearheading of assault by Commando-type troops. It included on this occasion the 1st Special Service Force which had been formed in June, 1942, as part of the American/Canadian

PLOUGH FORCE intended to land in the Japanese-held Aleutians but used instead to fight in Italy.

After the guns faded in Normandy came the swansong of amphibious raids off the French coast – Operation RUMFORD, designed to investigate the Ile d'Yeu on the night of 25/26 August, carried out by HMS *Albrighton* (Lieut J. J. S. Hooker, RN) and executed by five Frenchmen and a Briton under Lt W. Dauppe (all of 10(IA) Commando) who went ashore in a dory to find that the Germans had departed the previous night.

CHAPTER 28

Hit and Miss in the Far East

Throughout the Second World War the schism between those who campaigned in the East and the Pacific and those who fought in Europe remained open and divisive. Not only did the US Army concentrate its fullest attention upon Europe, it tended to allow its South-West Pacific component to wage a war of its own in alliance with the Australians, the New Zealanders and the US Navy. That suited General MacArthur, whose mission of vengeance against Japan was all-consuming. It also led to improvizations which unified co-operation between Services and Allies might have averted. Similarly, the British forces in India, Burma and the Indian Ocean often regarded themselves as 'forgotten' by London, at least until Mountbatten was sent out to form a new South-East Asia Command in October, 1943. Meanwhile the US Navy, of its own choice playing only a supporting role in Europe, sometimes lost contact with developments taking place there and went its own way in splendid pursuit of its own greater glory.

For example, shortcomings in the Solomons apparently failed to fix in Admiral Turner's mind the crucial importance of beach reconnaissance, pilotage and obstacle clearance. The reckoning, as mentioned on page 173, came during the successful but costly invasion of Makin in November, 1943, which he considered 'my poorest appraisal of beach areas for a landing during the whole war . . . The Red beaches were just plain stink profumo. That's why I pushed the development of Underwater Demolition Teams (UDT) so hard.' This amazing admission indicates how Turner was not only unaware of the techniques already practiced by COPP and their kin for TORCH, HUSKY, BAYTOWN and AVALANCHE, but was also in ignorance of US Navy work for over a year at Fort Pierce, Florida. Already created for Europe were Beach Jumper Teams equipped with powerful demolition devices, such as REDDY FOX, a 50 – 100 foot long pole, filled with 28 lbs of tetrytol, which could be floated into position, sunk and then detonated, and HOT DOG, a smaller version of REDDY FOX.

Be that as it may, Turner, appalled at the difficulties of pushing Amtracks through unbreached reefs and enemy booms and barricades at Makin, now opted for what he called 'swimming scouts'. In a letter to Admiral King on 26 December, 1943, he asked for the urgent formation of nine UDTs, and, a few days later, for the setting up of an 'Experimental and Tactical Underwater Demolition Station'. Needless to say this was easily and promptly arranged. Within four weeks UDTs, manned by Navy personnel, nearly all of whom were Reservists, were at work in the forefront of the action at Kwajalein (Operation FLINTLOCK). They swam ashore in daylight from LCVPs and LVTs, thoroughly protected by a typical Turner blasting operation as 'reef-hugging battleships' pounded the Japanese defences so hard that the demolition teams were undetected by a cowed enemy. The first assault waves on 1 February, 1944, met nothing to impede their landing.

UDTs had come to stay. At Saipan (Operation FORAGER) in June, 1944, they turned in a classic performance. Here Turner had them reconnoitre beach boundaries, blast gaps through the reefs and open channels for subsequent assault waves and the armada of landing craft and LSTs bringing in reinforcements and supplies. Without UDTs the whole schedule would have been set back and enemy resistance dangerously prolonged.

The attack on Guam, a month later, probably witnessed UDTs at the peak of their usefulness. Here they worked for three days and nights, closely protected by gun-fire, removing and demolishing elaborate man-made obstacles and blowing aside tons of reef. Extracts from the report of UDT 3 (Lieut R. F. Burke) give some indication of the variety, labour and danger of their task:

Operation delayed due to grounding of LCI 348 on reef. After attempts to remove the LCI, which taken under heavy mortar fire by enemy, it was decided to abandon it and crew was removed by UDT 3's boat No 4.

3 LCPRs sent to reef edge under heavy fire cover (sometimes within fifty yards of the swimmers) and smoke screen and launched five rubber boats. 150 obstacles removed using 3,000 pounds Tetrytol. . . . The enemy had placed obstacles in an almost continuous front along the reef. These obstacles were piles of coral rock inside a wire frame made of heavy wire net. Dispatched all UDT Boats to respective beaches to guide LCMs and LCTs with tanks ashore over reef.

Yet it is noteworthy that the complete abandonment of stealth and the three-day bombardment in support of the UDTs 'tipped off' Turner's plan to the enemy, prompting the Japanese commander to re-deploy his troops in those sectors where assault had been so clearly advertised.

Detached from European practices and US Navy and Marine expertise, and faced with the task of a major invasion of the Philippines, Lt General W. Krueger's Sixth US Army had to create its own equivalent of Amphibious Recon Patrols, Commandos and COPPs. Lacking Marines or OGs, Sixth Army called for volunteers who would scout ahead in parties of one officer and six enlisted men. Applications came from almost every unit and were given the evocative frontier title of 'The Alamo Scouts'. Within six weeks their own training centre had done its work and sixty-six physically fit and indoctrinated men were braced to the task of scouring coastlines and inland defences for enemy troops. They were instructed to find and report, but to avoid fighting except when trapped.

The Alamo Scouts were soon overtaken by the crowd. No sooner were they ashore on Leyte than they found themselves in company with Filipino guerrillas led by Americans. Within a few days or even hours of reconnoitring the beaches another specialized unit was close on their heels. 6th Ranger Bn was also a Krueger improvisation, trained to ruthless commando standards within a mere three weeks, because by now all the short cuts had been discovered by their predecessors in Europe. But they were recruited in a unique way, for Krueger simply nominated 98th Field Artillery Regiment for the job, placed it under the command of Lt-Col H. A. Mucci, the ex-Provost Marshal of Honolulu, and told him to replace those who did not want to volunteer from a long list of those from elsewhere who did. Miraculously and by sheer hard work, an artillery unit which had manned pack guns in the New Guinea campaign was turned into spearhead infantry and found itself nominated to seize, on 17 October, the islands of Dinagat, Suluan and Homonhon which lay across the approaches to the main assault area. Because prolonged occupation of the islands was not envisaged, these were not hit-and-run operations in the true sense of the term; although the orders issued had that flavour. Enemy radio installations and gun positions were to be destroyed, documents and codes captured.

When the time came to land there was but little opposition. At Sulunan the Japanese shot once, killing one Ranger, and then ran into the jungle where they were hunted down. Neither was there any resistance at Dinagat, where guerrillas had killed the enemy, with the result that Rangers were first to raise the Stars and Stripes again on the Philippines and free to erect the navigation devices which, on the 20th, guided the invasion fleet to its main assault position. Subsequently, in January, 1943, a Company of 6th Rangers, working with Filipino guerrillas and Alamo Scouts, won considerable credit and fame with a long-distance mission to rescue American prisoners of war from Cabanatuan Cavo, thirty-five miles behind the enemy lines. It was foot-slogging all the way with not a boat in sight, but it enabled 6th Rangers' group to hit a high spot in history by bringing some 500 fellow Americans safely out, ambushing and killing over 400 Japanese for the loss of only two Rangers and one Scout killed. Thereafter this unit continued to operate exclusively in the infantry spearhead role on land, in much the same way as had its sister battalions in Europe. It was a remarkable feat by an artillery unit to acquire so rapidly more skill and dash than that of ordinary infantry units with more experience in the art. Was it just the name 'Ranger' which inspired them? The fact remains that, when assigned the task of spearheading 37th Infantry Division in the assault on Manila's walled city, they were denied the honour because 'they had already had too much publicity'.

While the American Army fighting the Japanese improvised its raiding forces on the spot, Dutch, Australians and British built up theirs with ready-made bricks such as British Army and Royal Marine Commandos sent to India for use in Burma and elsewhere as spearhead units. Of the many operations attempted, most were inland, often across rivers. Here only those carried out independently at sea will be described, with pride of place given to the dedicated Australians, several of them 18-year-olds who had never before been to sea, who carried out Operation JAYWICK against shipping in Singapore harbour after a voyage of over 2,000 miles from Western Australia in an old Japanese-built fishing boat renamed *Krait*.

Major I. Lyon, Gordon Highlaners, and Lieut D. M. N. Davidson, RNVR, were the brains behind JAYWICK and it took them more than a year to complete its triumphant execution. Certainly it required a lot of imagination to swallow a plan which involved such a long journey through Japanese-dominated waters to launch three Folbots into a protected harbour with a view to fastening limpets on ships whose presence was no better known beforehand than that of the location of enemy defences. But JAYWICK was an act of faith carried out with an unavoidable lack of information by men to whom risk was second nature, against an enemy to whom such attack was unimaginable. Setting out from Exmouth Gulf on 2 September, 1943, and flying Japanese colours, *Krait* reached the 'thousand islands' of the Rhio archipelago in good order on 23 September and disembarked six men in three Folbot canoes who hid up on one of the islands. On the night 26/27 September they penetrated the encour-

agingly lax defences of Singapore Harbour. One canoe entered the inner
Keppel Harbour, the other one fixed limpets on shipping anchored off
nearby islands without serious challenge. At 0500 hours next morning all
six men, exhausted by hard paddling, were hiding on an adjacent island
listening to the thud of exploding limpets which accounted for seven ships
of about 33,000 tons, including a fully loaded 10,000 ton tanker. By good
fortune and much determination they managed to paddle for the next
three days to their rendezvous with the *Krait* and, after thirty-three days in
Japanese territory, returned to Australia, having survived investigation by
a rather uninquisitive enemy destroyer on the way.

JAYWICK ranks with FRANKTON and SUNBEAM A as among the
most successful of canoe operations, and was also perhaps the luckiest.
Both Lyon and Davidson were given to taking extravagant risks, venturing
forth with a minimum of intelligence and creeping up, as Davidson did, on
the tense crew of the *Krait* at the RV just to find out 'how well prepared
they were' and nearly being shot for his stupidity. Both were equally
obsessed with the idea of striking at Singapore, and that obsession led to
Operation RIMAU (TIGER), one that was even more perilously based on
chance, the chance that fifteen unreliable, electrically-powered sub-
mersible canoes (known as SLEEPING BEAUTIES) would be better
than Folbot canoes, and that a party of twenty-two men, carried in
cramped conditions aboard the submarine HMS *Porpoise* to the vicinity of
Singapore, could hijack a junk, transfer the SLEEPING BEAUTIES and
eleven Folbots to her and then raid the harbour.

Some measure of the wishful thinking which went into the planning of
RIMAU can be gauged from Dick Horton's description of the SLEEP-
ING BEAUTIES, which had only two speeds, full ahead at four knots
and half-speed.

How it was expected to cope with the tides off Singapore, which ran at
over six knots, had been left to fate. Steering and elevation was by
means of an aircraft type 'joystick' (like the Welman submarine) and on
a panel in front of the operator was a compass which was unusually
highly inaccurate.

Amazingly they managed to capture a 100-ton junk, *Mustika*, on 28
September and transfer everything to her in two nights' working, before
Porpoise cast off for another task. After that nothing went right. The
Mustika was intercepted by Malay police and the crew gave themselves
away. Lyon had her sunk and took to the Folbots in an attempt to paddle
the long distance to the pick-up point at Merapas Island. They might have

made it if the submarine assigned to make the pick-up (not *Porpoise*) had stuck to plan, but she did not and, again to quote Horton, 'no explanation of this has ever been given'. As it was, an intensive Japanese search gradually rounded them up, killing Lyon, Davidson and a few others, bringing eleven survivors to Singapore where one died of malaria and the rest were put on trial and finally beheaded on 7 July, 1945.

With the death of Lyon and Davidson, no more RIMAU-type amphibious operations were attempted. Dutch and Australian parties, most of the latter drawn from the Independent Companies, concentrated on the vital acquisition of information and the spread and support of clandestine activities in the Netherlands East Indies, New Guinea, Papua and Northern Borneo. They employed hit-and-run techniques but mostly left the hitting to guerrilla bands under SOE control, as did their counterparts in South-East Asia Command.

When Mountbatten assumed command of South-East Asia Command in October, 1943, he brought with him that vibrant dynamism for which he was renowned, plus the operational and administrative techniques he had developed as CCO. SEAC, he said, would deal directly with Combined Operations. To make sure, he co-opted several tried members of COHQ Staff. Without the same sense of personal involvement as MacArthur, Mountbatten's task in the Far East was still one of vengeance. Just as the Americans desired to reconquer the Philippines to wipe out the stain of the 1942 defeats at Bataan and Corregidor, so the British and Dutch were determined to recapture Burma, the Malay Peninsula and the Netherlands East Indies. But although many British viewed the capture of Singapore as an important stepping stone to the Philippines, the only strategic importance the Americans attached to the role of SEAC was the seizing of Upper Burma in order to open up land communications with China. As a result the maritime side of Mountbatten's task initially took second place to the extension of operations southwards. In consequence it was not until August, 1944, that the Small Operations Group (SOG) commenced what were, essentially, reconnaissance missions related to Operation ZIPPER – the projected invasion of Malaya which would come second only to OVERLORD in magnitude.

The Allies were all agreed that Colonel Donovan's OSS was to be prevented from taking a strong part in ZIPPER in the same manner as they were restrained from 'assisting' MacArthur and Nimitz. Fear of American interference in the delicate Indian political scene prompted Mountbatten to copy European methods by placing OSS under SOE, and then ensuring that neither organization received much priority or help. Relatively few agents were inserted to stimulate the activities of Anti-

Japanese Forces (AJF) and the flow of supplies was kept extremely low. Even at their peak in 1945, only 276 tons were delivered to SOE throughout SEAC, compared with 506 tons to Scandinavia and 1,147 to Yugoslavia. OSS agents took virtually no part in raiding (and in none at all of the amphibious type) since Operational Groups were excluded, as they continued to be within the commands of Nimitz and MacArthur.

Strict control was also imposed on the British Small Operations Group which began to assemble in Ceylon in April, 1944, under Lt-Col H. G. Hasler. Consisting, to begin with, of COPPs 7 and 8, which had arrived in India in the latter half of 1943, on 12 June it was 'officially formed' under Colonel T. T. Tollemache. It soon expanded to include four COPPs, three sections of SBS who were all Army Commandos, Royal Marine Detachment 385 and the Sea Reconnaissance Unit of long range swimmers, drawn from all three Services. Apart from the fact that R. M. Detachment 385 and the COPPs were not parachute-trained, the functions of the four types of unit overlapped, although the COPPs tended to specialize in tasks demanding thorough off-shore survey and navigation.

It is not the intention here to deal with the scores of raids classified as Force Commander Operations – that is, those carried out under Fourteenth Army, XV Corps or Force W which could be a beach reconnaissance, a fighting patrol, a 'snatch' of an enemy prisoner, or co-operation with local guerrilla bands. Mountbatten had specified in Operational Directive No 14 that the SOG would provide small parties of uniformed troops 'to operate against enemy coastal, river or lake areas', of which there were plenty in South-East Asia, and that they would 'NOT be qualified to work as agents'. First among the tasks they would undertake were 'Reconnaissance of enemy beaches, seaward approaches, beach exits and coastal defences'. Second, 'Small-scale attacks on objectives in coastal, river or lake areas.' Third, 'The provision of markers and guides for assault landings by larger forces which may be either seaborne or airborne'.

A beginning was made between 17 and 23 August by a COPP reconnaissance of beaches in the vicinity of the Peudada River in North Sumatra (Operation FRIPPERY). Carried by submarine, their task, ostensibly, was to assess suitability for a major landing. All that came of it was a submarine-carried demolition raid by SBS between 11 and 13 September with the railway bridge over the river as objective, – these were Operations SPRATT ABLE and SPRATT BAKER, of which ABLE came to nothing after the two-canoe party became split up, ran into all sorts of trouble ashore and returned, baffled, to the submarine. BAKER, under Major Sidders, also suffered from embarrassments. A corporal fell into the river from the bridge with a loud splash; there was a narrow shave when a Japanese bicycle patrol pedalled by; and the local natives, attracted to the scene, had to be restrained at gun-point in case they betrayed the canoeists while they laid the charge and fixed time pencils. Further delay, when time was already short, occurred to allow a train to pass. All in all it was a relieved party of SBS who paddled back to the submarine to learn later that one end of the bridge was in the water.

SPRATT BAKER was unique in the so-called Independent Operations by SOG in that it was the only one specifically designed to attack coastal objectives. A few were supply missions for guerrillas, of which CARPENTER III, carried out on 30 May, 1945, off the east coast of Johore by RM Detachment 385, was the biggest, involving a submarine and the landing of 8,000 lbs of stores and the evacuation of twelve men.

Reconnaissance was the major role, related to the projected invasion of Malaya across the Morib beaches and in the neighbourhood of Port Dickson by Force W and XXXIV Corps (Operation ZIPPER). Of several small operations, CONFIDENCE, on 9/10 June was alone crucial; the rest, COPYRIGHT, BABOON, BRUTEFORCE, CATTLE and BAKER, DEFRAUD, FAIRY, and SLUMBER were diversionary.

COPP 3, carried 1,200 miles to Phuket Island by submarine, executed BABOON on 8/9 March; its task the examination of beaches and a possible airstrip – for which purpose it included among its seven members an RAF officer. The beach survey was completed, but the canoe carrying the RAF officer overturned. His crew of two Royal Engineers was killed by enemy fire as they ran up the beach, and he was taken prisoner next day. The experiences of RM Detachment 385 attempting COPYRIGHT next day was equally hectic because the enemy were alerted, and eventually ended in tragedy. Having taken their beach samples, they were apprehended by Thai police, but fighting broke out and the men escaped into the jungle where they were hunted by both the Thais and the Japanese. One by one they were killed or captured as they tried to make their way to pre-arranged pick-up points, which the submarines kept under surveillance for the next nine days in the hope of finding them. Three were lucky enough to fall into Thai hands and spent the rest of the war as their prisoners. The two taken by the Japanese were removed to Singapore where their captors 'honoured' them by decapitation in the same manner as the previous Australian teams.

As a deception to BABOON and COPYRIGHT, BRUTEFORCE, consisting of four men and two canoes from RM detachment 385, were carried by Catalina flying boat to land on the Burmese coast at Ziggon on 29 March, their orders stating they should leave behind traces of their

presence. Nothing more was heard of them, however, and a search by
Catalina two days later was abortive. There does seem to have been an
exuberance about SOG deceptions. When it came to leaving traces of
their presence, their teams tended, in the opinion of those who had
experience of Europe, to overdo it a bit. The team from RM Detachment
385, under Lt A. L. Croneen, RM, which went by submarine to North
Sumatra on 15 April, simulated a battle on shore with Tommy-gun fire
and grenades, without, apparently, impressing anybody, for there was no
response. And CLEARANCE BAKER in West Siam was criticized for
leaving so much kit behind as to be unrealistic: in Europe only scraps were
thrown away to indicate a minor mishap.

How effective deception raids were must remain in doubt.
DEFRAUD, by ten men from RM Detachment 385 in the Nicobar
Islands on 18/19 April, certainly succeeded in bringing back information,
but its aim of engaging the enemy and inflicting casualties came to naught
for lack of enemy. FAIRY, in the Tavoy area on the same night, was called
off after the canoes had left the destroyers carrying them due to miscel-
laneous problems including the sighting of an unidentified motor boat.

As for CONFIDENCE, it can only be remarked that this was one of the
few essential beach reconnaissance which fell short of requirements,
despite the very considerable endeavours of the members of COPP 3
under Lieut A. Hughes, RNR, to complete the job. Taking eight men in
four canoes, he landed in two parties on the Morib beaches on 9 June.
Hughes's party managed to return to their parent submarine, HMS
Seadog, with sufficient evidence, it seemed, to indicate that the beaches
they had examined were adequate for a major invasion. But the party with
Captain Alcock, a Canadian, lost contact with *Seadog*, as well as among
themselves, and remained ashore, having discovered their beaches unsuitable. This had repercussions, for no further attempt was made to
examine the beaches for fear of compromising the main ZIPPER operation. As for Alcock and his men, their subsequent adventures amounted
to a saga in itself. Captured and reunited by a unit of Javanese AJF
guerrillas, they were handed over to a well organized, but suspicious band
of Chinese Communist AJF whose methods were, to say the least,
uncompromising and brutal. After a prolonged investigation of Alcock's
credentials, they were grudgingly recognized as allies, especially when it
became known that the Japanese were offering a reward of Malayan
$10,000, later increased to $100,000, for their capture. For their enlight-
enment, they were invited to witness the torturing of a spy and his
subsequent decapitation. They were told SEAC had been informed of
their survival, but during the next few weeks were almost constantly on the

move with the AJF unit, their health gradually deteriorating from mal-
nutrition and jungle sores. When contact was made by the AJF with
SEAC, it took a long time for arrangements for their rescue to be made by
Force 136, which was responsible for clandestine operations along with
OSS. It was September before they at last emerged, and by then the war
was over.

There is no doubt that the SOG filled an essential need in the same
manner as Amphibious Recon Patrols and the Alamo Scouts. The
information they provided could not have been acquired in any other
reliable way, and the price paid in lives for 174 operations was by no means
exorbitant – nine killed, five missing and two wounded.

Great good fortune also attended the ZIPPER landings at the Morib
beaches and close by Port Dickson in Malaya, since they eventually took
place without opposition on 9 September when the war with Japan was
over. If it had been otherwise the last major and prestigious amphibious
operation of the war might have beem catastrophic and not simply the
fiasco that it was. For as a result of inadequate reconnaissances and the
false conclusions drawn therefrom, the landing craft and men faced beach
conditions which somebody in the Royal Navy described as 'vile'. Many
craft became grounded too far out to permit unloading, while others
touched down on terrain which precluded rapid unloading. Scores of
vehicles were drowned and chaos reigned on congested beaches because
egress from them was extremely difficult through dense vegetation and
trees. A few yards inland narrow roads, bounded by deep ditches and soft
ground, prevented vehicles from getting off the roads without becoming
stuck, with the result that traffic jams of fearsome dimensions built up and
the tanks ripped the frail roads and their shoulders to shreds. Only men on
foot could move inland and it was fortunate for the unsupported infantry
that the Japanese tended to assist rather than resist. It was a strange irony,
indeed, that, under Mountbatten of all people, the culminating British
operation from the sea should be so badly prepared, and not so very
surprising that his despatches draw a veil over an episode most people
preferred to forget. ZIPPER's troubles were not the fault of the COPPs,
but the experience of CONFIDENCE was not lost on the Marines or
without significance for the future in their contacts with the AJF bands.
For these guerrilla bands were an enemy of the future who, during the
next decade, would challenge Britain for power in Malaya throughout
long-drawn-out operations in which Marine Commandos would play an
important role.

CHAPTER 29

Beginning Without End

At the end of an all-embracing war in which a greater number of revolutionary methods had burgeoned than any other in history, it was a telling paradox that the initial concept of hit-and-run raiding, performed by small groups, remained inviolate. This provided proof that when Clarke, Churchill and the Chiefs of Staff gave impetus in the summer of 1940 to pin-prick attacks they were on the right lines in the context of a situation in which Britain had lost the initiative. It also showed that when the Chiefs of Staff repudiated small raids in favour of larger-scale ones, they postponed the moment when some form of initiative through attack could be resumed. Had it not been for the innovative and aggressive drive of Keyes, Roosevelt, Mountbatten, Donovan, Turner, Carlson and Laycock, it is extremely likely that conventionally educated politicians, sailors, soldiers and airmen would have been content to conform to past practices and allow the war to develop on classic lines, as the Germans, to a marked extent, actually did. And if that had been so, the contributions by such dashing and ingenious fighting men as Clarke, Courtney, Pinckney, Clogstoun-Willmott, Lovat, March-Phillipps, Appleyard, Edson, Kennedy and Boyd would have been relegated to the anonymous masses where they might have been suppressed without playing a constructive part through the superior, intellectual thuggery they were permitted to practice. And let it be remembered that a good University degree or the highest secondary school qualifications were by no means oddities among a company of men, several of whom read the Classics on their way to action.

This is not to claim that amphibious hit-and-run raids in themselves won the war or even possessed major significance. But it does suggest that an outstanding individual at any level in a military organization and in combat has a vital part to play in forcing a conclusion without resorting to massed slaughter. For if there is a single major lesson to be drawn from the sum total of amphibious raiding operations during the Second World War it is their comparatively low cost in lives set against results achieved, particularly if one includes within those achievements the enormous dividends accruing from the solution of the problems of major seaborne invasions upon which nearly all Allied campaigns were founded. Looking backwards to the cataclysmic days of 1940, the survivors of 1945, who had seen Combined Operations through from the beginning, must have been amazed by what had been done in the time. Who, among those who went ashore near Boulogne for the rag-bag Operation COLLAR in June, 1940, could have envisaged the storm of repeated and successful visits to the same area in the HARDTACK and TARBRUSH sequence of raids in 1943 and 1944? What confidence could there have been in the infant Commandos in the autumn of 1940 when senior naval and army officers were sincerely doing all in their power to strangle them in the cot? How could anybody in those early days have imagined that, from the hotch-potch assembly of a few assault craft and transport aircraft, would emerge the armadas of purpose-built ships, craft and aeroplanes, along with their attendant support organizations, demanded with such foresight and verve by Keyes and the small Directorate of Combined Operations?

The fact is that from the enforced initiatives of 1940 there emerged fundamental changes in political and military systems and equipment which imposed a profound influence upon defence development in the war's aftermath. The institution of DCO obliged individual Service Departments to function as members of a team along with the gradually enforced abandonment of their traditional go-it-alone habits. The imposition of joint and inter-Service planning and executive rules not only spread outwards to all levels of the British military machine, but were exported across the Atlantic to infect the Americans whose departmental fissions were even more pronounced and motivated by jealousies than those of Britain. Even if, by 1945, a perfect world of ideal harmony based upon unadulterated co-operation between allies and among the multitude of organizations and people had not been achieved, the habit of working together towards an agreed goal was implanted.

There is no better historical example of collaboration among allies on a vast scale than that of the Anglo-American alliance of the Second World War. Nor is it without significance that extensive cementing of that alliance at ground level was performed by the arbiters of raiding as they endeavoured to initiate offensive operations when the defensive was about all that seemed possible. Very likely the British enthusiasm for raiding was of importance in overcoming American reticence in that field. Of decisive importance is the likelihood that Churchill's and Mountbatten's prodding were essential in thrusting their allies towards the Commando idea and a willingness to adopt so rapidly the improved joint-Service systems. Indeed, it has to be asked if the war might not have been prolonged if this had not been so. But it is yet another example of the inspiring nature of American open-mindedness to innovation that they followed the Commando concept, and not only copied but produced, in enormous war-winning numbers, British-invented LSTs, LCTs and LCIs without which the major invasions would have been impossible. The point is that the widespread and diverse consultations and contacts inherent in combined collaboration set up systems of thought through which the participants reached sound solutions with mutual concurrence. As good an example as any of this give and take process was provided by the rationalization of different British and American approaches to beach assault methods. It was significant that the British, with their pronounced objections in 1941 to the American doctrine of daylight assault supported by overwhelming bombardment, could adapt this method a year later; and that the Americans, in their turn, came to appreciate and employ the British technique of stealthy landing by night.

It called for immense courage for men to embark upon courses which diverged so acutely from strongly-held doctrine and method. So it is proper to indicate those who were most influential in making the greatest changes. Churchill, despite the incontrovertible evidence of his doubts and vaccillations concerning amphibious operations, comes at once to the top in seeking new ways, as does Roosevelt, despite his tendency, like Churchill, to innovate without due regard to feasibility. It must never be forgotten that it was often their task to compel conservative subordinates to take risks in order to make progress, and that striking sparks from the complacent was often essential to generate the initiative demanded. In these conditions, and inevitably in a world in which the publicist often reigns supreme, heroes assume dominant importance. On both sides of the Atlantic Mountbatten stands out uniquely as an undisputed leader. No other officer quite equalled him in achieving such breadth of influence on statesmen, admirals and generals. Not only was he at home in the corridors of power, he also had a motivation spurred by bitter and recent experience of being shot at in the most direct and intensive way. But while it is correct to credit him with bringing Combined Operations to the pitch that they reached worldwide, it is equally wrong to overlook the man who preceded him and set the stage.

Sir Roger Keyes warrants far greater praise than it has been his lot to receive, to off-set the damnation to which he has been consigned by his peers. His critics overlook the fact that the Americans regarded Keyes's unique experience of amphibious raiding with the respect which was his due, and also forget that the foundations of the organization Mountbatten took over were laid by Keyes. From Keyes in the summer of 1940, before Churchill and the Chiefs of Staff diverted him on to the track of the falsely conceived larger raids which were his downfall, came the driving force behind small raids as a preliminary to invasions. Urged on by him, too, was the wave of ideas leading to the development of commandos along professional lines, the creation of a parachute force, the raising of Small Boat raiders, the impulse to design and build an entirely new range of landing ships and craft, the investigation and development of gliders, helicopters, parachutist-carrying aircraft and beach-landing devices, and, withal, the techniques required to operate this paraphernalia once it had been built and delivered. Reshuffle DCO as Mountbatten did when he took over in 1941, he had to thank Keyes for providing something worth organizing, and subsequently appreciate that the difficulties he encountered were often best overcome by solutions similar to those employed by Keyes, even if in a more subtle manner.

Consider, finally, the highly publicized Donovan and the unfairly underrated Turner, to both of whom America and the Allies owe a greater debt than history has yet paid, because they were controversial and often exposed to public denigration out of context. Seen amid the testing circumstances of their day and with the jobs they were invited to perform, they were shining examples of strong leaders in the controversial Keyes mould. They were innovative and reasonably loyal to the demands of their superiors. They got things done and bruised sensitive people on the way to their goals at a moment in history when there simply was not the time available to tread delicately round every obstruction. The pursuit of popularity is not always the criterion of success, particularly in desperate times. Donovan trod on toes when he created in OSS a vast and radically new organization which was automatically pitted against strong vested interests, and still managed to include within it a substantial 'commando' type section, the OGs, which performed more amphibious hit-and-run raids than the entire US Marine Raiders and Army Ranger battalions combined. Turner, apart from leading major Amphibious Forces with stupendous effect in nearly all the US Navy's Pacific invasion, has to his credit an innovation of which hardly anything is known to this day – the creation of the joint Army, Navy and Marine section to handle Amphibious Warfare at the centre, which was the closest any American department got to COHQ.

Regardless of immense courage and determination by individuals, it has to be repeated that it was large fleets and armies which won the war, not mosquito stings. On the other hands the fleets and armies would have been in greater difficulty without raiding forces and, one way or the other, would have been compelled, as Sixth US Army was, to raise something like them. The raiders' closing balance sheet, to be acceptable, had to show a clear profit, but the main trouble in that sort of exercise lies in the fact that nearly all the assets are unquantifiable.

Opponents and supporters of raiding, in all its forms, naturally tended to adopt extreme positions of justification. The opponents listed inactivity and failures as proof of wasted effort, and reinforced that contention by pointing out that élite forces would have been put to better use in direct involvement with main forces on the principal battlefields. The supporters extolled the benefits of dramatic successes, linking their morale-lifting attributes with raiding's inestimable value as distractors of enemy effort. As is common in such arguments, the truth probably lay somewhere midway. Raiding forces did deflect key personnel with vital leadership potential from the expanding citizen forces which accordingly suffered in their development and combat worthiness; they also consumed industrial resources which might have been put to better use. Equally there is no doubt that the activities and threat of raiding forces compelled the enemy to waste a disproportionate quantity of effort and material in countering them. At the time it was hardly possible to establish whether the effort was worthwhile, and this naturally induced doubts and uncertainty. Only after the war, and spread over a very long period, has enough been divulged to form a more precise judgement. Only recently has it been possible to understand with reasonable certainty the impact of raiding upon enemy commanders as they strove to cope with shadows gathering like a sinister cloud, and this is chiefly because the disclosure of how many secret plans and codes were snatched from the enemy during raids has been delayed. This information adds immeasurably to the profit side of the account.

Intangibles, such as the eternal interaction of one activity upon another, have also to be entered into the tally of strategic, tactical and technical benefits and expenses. Inescapably each raid, no matter its size, overlapped elsewhere and called for overheads. The creation of co-ordinating and intelligence-seeking joint-Service organizations on an unprecedented scale was all part of the profit and loss account in which had to be incorporated departments such as COHQ, SOE, OSS and the expanded offices of State set up to deal with Allied and inter-Service matters. Waste there undeniably was, but the revolution in a mutual co-operative spirit which spread outwards and in all directions was frequently justified by improved performances. Open-minded discussions in their clash with old-fashioned, set positions were often productive of new ideas of war-winning potential. The release of pent-up inventiveness, encouraged by Keyes, Mountbatten, Donovan and their like in the debate with Departmental Heads was the detonator of an explosion of enthusiastic, impetuous and patriotic youth who wanted to prove their manhood and get on with the war in an original manner. To those who believe that no nation worth its salt can survive unless its people are prepared to delve and sacrifice willingly for its welfare, the example set by the offspring of commandos – the Airborne Forces, SBS, Raiders, Rangers, SAS, OGs with their many off-shoots – will always be an inspiration underlining their belief that the power of the free individual is an essential ingredient to motivate supervisory bureaucratic organizations.

Yet, of necessity at the heart of all combined operations, lay the requirement for multi-purpose organizations to co-ordinate the activities of the long-established ministries and headquarters whose autocratic, self-preservation was overdue for revision in order to keep pace with modern technology. Perhaps it was symbolic that, within the Anglo-American alliance, it was the example set by Britain's COHQ which persuaded the Americans to leap-frog into the lead after the war. For too long the US had suffered from the ludicrous and wasteful rivalries afflicting the Navy and Army Departments, and the move in 1947 to set up a central Department of Defense, to supervise them and the newly formed Air Force, came not a moment too soon as the threat of World War III loomed up. So it is no credit to successive British governments that it took them another 15 years to form their own Ministry of Defence, although entirely logical that it should be the second Chief of Defence Staff, Admiral of the Fleet Lord Louis Mountbatten who, by a characteristic exercise of power, pushed them over the brink.

Finally, consider the relation of small-scale operations to those of vast dimensions, and accept for argument's sake, that it was not until the Americans had attained a gigantic preponderance of material and trained men that they, like the British, felt compelled to invest in smaller scale raiding forces to attempt recapture of the initiative. That is a lesson none but the mightiest of powers should forget – that nations with restricted or attenuated military means cannot afford to ignore the importance of possessing a highly trained élite in preference to a semi- or completely incompetent conscripted mass. Then relate that argument to the results of innumerable campaigns and battles, fought since 1945 and watch which way the pointer swings. In sum, the achievements of those who waged hit-and-run raids was not the impact they made at the time so much as the ideas they promoted and the foundations they laid for future warfare.

BIBLIOGRAPHY

Many Official Histories, in addition to those included below, have been consulted, as have public archives in Britain and the US.

Anon, *History of the Combined Operations Organisation 1940–1945*, Amphibious Warfare HQ, 1956.

J. E. A., *Geoffrey*, Blandford, 1947.

Churchill, W. S., *The Second World War (6 Vols)*, Cassell, 1948.

Crowl, P. A. & Love, E. G., *Seizure of the Gilberts and Marshalls,* US Dept of Army.

Darby, W. O., *We Led the Way,* Presido Press, 1980.

Dyer, G. C., *The Amphibians Came to Conquer (2 Vols),* US Dept. of the Navy, 1969.

Feldt, E., *The Coast Watchers*, OUP, 1946.

Fergusson, B., *The Watery Maze*, Collins, 1961.

Foot, M. R. D., *SOE in France*, HMSO, 1966.

Fraser, D., *Alanbrooke*, Collins, 1982.

Greenhous, B., *Semper Paratus*, RHLI, Canada, 1977.

Haggerty, J. J., *A History of Ranger Battalions in World War II*, Fordham University, 1982.

Hinsley, F. H. and others, *British Intelligence in the Second World War (3 Vols)*, HMSO, 1979.

Holman, G., *The Little Ships*, Hodder and Stoughton, 1943.

Horton, R., *Ring of Fire*, Cooper, 1983.

Hough, F. O. and others, *History of the US Marine Corps (5 Vols)*, US Marine Corps.

Jones, R. V., *Most Secret War*, Hamilton, 1978.

Kennedy Shaw, W. I., *Long Range Desert Group*, Collins, 1945.

Ladd, J., *Commandos and Rangers,* Macdonald and Janes, 1979.

Lane, R. L., *Rudder's Rangers,* Ranger Assoc, 1979.

Macksey, K., *The Partisans of Europe in World War II,* Stein and Day, 1975.

Maund, L. E. H., *Assault from the Sea*, Methuen, 1949.

McLachlan, D., *Room 39*, Weidenfeld and Nicholson, 1968.

Miller, J., *Cartwheel: The Reduction of Rabaul,* US Dept. of Army, 1959.

Peniakoff, V., *Popski's Private Army,* Cape, 1950.

Pitt, B. (Ed), *Purnell's History of the Second World War,* BPC, 1966.

Ryder, R. E. D., *The Attack of St Nazaire,* Murray, 1947.

Saunders, H St. G., *The Green Beret,* Joseph, 1949.

Saunders, H St. G., *The Red Beret,* Joseph, 1950.

Smith, B. F., *The Shadow Warriors,* Deutsch, 1983.

Updegraph, C. L., *US Marine Corps Special Units of the Second World War,* US Marine Corps, 1972.

Wynyard, N., *Winning Hazard,* Sampson Low, 1949.

INDEX

DATE			